AMERICAN
SHOCKWAVE

AMERICAN
SHOCKWAVE
Entrepreneurial Capitalism
and its Global Impact

Kim Ezra Shienbaum

PRAEGER

Westport, Connecticut
London

Library of Congress Cataloging-in-Publication Data

Shienbaum, Kim Ezra.
   American shockwave : entrepreneurial capitalism and its global impact / Kim Ezra
Shienbaum.
      p. cm.
   Includes bibliographical references (p.   ) and index.
   ISBN 0–275–97483–9 (alk. paper)
      1. Industrial policy—United States.   2. Capitalism—United States.
   3. Entrepreneurship—United States.   4. Deregulation—United States.
   5. Technological innovations—Economic aspects—United States.   6. United
   States—Foreign economic relations.   I. Title.
   HD3616.U46S45   2002
      330.12'2'0973—dc21   2001133080

British Library Cataloguing in Publication Data is available.

Library of Congress Catalog Card Number: 2001133080
ISBN: 0–275–97483–9

First published in 2002

Praeger Publishers, 88 Post Road West, Westport, CT 06881
An imprint of Greenwood Publishing Group, Inc.
www.praeger.com

Printed in the United States of America

The paper used in this book complies with the
Permanent Paper Standard issued by the National
Information Standards Organization (Z39.48–1984).

10 9 8 7 6 5 4 3 2 1

Copyright Acknowledgments

The author and publisher gratefully acknowledge permission for use of the following
material:

Excerpts from Steve Beitner. *Agilent Technologies Annual Report*. Agilent Technologies, 1999.

From *The Rise and Fall of the Great Powers* by Paul Kennedy, copyright © 1987 by Paul
Kennedy. Used by permission of Random House, Inc.

Excerpts from Paul Kennedy, *The Rise and Fall of the Great Powers*. London: HarperCollins
Publishers, Ltd., 1987.

This book is dedicated to
Clara and Isaac

Contents

Preface

Many Americans have a sense that their economic landscape has changed dramatically in recent decades and have coined various terms to denote this change. The New Economy is one of them. Yet this term obscures as much as it explains. Most of us really don't have a good sense of what is "new" about the New Economy or how this change occurred. Clarifying the distinguishing features of the New Economy, and explaining how it began, may provide valuable clues about how, when, and whether it will end, and what it portends for the future.

Insights into the New Economy, I believe, become much clearer through the lens of political science rather than economics and, in any event, economists have pretty much dissected the evidence at hand. Thus, I have written *American Shockwave: Entrepreneurial Capitalism and its Global Impact* with only one modest goal in mind: to bring order to the obvious!

American Shockwave makes the case that, beginning in the late 1970s and early 1980s, the federal government, not the private sector, played a catalytic role in fostering innovation, entrepreneurship, and competition—three key features of the New Economy crucial to the success of the American brand of capitalism. Without a definitive federal role in shaping the landscape of the New Economy by setting the terms of engagement (more competition) and by laying the groundwork (giving strong incentives to entrepreneurial innovators while dismantling regulatory protections for more established companies) it might never have emerged at all. The fact that it did, I maintain, has altered the very nature 'of U.S. capitalism, creating a new economic model—"entrepreneurial capitalism"—unique to America.

The book's central argument placing Washington at the epicenter of the New Economy will undoubtedly fuel strong objections from those who believe that the real foundation of American economic success lies in private sector initiative. Even readers sympathetic to public policy intervention will ask pointed questions. Why did the federal government get involved in supporting entrepreneurial innovation? How could such a transformative role go publicly unnoticed and unacknowledged for so long? Under what possible conditions would Republicans have lent their support to public policies of this sort? Why did this role not unleash a pork barrel feeding frenzy? Wasn't choosing "winners over losers" the fatal flaw of now discredited European and Japanese industrial policies? Above all, isn't the New Economy premised upon less government intrusion and more reliance on market forces? Readers can expect to find answers to all these questions in the pages that follow.

American Shockwave should not, at the outset, be dismissed as yet another "ivory tower" book written by an academic with a pro-government/antibusiness bias. Quite the contrary. As a private investor I strongly believe that the private-sector response to the challenging, if not brutal, environment of entrepreneurial capitalism has been nothing short of heroic. The very fact that such strong medicine administered by the federal government didn't knock corporate America off its feet, but instead energized long-established companies such as GE and IBM to adapt, is ample evidence of its resilience. Battle-weary CEOs still reeling from the aftershocks this new economic model has imposed, as well as the shell-shocked private investment community, already recognize that under the rules of the New Economy, advantages such as a proprietary technology or a market dominant position are temporary as accelerating rates of entrepreneurial innovation challenge the resources of even long-established giants. This book explains how this happened and identifies who was responsible for changing the rules of the game!

Under what conditions might the New Economy (and the entrepreneurial capitalism that undergirds it) be in jeopardy? Would a secular bear market in the technology sector, for example, end it? These questions were raised during the 2000–2001 bear market when the Nasdaq, home to most of the newer technology companies, underwent a horrifying decline brought on by technology overcapacity and inventory buildups in a slowing economy, severely shaking investor confidence.

If the New Economy had been solely a consequence of private sector initiative funded exclusively on the basis of investor confidence, then "investor fright" during bear markets might end it. New entrants with innovative breakthroughs will find it harder to get private funding at any stage. Indeed, during the most recent bear market, private venture capital investment in startups fell by 31 percent in the fourth quarter of 2000 and, in the first quarter of 2001, by 60 percent from the previous periods. The initial public offering (IPO) market also shrank precipitously. During the first quarter of 2001, only 21 companies went public, compared with 123 for the same period a year earlier.

The argument of *American Shockwave*, however, implies that Washington has been the "public venture capitalist" of first and last resort for quite some time. By contrast, it was only in the mid- to late-1990s that private venture capital "took off" and the equity markets really opened to the youngest new entrants. Frankly, the private sector, particularly with respect to early stage technology and biotechnology investments, must be considered "hot money," subject to extreme mood swings and quick to take flight at even the hint of adversity. Thus, even after investor confidence eventually recovers from periodic bear market shocks, the history of the last twenty-five years suggests that the federal government should continue its efforts to foster innovation, entrepreneurship, and competition. If it does, then the New Economy will survive and the world will remain spellbound by the intensity and range of American innovation and enterprise.

Many people provided help and support for this project. I would like to single out and thank the staff at Senator Arlen Specter's office, who provided me with multiple Congressional Research Service reports, most archived and some dating back to the 1970s. Answering this particular request of a constituent must have been a monumental task, but it was handled expeditiously and I remain grateful. I am also grateful for the opportunity to have met, as host of my Rutgers radio series, several people not normally in a college professor's orbit who appeared as my guests: George Gilder shared his excitement and considerable knowledge about technology innovation after taping a show; David Thompson, founder and CEO of Orbital Sciences, informed me about federal support for entrepreneurial companies like his own which depended—indeed, initially survived—on public seed capital, while Dr. Philip Schein, former CEO and founder of U.S. Biosciences (which merged with MedImmune in 1999), made me aware of his company's development of old Defense Department biotechnology patents.

I also wish to express my gratitude to Shirley Masters, former president of the Susquehanna County Chamber of Commerce, for making me aware of the Electronic Commerce Resource Center at the University of Scranton and for her efforts in arranging interviews with Elizabeth Zygmunte and Andrea Mulrine there. I would also like to thank Elizabeth and Andrea for making extensive personal presentations of their work and for educating me about the origins of the Electronic Commerce Resource Centers (ECRCs).

Several colleagues must be mentioned as well. I am particularly grateful to John Ward at West Chester University for his strong encouragement during the very earliest stages of this project and to many of my colleagues in the Political Science Department at Rutgers–Camden. Arthur Klinghoffer, as chair, carefully read a first draft of the entire manuscript and was generous in his praise and helpful with his comments. So, too, were Alan Tarr and Shaheen Ayubi. Russell Harrison helped me organize my charts and graphs. I'd also like to thank Karen McGrath, our department secretary, for her efficient help at various stages of the project.

I would be remiss if I did not make special note of the assistance provided me by a number of my students, many of whom volunteered their services. Of particular note are Jackie Pasquin, who unearthed the unpublished paper by Josh Lerner on the Internet in 1997 and helped research Chapter Five; Peter Romeo, who not only made numerous trips to the Paul Robeson Library on my behalf but served as a sounding board for my ideas; Dung Nguyen, who unearthed information on technology innovation legislation; and Deanna Malatesta, who brought to my attention the Rand Corporation's RaDiUS project and other important materials. Lou Ferrara kindly offered his help with some of the charts. Their efforts helped make this project fun and moved it along more rapidly than otherwise might have been possible.

I am greatly indebted to Michael Hermann, my editor at Greenwood/ Praeger, for his unwavering support for *American Shockwave* and his help in bringing the project to rapid completion with considerable charm and grace. My thanks go also to Lori Ewen, my Production Editor, as well as all the others at Greenwood/Praeger involved in bringing this book to publication. Last, but not least, I must thank my long-suffering family and friends who permitted me the indulgence of believing my work was important.

Kim Ezra Shienbaum
New Milford, PA

CHAPTER 1

An Overview

America triumphantly entered the twenty-first century on the wave of the longest peacetime expansion in its history,[1] dramatically reversing an economic decline that had become embarrassingly apparent by the late 1970s and early 1980s. The process of resurgence,[2] in my view, transformed more than the American economy. It radically changed the very nature of American capitalism and created something entirely new. I have chosen to call it "entrepreneurial capitalism," not only because of the unprecedented and accelerating rate of entrepreneurial innovation,[3] but because the rules of this New Economy have been remade to favor new entrants as never before.

Yet even as the New Economy continues to be hotly debated worldwide as a suitable model for other nations to follow—a debate which will, no doubt, continue for some time in the absence of any other successful contemporary economic role models[4]—its dimensions have yet to be systematically explored or its genesis convincingly explained.

Advocates of the New Economy[5] have staunchly assumed economics, not politics, to have been the key to its emergence; hence the private sector has received all the plaudits.[6] To the extent that government and public policy generally have been accorded any role in America's economic resurgence, it has been attributed variously to sound fiscal and monetary policy in the late 1990s or to regulatory reform in the 1980s, which reduced the role of government, setting the private sector free to innovate, restructure, and enhance productivity.[7] Others trace the vigor of the New Economy back to Reagan-era tax cuts and still others to the postwar global economy that produced competitive pressures which, they claim, forced the private sector to initiate change independent of public policy.[8]

While all these explanatory factors are no doubt important contributors and necessary conditions for the transformation of the American economy, they are simply not sufficient to explain the timing and magnitude of change or the explosive unleashing of entrepreneurial forces. *American Shockwave* makes the case that their release was neither accidental nor a fortuitous consequence of government getting out of the way.

On the contrary, the federal government was the prime mover of entrepreneurship, competition, and innovation—the three key features which have led to the success of the American brand of capitalism. Washington must be placed squarely at the epicenter, as the catalyst, of this economic revolution. Indeed, the core feature of entrepreneurial capitalism, and one that distinguishes it from the nineteenth century laissez-faire model or from anything that has gone before, is the degree to which the federal government has been actively involved in its creation, facilitation, and maintenance.[9]

This view differs from the common perception that a central feature of the New Economy has been a passive retreat by the American government, which was the first worldwide (followed by Great Britain under Margaret Thatcher) to dismantle regulation, encourage privatization, and embrace free trade and the global economy. To be sure, deregulation, privatization, and free trade are the minimum requirements for entrepreneurial capitalism to emerge. They are necessary but they are not sufficient in and of themselves to account for the ferocious vitality of the American economy.

In fact, what happened was that the federal government began to act in ways it had never done before. In assuming the role of catalyst in the transformation of an economy in relative decline, it committed itself to injecting competitive forces into the domestic economy by actively supporting new entrants with commercially viable new products and services, especially in the areas of high technology and biotechnology. Their entry was facilitated by a variety of policy incentives that created opportunities and niches for young companies, protected new entrants, and, where necessary, funded new technologies and the entrepreneurial companies that created them. Hence, a strong case can be made that federal innovation policy actually increased the rate of innovation in the economy. Indeed, Josh Lerner, professor of entrepreneurial finance at the Harvard School of Business, went so far as to describe this new *sub rosa* federal role as one of a "public venture capitalist."[10]

This underscores my view that government did not merely get out of the way. It actively changed the rules and terms of its economic engagement. Without these changes in Washington's policy priorities, it is our contention that the transformation of the American economy would have been severely retarded or might never even have emerged. I believe that the innovation of the U.S. economy, a hallmark of entrepreneurial capitalism, has been a consequence of just the right mix of encouragement for the entrepreneurial sector combined with deregulation and vigorous antitrust enforcement. The core task of this book, then, is to reevaluate the hitherto underemphasized role of the federal government in bringing about this significant change and to identify the unique mix of public policies that underwrote commercially viable technology innovation with strong support for the entrepreneurial companies that generated it, in the process helping to transform the American economy into the world's most competitive.

For those who believe that economic performance occurs independently of politics and that in the case of the New Economy private sector initiatives such as "management improvements," "technological innovations," or "corporate restructurings" were more important causative factors, Nobel prize-winning economist Douglas North's observations are pertinent. As an institutional economist and in books such as *Institutions, Institutional Change and Economic Performance*, he has made a strong case that political institutions undergird economic ones. Certainly economic theory changed in the late 1970s and 1980s, becoming less supportive of "regulatory" capitalism, but it was not until these changed beliefs were embodied in new rules of the economic game (and specifically spelled out in new policy priorities) put in place by political institutions that economic change occurred. Corporate restructurings and other private sector adjustments reflected, rather than initiated, those changes.

In fact, to leave out Washington's role in altering the policy priorities that have led to America's strong economic performance is to leave out an important piece of the puzzle. For example, the acceleration in private sector venture capital to finance new technologies from the mid- to late-1990s onward was, in fact, preceded by the national commitment to maintain and extend U.S. global leadership in innovation exemplified by the High-Performance Computing and National Research and Education Act of 1991, sponsored in the Senate by Al Gore,[11] as well as by other federal technology innovation legislation dating back to the 1980s. To believe otherwise dangerously points other nations seeking to emulate us in the wrong direction. Indeed, if "entrepreneurial capitalism" is ever to become a model for the developed and developing world, it is critical to understand the conditions under which it emerged and the public policies put in place to bring it about.

Admittedly, attributing such a transformative role to the federal government is a bold assertion. Even Peter Eisinger in his ground breaking book *The Rise of the Entrepreneurial State: State and Local Economic Development Policy in the United States* did not make such a claim. Eisinger instead argued that state governments, but not the federal government, had responded to declining U.S. competitiveness abroad, and he was the first to explain why they had been compelled to intervene:

International competition in the marketplace, a phenomenon that began to take serious shape in the 1970s put a premium on product innovation and technological pioneering . . . The entrepreneurial state is a response to increasing technological complexity and to the great international forces whose mastery eludes the capacity and resources of most individual private entrepreneurs.[12]

Moreover, Eisinger had explicitly stated that American government at the national level played no comparable role as entrepreneurial agent, limiting itself to using the "blunter tools of macroeconomic tax and spending policy and monetary controls" to stimulate competitiveness.[13] Thus, he had concluded that "much of the effort to shape the American economic future . . . devolved to the *state* capitals" (emphasis added) and by the 1970s "*states and communities* began to intervene in markets where even individual entrepreneurs feared to go" (emphasis added).[14]

It is important to note, however, that Eisinger's book was researched in the 1980s and published in 1988 before the full dimensions of federal activity became as clear as they did by the 1990s, and I contend that government at the national level, in fact, adopted a far bolder role than even Eisinger had discerned a decade earlier. I propose that policy makers at the national level stepped outside of the orthodoxy that their primary job was to act indirectly, through fiscal and monetary policy.

This assumption raises new questions. What factors led Washington to assume a more direct role in altering economic outcomes beginning in the late 1970s and early 1980s? Given America's ideological commitment to the position that free markets are, in and of themselves, more reliable generators of growth and entrepreneurial activity than government involvement, how were public policies aimed at ensuring access and funding for entrepreneurial innovators put in place without arousing fierce opposition both within Congress and, equally important, outside it? How did the "big picture" of federal involvement in such a massive undertaking escape both public notice and the usual "pork barrel" pressures? While these important questions must be addressed immediately, they will be explored at much greater length in the chapters that follow, chapters in which the policies themselves will be identified, examined, and analyzed.

It is crucial to recognize at the outset that the ways in which the federal government intervened, and its reasons for doing so, differed from those of the state governments—as well as the governments of other nations responding to the same competitiveness concerns. The defining features of the policy response at the federal level can be summed up as follows:

National security not economic development.

Ad hoc incrementalism/administrative pluralism, not national planning.

New entrants, not "national champions."

NATIONAL SECURITY, NOT ECONOMIC DEVELOPMENT

By the late 1970s, policy makers had become alarmed by America's declining competitive position because they recognized its implications for national security. Economic underperformance posed serious risks to its postwar global leadership position and, left unchecked, could undermine it. Gradually Washington became aware of the hand wringing in academic circles about the parlous state of the American economy, which dominated discussion and scholarship[15] throughout the 1980s, even until the early 1990s. America, these alarmists warned, seemed to be descending into a decline similar to that experienced by Great Britain at the end of the Second World War. The only question being actively debated was whether that decline would be as precipitous as England's had been, or whether it could be managed and slowed. If not, America would unceremoniously have to join the ranks of other "declining hegemons" and relinquish its postwar global leadership position, an issue eventually brought to the forefront of public attention by Paul Kennedy in *The Rise and Fall of the Great Powers*, published in 1987, as well as by others.[16] A series of Congressional Research Reports published during the 1980s, citing these scholarly concerns, demonstrates that it was not merely an academic debate, but one brought to the explicit attention of Congress.[17]

In other words, it was not declining competitiveness per se, but its impact on America's global leadership role that led Congress to act. That the *raison d'être* was primarily national security explains how public policies supporting entrepreneurial innovation and increasing competition were put in place without arousing fierce opposition. Nothing less than concerns about national security could have garnered the strong support of Republicans and de facto furthered the goals of some Democrats who may have been sympathetic to an industrial policy but recognized the futility of pushing forward such an agenda at such a time. Thus, a bipartisan consensus was forged out of a mutual concern for national security, which then became the basis for federal policies to boost technological innovation.

This observation has been confirmed by Kenneth Flamm's study of the

Figure 1.1
Federal Obligations for R&D (Defense vs. Total)

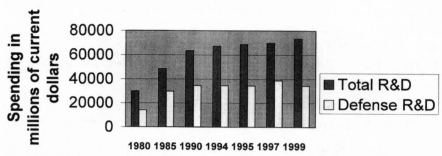

Source: U.S. Department of Commerce: Bureau of the Census: Statistical Abstract of the U.S. (2000).

computer industry whose rapid development, he claimed, was hastened by the military's need for powerful information processing capacity:

Since the mid-1950s, the only politically acceptable way to support the technological development of U.S. industry is to declare it militarily strategic. Rather intricate contortions have sometimes been required to justify military expenditures that are fundamentally intended to build up the general level of industrial and scientific capacity in the U.S. economy.[18]

This focus on national security as a justification for government support of technological innovation is reflected by the fact that federal Research and Development disbursements, always disproportionately allotted to the Department of Defense, increased from 46 percent in 1980 to 60 percent of the total given to all departments by 1985[19] (See Figure 1.1). Only later, after the collapse of the Soviet Union, did the national *raison d'être* for government support expand to include national economic security. This contrasts with the actions of the state and local governments, which, as Eisinger noted, had made economic development their exclusive and explicit priority.

Thus, by the 1980s the federal government had become a facilitator and participant in the market economy to a degree unaccustomed in America and inexplicable in conventional ideological terms. That it occurred at all— and began to accelerate under a Republican president, Ronald Reagan— reveals the extent to which Congress had become alarmed by America's global underperformance. This explains its readiness to accept the argument that fundamental changes in policy direction were necessary on grounds of national security. Without fully realizing it, members of Congress and successive presidents were "reading from the same page." Of course, this implicit consensus was never formalized or publicized. But an understanding emerged that something drastic had to be done, for the sake of national security if for no other reason, to reverse America's economic decline.

AD HOC INCREMENTALISM/ADMINISTRATIVE PLURALISM, NOT NATIONAL PLANNING

By placing the federal government at the forefront of structural economic change, I in no way mean to imply that its role was deliberate in the sense of an "industrial policy" or a "national plan." Far from it. The legislative, administrative, and judicial rulings that changed the rules of the game were put in place in piecemeal fashion, at different times, under different administrations over a twenty-five year period. The process of policy change began hesitantly in the waning years of the Carter Administration, grew more vigorous, acquiring intellectual conviction during the Reagan era, and accelerated in the 1990s under Clinton when its economic benefits became more clearly visible.

Still, there was no grand plan, no single architect, and no "industrial policy." The policy response was, in fact, uniquely American. It came about through a series of bipartisan, incremental adjustments to the realities of global competition, a consequence of American-led postwar commitments to free trade and to the institutions it had created to maintain and extend market economies. It took some time before successive congresses and presidents came to the gradual, but alarming, realization that comprehensive structural adjustments would have to be made before America could become globally competitive with its new economic rivals, especially Germany and Japan. This concern became more urgent as national security concerns heightened during the Reagan era.

Yet, despite the bipartisan incrementalism of the American political process, these policy changes had enormous transformative consequences for the American economy. As social policy writer Malcolm Gladwell reminds us in *The Tipping Point: How Little Things Can Make a Big Difference*, small changes feed on themselves, causing people and institutions to behave differently, ultimately crystallizing into huge shifts.[20] That describes precisely what happened here. However, since there was no national plan, the "big picture" of the impact of these incremental policy shifts, which propelled the U.S. economy into an era of entrepreneurial capitalism, went unnoticed.

There were other reasons Washington's policy response did not attract public attention and the usual "pork barrel" pressures. For one thing, the pluralism in the administration of these policies was as uniquely American as their ad hoc and incremental creation had been. The administration of federal R&D expenditures is a case in point. According to RaDiUS, the first comprehensive database of R&D in the United States, as of June 2000 the number of records in each level were as follows:

Figure 1.2
Number of Records in Each Level of RaDiUS

Level 1—24 agencies

Level 2—170+ bureaus

Level 3—1,550+ programs

Level 4—4,720 projects

Level 5—395,693 awards[21]

It took several years before what may have looked like wasteful duplication came to be recognized, paradoxically, as a strength, not a weakness. Josh Lerner, in his article "The Government as Venture Capitalist: The Long Run Impact of the SBIR Program," published in the *Journal of Business* in 1999, validated this insight. Noting that the funding for each grant was comparatively small and that funds were allocated by a number of government agencies, he suggested that the pluralism itself insulated any particular agency from political interference.[22]

There will still be those who question how federal policies involving the disbursement of millions of dollars in public funds to entrepreneurial companies could have escaped the attention of corporate lobbyists. Surely they would have put pressure on members of Congress to exert political interference on behalf of their more established constituents?

Peter Eisinger's book, even though it was aimed exclusively at the state level, offers some a clue:

The advent of the entrepreneurial state has gone almost unnoticed . . . But this is perhaps not surprising: the initiatives that define this new intervention are small, technically complex and difficult to evaluate . . . Furthermore the problems of the entrepreneurial state are not the products of mass political demands or the subjects of extended media debate or party platform planks. They appear instead to be technocratic experiments, emerging from the nexus of research institute, academic and bureaucratic connections to achieve highly general and almost universally popular employment goals articulated most often by political chief executives.[23]

Thus, the complex nature of the disbursements prevented them from becoming visible "red flag" issues that might have attracted the attention of the public, the media, or lobbies representing more established companies. Relegated to the realm of the technical, they became part of what one academic observer, John W. Kingdon, called the "hidden agenda."[24]

INNOVATIVE NEW ENTRANTS, NOT "NATIONAL CHAMPIONS"

If it seems obvious with hindsight that to increase global competitiveness it is first necessary to increase domestic competitiveness, it was not as obvious thirty years ago. At that time all the other industrialized countries, even pre-Thatcher Great Britain, decided to improve their global competitive positions by limiting domestic competition in key technologies, instead focusing their efforts on selecting and supporting national champions, even nationalizing them as France and Britain did.

Washington, on the other hand, did not attempt to choose winners over losers but instead set up an incentive structure that rewarded innovative new entrants. Why? DARPA reported that by the 1980s "studies sponsored by the National Science Foundation and others had found that small technology companies created 2.5 times as many innovations per employee as large companies."[25] Simultaneously during this period, the focus of antitrust policy became more clearly articulated to protect consumers over producers (and under the Clinton Administration even broadened to protect competitors over market-dominant companies) while regulatory protections were removed from established companies.

Thus, while America took the path of enhancing domestic competition as a precursor to enhancing the international competitiveness of U.S. companies, thereby shoring up our global leadership position, our rivals put in place industrial policies in which their governments sought to alter market outcomes by identifying and supporting winners over losers. In fact, entrepreneurial competitors were even suppressed. The end result was to make their economies less competitive than ours.

Once again, the computer industry exemplifies this trend. In the 1950s and 1960s West Germany, France, Britain, and Japan all embarked on crash programs to build their computer industries. Kenneth Flamm in *Targeting the Computer* explains:

Consolidating all computer production into one favored "national champion" was a popular solution. The hope was that by creating a smaller, national, "scale model" of IBM, the European markets dominated by IBM would be recaptured ... And it was a losing strategy in Europe ... Worse yet, no support was given to new entrants to go after new markets in a manner that was to prove successful in the United States.[26]

The British policy thrust in the pre-Thatcher era, according to Ian Hendry's *Innovating For Failure: Government Policy and the Early British Computer Industry* also differed from ours:

In both countries the great majority of sponsorship was directed towards established firms, but in America, government-funded development contracts also provided a starting point for entrepreneurial ventures.... There was nothing to compare with this phenomenon in Britain and when an entrepreneurial new venture to manufacture computers was set up in the 1960s ... the government went out of its way to discourage it.[27]

REVIEW OF THE LITERATURE

The contributions of all authors can only be judged in the context of prior scholarship and *American Shockwave: Entrepreneurial Capitalism and its Global Impact* is no exception. The New Economy is one area that has attracted furious debate, particularly during the past decade. The works selected as the focus for discussion are representative of the scholarship of this period and fall into two distinct camps. One believes in the New Economy, traces its emergence to the retreat of government, and views this as a positive development. The other does not accept the existence of a New Economy, and instead compares this period with turn-of-the-century unfettered laissez-faire capitalism. This school of thought is far less sanguine than the first. The current abdication of government to market forces, they predict, will ultimately have catastrophic consequences for the American economy. *American Shockwave* uses the ongoing debate as a starting point for discussion. However, by accepting that a new economic paradigm—entrepreneurial capitalism—has indeed emerged, yet identifying the federal government rather than the private sector as the catalyst, it sets itself apart from both prevailing scholarly camps.

To put the thesis presented here in the context of this prior scholarship, I am not the first to have noted profound changes in capitalism. Sten Thore's *The Diversity, Complexity and Evolution of High-Tech Capitalism*, published in 1995, observed:

The last quarter of this century has witnessed the emergence of a new economic order ... It is the capitalism of a new kind of turbulent American entrepreneurship. The emerging economic order is a new kind of capitalism that neither Adam Smith nor Karl Marx foresaw.

Yet Thore offered no insights as to its genesis, diffidently stating:

There exists no accepted name for this new order. In this book I shall use the labels "creative capitalism" and "high tech" capitalism. Those terms are tentative and may not be the terms that historians and economists eventually settle for.[28]

More important, Thore did not view this new form as distinctly or uniquely American, as argued here, but instead saw similarities with the capitalism of the Asian "tigers," observing: "The new capitalism is also the capitalism of the economic power-houses of the Far East."[29] All that, of course, was written before the Asian collapse of 1997 and 1998 made crystal clear the differences between "entrepreneurial capitalism" and the Asian model of "authoritarian" capitalism.

Some years earlier, Alvin and Heidi Toffler's *Creating a New Civilization: The Politics of the Third Wave* (1995) pinpointed, with prescient accuracy, the defining characteristics of this emerging new model. Unlike the Second Wave—which was based on conformity, uniformity, and bureaucracy—the Third Wave was flexible, fast paced, decentralized, and information rich.[30]

Yet this view—that American capitalism has assumed a new form—has not gone unchallenged. Some observers remain skeptical about the New Economy and argue that we are, in reality, returning to an earlier era of "unfettered capitalism" typical of the laissez-faire nineteenth century era, with the federal government abdicating its regulatory responsibilities. Far from going forward, these observers argue, generally from the vantage point of the political left, we are going backward, and they predict catastrophic social and economic consequences.

Typical of this school of thought was Robert Kuttner's *Everything For Sale: The Virtues and Limits of Markets* (1997), an impassioned reminder of the vital role of government in American economic history. The author lamented that Democrats beginning with Carter and personified by Clinton had become, albeit ambivalent, advocates of an unfettered free market: "The ideal of a free, self-regulating market is newly triumphant. The historical lessons of market excess, from the Gilded Age to the Great Depression, have all but dropped from collective memory . . . Government stands impeached and impoverished."[31]

In *The Future of Capitalism* (1996), Lester Thurow had expressed a similar fear that "survival of the fittest capitalism" stood alone today, "driving the forces of competition off the playing field," making it unable to find solutions to the ills of the next century.[32] Reinforcing the point that unfettered market forces, galvanized by free trade, are creating a grim present and a catastrophic future—as they did in the early part of the twentieth century leading to the Great Depression—was Donald Barlett and James B. Steel's *America: Who Stole the Dream?*[33] (1996). More recently, in *False Dawn: The Delusions of Global Capitalism* (1998), British academic John Gray feared that having "proletarianized" the middle classes, American-style laissez-faire capitalism was being proffered by "the Washington consensus" to governments abroad, where it would most likely lead to political ruin amid the destruction of social cohesion.[34] Edward Luttwak's *Turbo-Capitalism: Winners and Losers in the Global Economy* (1999), while appearing to suggest that this form of capitalism was something new, in fact described it as a "retreat of government," which implied a return to laissez-faire capitalism. Moreover, he, too, expressed concern about the "social inefficiencies" this form of capitalism has produced: broken families, increased crime, and the like.[35] And there are some economists, Paul Krugman among them, who, while they may not believe America is returning to the nineteenth century, explain the new economic prosperity as a temporary cyclical phenomenon and not a consequence of fundamental structural change. Writing in *Foreign Affairs* in 1998, Krugman claimed that "nothing fundamental has changed . . . Come the next recession, all this triumphalism will seem silly."[36]

My view is that this phenomenon is not temporary because it has been caused by structural changes that are permanent (unless the political consensus that produced them evaporates and relevant public policies are repealed) and that we are not "going back to the future" to an era of weak government and monopolistic corporations. The reality is the opposite: We have entered an era of unrelenting competition, both global and domestic, with American government playing a dominant role in setting the rules of the game. Abroad, our government has been underwriting the global institutions which ensure the rules are enforced so that world markets become, and remain, open and liberalized. At home, merger activity notwithstanding, government is actively policing competitive forces and, where necessary, underwriting them. Indeed, a vital feature of "entrepreneurial capitalism" is the degree to which the federal government has committed itself to maintaining competitive forces by redefining its mission to do so as a necessary condition of national security! Thus, Section 2A of the Small Business Act of 1997 (Public Law 85–536) stated: "The preservation and expansion of . . . competition is basic not only to economic well being, *but to the security of this Nation*" (emphasis added).

Identifying the actions of the American government as the causative factor in a new economic era does, however, lead to a different set of criticisms, raised this time by observers from the political right. Those observers, including the Tofflers and Sten Thore, who had acknowledged a new era, offered no clear answers about how this change occurred. They were certain of only one thing: American government was not the agent of change but possibly an impediment to it. Indeed, they cautioned that government must adapt itself to these new circumstances. Thus, Newt Gingrich, in a foreword to the Tofflers' book, emphatically stated: "The gap between objective changes in the world at large and the stagnation of politics and government is undermining the very fabric of our political system."[37]

With former House Speaker Gingrich himself unwilling to credit the federal government as the agent of structural changes that altered the economy, American business has been more than willing to step up to the plate and accept responsibility for transforming the American economy with bold restructurings and massive investments in technology throughout the 1980s and 1990s. David Hale, economist for the Zurich Group of financial companies, exemplified corporate America's view of its critical contributory role: "As in the period immediately before World War 1, the previous high point of globalization—there is a widespread belief that business and corporate leaders, not politicians, are the dominant personalities reshaping the global economic order."[38]

Indeed, he even went on to assert that "many believe that politicians have become irrelevant to the process."[39] This view was validated by Robert McTeer, president of the Dallas Federal Reserve Bank, who gave a televised speech on January 27, 2000, summarizing the relevant factors in the New Economy: "Add to technology and globalization, deregulation in most of the world, and privatization, and the replacement of the heavy hand of government with Adam Smith's invisible hand of the marketplace, and you've got what I would call a new paradigm."

Economists are not alone in crediting business with generating massive change. Corporate heads, who are all too familiar with the demanding environment of entrepreneurial capitalism because they must navigate its ever changing and highly competitive waters to survive, have been quick to argue that they were the instigators of change. Entrepreneur Mortimer Zuckerman's article, "A Second American Century," published in the prestigious journal *Foreign Affairs* in 1998, suggested that American prosperity derived from a series of unique structural advantages that were put in place by corporate America and reinforced by a unique culture of individualism.

Academic commentary from some quarters reinforced the view of business leaders that government was the least important force in generating change, and even possibly a loser to corporate initiatives. Daniel Yergin and Joseph Stanislaw's *The Commanding Heights: The Battle Between Government and the Marketplace That Is Remaking the World* (1998) crystallized the argument that there has been a global shift of power away from government and towards market forces in recent years.

No doubt corporate America did its part, adapting heroically in many cases to structural change imposed upon it. But it was emphatically not the instigator of those changes. Placing it first would be like putting the cart before the horse. In fact, I must repeat my case: The catalyst for economic transformation was American government at the national level. It created the structural underpinnings for this new form of capitalism. Entrepreneurial capitalism is a consequence of politics, not economics.

This, then, is a book about the role of government at the national level in recreating the economic realities of late twentieth century America, and it is written by a political scientist, not an economist. It is the first book to offer an explanatory framework for understanding the transformation of the American economy from an era of "regulatory capitalism," spanning thirty years from the Great Depression to the late 1970s, to a new model: entrepreneurial capitalism. It is also the first to place government at the center rather than at the periphery of profound economic change. It is offered as a work of analysis and synthesis, building upon and amplifying the excellent work of other more specialized contributors such as Kenneth Flamm, who examined government's role in the early computer industry, or Peter Eisinger, who analyzed state and local economic development policy.

Now that we have set out the main arguments to be developed in *American Shockwave: Entrepreneurial Capitalism and its Global Impact* we are in a better position to address some of the concerns bound to be raised by critics. I recognize that the central argument of this book may be controversial, even unacceptable, to observers on both sides of the political fence. Hence, a few brief comments in defense of my hypothesis may be appropriate at this point.

The political right might strongly object to any set of arguments that portray government as an effective agent of positive transformative change since they view the resurgence of the American economy as primarily market driven and private sector led. They will undoubtedly call attention to the fact that in 1998, for example, two-thirds of total R&D spending came from the private sector and only one-third from the federal government. I would remind them, however, that private sector R&D lagged government R&D expenditures during the 1970s, that it was practically even with federal R&D expenditures from 1980 until 1990, and only exceeded federal R&D expenditures from the mid-1990s, after the technology revolution was already underway[40] (See Figure 1.3).

More important, private venture capital commitments, a more likely source of investment in innovation than corporate R&D, had been a modest $2.2 billion in 1980 and took thirteen years to double. It was only from 1994 to 1999 that venture capital commitments expanded almost sixfold to approximately $46 billion in 1999.[41] Even today, the largest single source of early-stage seed capital for high-technology startups is not the private sector but government set-asides for the SBIR program administered by DARPA, according to that agency's own estimates[42] (See Figure 1.4).

Clearly, high-risk technology and biotechnology innovators have benefited hugely from early-stage federal support, particularly during periods when private sector investment has lagged because the payoffs appeared too distant. A fair accounting of the federal government's role might concede, for instance, that the Netscape browser built on the NSF-funded Mosaic project at the University of Illinois' National Center for Supercomputing Applications or that the joint government-funded Human Genome Project, begun in 1990, laid the groundwork for Celera Genomics' remarkably rapid breakthrough in sequencing human DNA in only two years.

Figure 1.3
R&D Expenditures Government vs. Industry

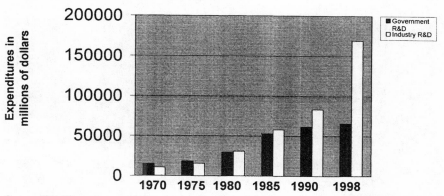

Source: U.S. Department of Commerce: Bureau of the Census: Statistical Abstract of the United States.

The scientific community itself, while applauding the Celera gene research as more complete and easier to use, acknowledged the head start provided by the Human Genome Project. But there are also market sectors where profitability is not assured yet where research and development are vital. Markets for space-related goods and services, space-based industrial facilities, and materials processing, in particular, remain futuristic even in the commercially driven "New Space Age." In its infancy the commercial potential of space was researched and funded by departments and agencies of the federal government, especially NASA, which still plays a large role today. In the biotechnology sector, efforts to develop vaccines for distant but alarming diseases such as the ebola virus have not attracted any interest from private sector pharmaceutical companies. The military has funded all research being conducted at government laboratories. And at a time when insect-borne diseases such as the West Nile River virus are becoming rampant in the United States, the private sector has ignored "bio-bug," R&D viewing it as unprofitable because it may not be patentable, leaving it to several agencies of the federal government (and some private foundations and farm groups) to fund and conduct research in this critical area.[43] The terrorist attacks of September 11, 2001 simply underscore the need for continuing federal incentives in high risk areas, such as power technology and security technology innovation and for bio-warfare detection and treatment.

On the other hand, the political left, which strongly opposed the defense build-up of the 1980s, may be puzzled to learn that national security served as the "back door" rationale for government action to boost national competitiveness through technology investments, since

Figure 1.4
Private Sector Venture Capital Commitments by Source 1980–1999

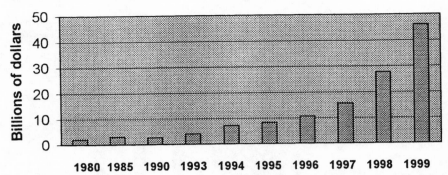

Source: U.S. Department of Commerce: Bureau of the Census: Statistical Abstract of the United States.

the "front door" rationale of industrial policy used by rival nations would have met with strong Republican and even many Democratic objections. The left may also be puzzled to learn that the Department of Defense's Advanced Research Projects Agency (DARPA) played a major role in funding the technological innovation generated by entrepreneurial companies, which has fueled our economic metamorphosis.[44] For example, provisions specifically facilitating and encouraging technology transfer to small businesses were inserted into several Defense Authorization Acts. DARPA, because it received the lion's share of funds, played a major role in making disbursements to small technology companies under the Small Business Innovation Research Program established in 1982 as well as the Small Business Technology Transfer Program enacted in 1992, even though both programs were administered overall by the Small Business Administration.

A Brief Preview of the Book

Here is a brief preview of what readers can expect to learn from subsequent chapters. With entrepreneurial capitalism defined as an intensely competitive environment marked by the federal government's commitment to supporting an accelerating pace of entrepreneurial innovation, Chapter Two examines in detail the differences between entrepreneurial capitalism and the early twentieth century laissez-faire model with which it is frequently compared, particularly by observers such as Edward Luttwak, who view the wave of corporate mergers in fields such as banking, oil, and automobiles as evidence that we are returning to an earlier era marked by monopolies and a retreat of government. The differences between laissez-faire capitalism and entrepreneurial capitalism are summed up by this comment, which owes much to the insights of the Tofflers:

We have shifted over the years from a stable to an unstable business environment, a protected to an unprotected market, centralized to decentralized management, economies of scale to "de-massification" and customization, to minds replacing machinery as assets and from a vertical to a "virtual" corporate model.[45]

The environment of entrepreneurial capitalism, unlike capitalism of the nineteenth century, is kaleidoscopic. Technological innovation has produced constant change so that established companies have had to become fast, flexible, and entrepreneurially minded in order to survive against agile new entrants, with no competitive advantage ever secure. Indeed, the pace of change has become so rapid that entrepreneurial companies less than twenty years old—like Dell and Microsoft—have begun to be considered "old" technology companies.

The chapter goes on to examine the various strategies used by successful private sector corporations as they adapt to the rapid changes imposed by new entrants, initially given access to the economy by the federal government's commitment to actively maintaining competitive market forces, and, where necessary, underwriting the competition. The private sector accommodated these new entrants, but we cannot underestimate the natural preference for established companies and their investors to seek predictability and stability by acquiring proprietary technologies, erecting barriers to entry, establishing dominant market share, and building brand images sufficient to deter, or at least diminish, competitive forces.

Chapter Three explores the genesis of entrepreneurial capitalism and locates its intellectual roots. They can be traced to the period after World War II, an era recovering from the ruins of trade protectionism run rampant, particularly after the Smoot Hawley Tariff Act of 1930 choked off global trade between America and the rest of the world. Determined to prevent such ruinous protectionism from ever again gaining a foothold, American leadership led the Allies to put in place the structural foundations for globalization in 1944, including institutions such as the International Monetary Fund and World Bank, whose primary missions were to shore up and develop economies in order to facilitate free trade. Those institutions were joined in 1948 by GATT (the General Agreement on Tariffs and Trade), which in 1995 became the World Trade organization, and by moves instigated by America encouraging European integration and a multilateral trading system, which led to the creation of the OEEC, now the OECD, designed to liberalize trade and foster economic development. Thus, "globalization" was not an impersonal exogenous force to which corporations had to adjust, but a deliberate consequence of political ideas and policy choices made by the Roosevelt and Truman Administrations after World War II and imposed upon them as well as on the rest of the world.

The chapter goes on to analyze why, having laid the groundwork for a global economy, America failed to prepare for its inevitable consequence: the injection of intense global competition into a domestic economy that proved ill prepared to compete. Many factors were to blame, including America's preoccupation with the Cold War and its own economic strength in the early postwar years in the absence of competition from war-ravaged Europe. America was abruptly forced to reexamine its declining competitive status following the Soviet's launching of Sputnik in 1958 and economic competition from the "miracle" economies of Japan and Germany. Then, between the 1960s and 1970s, America suffered an even more severe relative decline following the Vietnam debacle and the rise in oil prices in the 1970s.

There is mounting evidence that the policy changes that ultimately produced "entrepreneurial capitalism" were preceded by intense academic discussion and concern over declining U.S. economic performance. The findings of a Harvard Business School Colloquium, published in 1985, typified these concerns by warning that the United States had been losing its capacity to compete in the world economy over the last fifteen years (1970–1985) and that it needed to reexamine and modify its basic economic strategy. This academic soulsearching reached the informed public in books such as Paul Kennedy's *The Rise and Fall of the Great Powers* (1987), which predicted the ascendancy of Germany and Japan, suggesting ways in which America's decline might be slowed. Kennedy's efforts had been preceded by Mancur Olson's *The Rise and Decline of Nations* (1982), which offered reasons why certain economies became ossified. These academic concerns were ultimately made known to policy makers in Washington, forcing them to forge a political consensus for fundamental structural reform clearly evident by the late 1980s and 1990s. This is not to imply that American government, with its fragmentation and permeability, moved as one. Contradictory forces then, as now, were simultaneously pulling it in different directions. As late as 1997, economist Paul Krugman remained a naysayer, expressing a grim prognosis in *The Age of Diminished Expectations: U.S. Economic Policy in the 1990s*. Nevertheless, a clear line of policies did emerge that brought about entrepreneurial capitalism, the development of which is tracked in the next two chapters.

Chapter Four, "Legislating Entrepreneurial Capitalism," has as its goal an explanation of how this new model emerged and the public policies that made it a reality. Before turning their attention to the mechanics of economic revival, Congress and the President began the task of disman-

tling "regulatory capitalism." Enhancing competition became the goal.
Thus, on the one hand we will show the progression of reforms repealing
economic (but not social regulation) and, on the other, the enhanced role
of both the Anti-Trust Division of the Justice Department and the Bureau
of Competition at the FTC. The chapter begins with an examination of
the Domestic Council's 1977 report "The Challenge of Regulatory Reform" as Jimmy Carter took office. Deregulation gained momentum under Ronald Reagan and was legitimized as a bipartisan goal with Bill
Clinton's battle cry: "The era of big government is over!" In his January
2000 State of the Union Address, he trumpeted progress toward that goal
by stating that we now had the "smallest federal work force in forty
years." The chapter proceeds to identify the key legislative milestones
enacted to help meet the goal of enhancing American global competitiveness, beginning with the Stevenson–Wydler Technology Innovation
Act of 1980, the Bayh–Dole Patents and Trademarks Amendments Act
of 1980, and the Small Business Innovation Development Act of 1982,
and extending into the technology innovation legislation enacted during
the Clinton Administration. The strategy, as we shall see, was to utilize
the powers of the federal government to facilitate new entrants into the
economy and to underwrite the technological innovation they generated
until private capital became available or in areas deemed too risky even
for venture investors. Beneath this supportive policy climate entrepreneurial capitalism was nurtured. Not until the mid-1990s did the private
sector fully seize and extend the opportunities created.

Chapter Five, "Financing Entrepreneurial Capitalism," analyzes in
greater detail the variety and extent of federal investments in commercially viable, but high-risk, technologies that the private sector at the time
did not have the resources to support. By shifting its support from basic
to applied research, government vastly accelerated the process of commercially viable high-technology and biotechnology investment. Though
the best known breakthrough federal investments produced the Internet
and the Human Genome Project, many others occurred as a result of
expanded federal R&D spending that far outmatched private sector
R&D; through grants and subsidies that turned government into a "public venture capitalist"; by permitting private companies access to
federally funded patents; and through federal pioneering of more efficient business practices that took years to be adopted by the private
sector. For example, Internet based procurement was adopted with much
fanfare in 1999 by General Motors and Ford, yet the federal government
had begun to use this process, via DARPA, more than a decade earlier.
Direct federal investment in new technologies was always meant to be
transitional, the ultimate goal being to stimulate private sector activity
and to encourage the expansion and diversification of capital markets
which, like the Nasdaq created in 1971 or the ACE Network created in

1997, supported primarily younger companies. Simultaneously, but often grudgingly, successive Congresses made changes to the tax code to provide R&D tax credits to the private sector and to lower the capital gains tax to provide incentives for venture capital formation, which ultimately exploded from hundreds of millions in the 1980s to $20 billion in 1998, increasing to more than $46 billion in 1999.

The most critical factor in the emergence of entrepreneurial capitalism, however, was that the federal government now made it a policy priority to include new entrants in all phases of its enhanced technology initiatives, from training new vendors to use web-based procurement methods to setting aside funding and subsidies for young companies to granting contracts. For example, while established defense contractors such as McDonnell Douglas continued to receive federal contracts, so did young companies like Orbital Sciences, with pioneering technologies in the field of satellite delivery systems.

The incentives giving strong encouragement to the entrepreneurial sector stood in direct contrast to both Europe and Japan, which preferred policies discouraging new entrants in favor of subsidizing "national champions." That the rules of the game put in place by government for the first time now favored, protected, and supported new entrants into the economy cannot be overemphasized as a key factor explaining the technological dominance and economic performance of the United States relative to other industrialized economies, even though it took twenty years for the economic impact of these structural reforms to become clearly evident.

Chapter Six, "The Global Impact of Entrepreneurial Capitalism," examines entrepreneurial capitalism in the context of the embedded culture and history of America, comparing it with European and Japanese cultures, which have supported "managed/state guided capitalism" involving more frequent and coordinated government intervention in the economy. Even as Europe and Japan adapt to more deregulated and less protectionist environments, this chapter assesses the probabilities that they will fully implement the Anglo-American model to admit new entrants into their economies to the extent we have done. In Germany, for example, "unfair competition" laws have long served to protect established companies from new competitors in domestic markets such as retailing, much as tariffs were used to keep out foreign competitors. The chapter also assesses the extent to which they will be able to tolerate the adverse consequences of the shift to more competitive and less socially protective societies. France and Germany, in particular, have found several aspects of the adversarial style of entrepreneurial capitalism too harsh for their more consensual styles of managed capitalism (a lack of protections for labor, for example) and their leaders, Jospin and Schroeder, both socialists, have given voice to these concerns. Japan, too, is struggling amidst corporate restructurings, job losses, and reevaluations of established business practices such as longstanding relationships with vendors and suppliers.

The final chapter, "Backlash: The Limits of Entrepreneurial Capitalism," analyses the emerging forces that could derail the economic revolution. Two in particular will be analyzed: (1) the antiglobalization movement and (2) the undermining of investor confidence in technology investments, either through a prolonged secular bear market in technology stocks or by excessive regulatory intrusion into market-dominant companies such as Microsoft. The forces of globalization, as well as entrepreneurial innovation, are necessary to bolster the competition crucial to the existence of the New Economy.

Even if the full dimensions and genesis of entrepreneurial capitalism are not yet fully understood, there is a growing backlash in the United States against the perceived effects of globalization, such as the loss of jobs to less developed nations or competition from cheaper foreign goods. Technological change, too, has become so rapid that job obsolescence and job insecurity has spread to the middle class as well as to working Americans, increasing the possibility of a political backlash.

This anxiety found political expression among the political right through Patrick Buchanan, whose year 2000 bid for the presidency was made through Perot's Reform Party, which from its inception emphasized trade protectionism to protect Americans from job losses. It was also a policy endorsed by the unions, by Ralph Nader's Green Party in the Year 2000 presidential election, and by some elements of the Democratic Party. If the backlash from both the political left and the right grows, the future of America's commitment to free trade and globalization could be in jeopardy. Although globalization did not in and of itself produce entrepreneurial capitalism, it did introduce exogenous competitive forces into the American economy and, by doing so, provided the impetus for government to initiate structural change. Hence, "mobilization against globalization" here in America could undermine the underpinnings of entrepreneurial capitalism.

The chapter continues by assessing the likelihood that a global backlash against globalization in general, and entrepreneurial capitalism in particular, may intensify. These possibilities have been examined by several recent books, including John Gray's *False Dawn: The Delusions of Global Capitalism* and Edward Luttwak's *Turbo-Capitalism: Winners and Losers in the Global Economy*. Both authors correctly predicted the growing international opposition not only against global free trade but against American-style capitalism that has since emerged. In November 1999, the annual meeting of the World Trade Organization (WTO)—held in Seattle to discuss a fresh round of trade liberalization—was disrupted by an army of ragtag 1960s-style protesters who attracted a strong response from police in riot gear armed with tear gas. While the protests did not crystallize against globalization per se, they attracted union members protesting the loss of jobs, environmentalists, human rights activists protesting "corporate greed," consumer groups protesting genetically modified food, right-wingers protesting the loss of American sovereignty, and even some who feared world domination by America! Michael Moore, then Director of the WTO, characterized them as "dark forces" of tribalism and separatism, and one of the WTO participants was forced to declare that "trade is the ally of working people, not their enemy."

Should these disparate forces coalesce internationally (and unions worldwide believe they have found a unifying theme) they may, in the twenty-first century, serve to reinstate "back door" protectionism. The World Social Forum, inaugurated in Porto Alegre, Brazil, in early 2001 as a counterpoint to the World Economic Forum, may prove to be the catalyst. Protectionist forces, after all, did win out globally during the first third of the twentieth century, with ruinous consequences. Thus, if a new wave of international protectionism emerges, it could undermine globalization, which would, in turn, reduce the competitive pressures that served as the raison d'etre for alterations in public policy that ultimately produced "entrepreneurial capitalism." Ominously, the Clinton Administration had supported the injection of union and environmentalist concerns into trade negotiations, thereby alarming developing nations, who feared they might undermine further extensions of trade liberalization to the Third World.[46]

The chapter goes on to scrutinize a second factor with the potential to undermine entrepreneurial capitalism: namely, the possibility that private sector confidence in making high-risk investments in the technology and biotechnology sectors could be undermined by a prolonged bear market. It is still too soon to predict the impact of the ugly bear market of 2000–2001 that led to the unraveling of overstretched market valuations, particularly in the technology sector, after a series of interest rate hikes by the Federal Reserve Board deliberately slowed the economy. Furthermore, overbearing or misguided regulatory intrusions into the operations of market-dominant companies—which in reality face intense competitive pressures caused by entrepreneurial innovators, similar to the Microsoft antitrust case—might also have a dampening effect on investor confidence. Under these circumstances, the availability of private sector capital and access to receptive equity markets could shrink, resulting in a lessening rate of entrepreneurial innovation—hence competition from new entrants—thereby undermining entrepreneurial capitalism.

Entrepreneurial capitalism emerged in the 1980s because the federal government created the necessary conditions. Alarmed by America's declining global competitiveness, it made a strong commitment to accelerating the pace of public investment in high-risk technologies, simultaneously mandating access and funding for new entrants. During the 1990s, the continued pressures of global competition—and the development of diversified capital markets—enabled the private sector to extend the wave of entrepreneurial innovation initiated by the federal government's prior investments in high technology and biotechnology. I can only speculate that should a new wave of protectionism cause competitive forces to lessen, or should technologically innovative young companies become starved of access to private capital, entrepreneurial capitalism itself will be at risk. In the latter case the federal government will, no doubt, ride to the rescue. To do less would jeopardize America's preeminent global economic leadership position. These possibilities, however, remain at this point in time far in the future.

CHAPTER 2

Defining Entrepreneurial Capitalism and its Impact on Corporate America

INTRODUCTION

Entrepreneurial capitalism, fully established in America by the end of the twentieth century and defined by an accelerated and unprecedented rate of entrepreneurial innovation, shattered every rule that older, more established corporations had relied on to protect market share. Barriers to entry came crashing down; proprietary technologies were replaced by novel "disruptive" ones offering faster, cheaper solutions; companies with dominant market positions found themselves challenged by new competitors in newly created "spaces"; technology companies experienced "product cycle compression," and even mass market product brand names lost their luster.

The disruptive impact of entrepreneurial capitalism—volatile unpredictable and dynamic—was felt slowly at first. New entrants entered the economy at an accelerated rate only after a policy climate conductive to economic change was built within the federal government, starting in the late 1970s. Once convinced of the need to inject competitive forces into the economy in order to reverse grinding economic decline, Washington's policy response, beginning in the 1980s, was to dismantle regulatory protections for established companies while incrementally introducing a variety of incentives strongly supportive of technologically innovative new entrants. Thus, the rules of the economic game were changed for, but not by, corporate America. In reality, the infusion of competition and exposure to truly open market forces shocked the corporate establishment. While they had paid lip service to market competition, they had sought shelter from its effects, either through regulation or the efforts of highly paid lobbyists.

Now, however, competitive forces, jump-started by the infusion of public seed capital and by deregulation, multiplied exponentially as the private sector found the confidence and the resources to fund young companies on its own. Initially it was the junk bond financing pioneered by Michael Milken in the 1980s that gave life to upstarts such as MCI. As junk bonds became vulnerable to scandal, diversified sources of equity capital gradually became available to the private sector.

As the new century began, there appeared to be a new-found tolerance, indeed an appetite, for risk, and the amount of venture capital available to finance startups grew explosively while ever-younger companies went public. Corporations established venture capital units and even individual investors clamored to become venture capitalists. Publicly listed business incubators such as CMGI and Internet Capital Group initially found a receptive welcome in the stock market, while companies like Friedman, Billings, and Ramsey vowed to put the "public" back into initial public offerings.

As a result, an economy newly awash in venture capital experienced whirlwind change, which catapulted the private sector into a vast, kaleidoscopic and never ending free-fire zone. No industry or sector was immune. The most successful companies faced up to the challenges of entrepreneurial capitalism and went on to transform themselves into global titans. Those choosing not to acknowledge—or unable to respond quickly enough—to this new environment faced a grinding decline and eventual extinction.

A brief respite from the flood of new entrants going public was afforded by the Nasdaq plunge of 2000–2001, when a slowing economy and technology overcapacity caused an ugly bursting of the "tech bubble." In the ensuing debacle, some 210 Internet companies went out of business in the first two months of 2001 alone, venture capital commitments slowed, and initial public offerings[1] dried up. Nevertheless, those tempted to view the events of 2000–2001 as presaging a permanent respite from entrepreneurial competition may eventually recognize the "tech wreck" as an event more cyclical than secular.

After determining whether or not "entrepreneurial capitalism" in fact exists, this chapter will proceed to describe entrepreneurial capitalism in more detail, determine its impact on established companies, and examine precisely the ways in which corporate America adapted. Subsequently Chapters Three, Four, and Five track, analyze, and evaluate the catalytic role of the federal government in unleashing these transformative forces.

Entrepreneurial Capitalism or Laissez-faire Capitalism?

First and foremost, is "entrepreneurial capitalism" really new?

It is important to recognize that not everyone is convinced that the economic environment has really changed. Skeptics vociferously argue that the "new" economy is dangerously like the old one of the late nineteenth and early twentieth centuries. "Laissez-faire capitalism," they charge, has merely been given a new name.

Historians, of course, will correctly remind us that 1890–1920 was as much a period of entrepreneurial innovation[2] as anything we see today. But other comparisons are on much shakier ground. Some have drawn parallels between the industry consolidations that took place in oil, tobacco, and steel during laissez-faire capitalism and the contemporary trend towards ever-larger mergers, especially during the 1990s. The Exxon–Mobil merger approved in November 1999 was, after all, the largest industrial combination in history—and it was followed by other mergers even greater in size and scope.[3] Comparisons have also been made between the 1890–1920 period, when government was far less active, and what some now view as a similar surrender to market forces in the 1980s and 1990s. John Gray, author of *False Dawn: The Delusions of Global Capitalism*, summed up these late twentieth century concerns when he wrote: "The present situation is comparable to that at the turn of the past century. It was a golden age of capitalism, characterized by the principles of laissez faire: so is the present."[4]

Nevertheless, there are grave dangers in making such comparisons without examining all the relevant structural differences between the two eras. The period of laissez-faire capitalism is different from that of entrepreneurial capitalism in several important respects as reflected by the chart below.

Chart 2.1
Structural Differences Between the Eras

Laissez-Faire Capitalism	Entrepreneurial Capitalism
**Antitrust in its infancy	**Antitrust now explicitly committed to protecting consumers. Expanded under the Clinton Administration[5] to protecting competitors over market-dominant companies.
**Protectionist trade barriers insulated "trusts" from foreign competition	**Global free trade/exposure to foreign competition
**No access to diversified capital markets for new entrants	**Access to diversified capital markets for new entrants.

**No federal government involvement   **Federal government provides incen-
in entrepreneurial innovation   tives and mandates access to new en-
                                                             trants.

A combination of all these factors made market competition by the 1990s much more intense than it had been between 1890–1914, a period which had led to the ruthless extinguishing of entrepreneurial forces, increased consolidation, and the emergence of monopolies. For example, when John D. Rockefeller, Sr. assembled Standard Oil in 1900, he merged with more than fifty companies, closing down over two-thirds in the process of establishing control. By contrast, the Exxon–Mobil merger in 1999 was justified in terms of increased market competition.

Moreover, the predicament of the steel industry today, compared with the absence of competition a century ago, further illustrates this point. U.S. Steel, assembled when Andrew Carnegie and J. P. Morgan joined forces in 1899, had achieved at its zenith a 70 percent market share in certain types of steel. Compare that with USX's predicament a century later, when the former U.S. Steel found its market share being eaten away by entrepreneurial mini-mills like Nucor, with twice its market capitalization. Robert W. Crandall of the Brookings Institution maintained that contemporary competitive pressures have increased as thirteen old-line integrated steel companies faced some forty U.S. mini-mills with 45 percent market share producing carbon steel for 40 percent less.[6]

The Economic Environment of Today versus Yesterday: A Closer Look

Business historian Thomas McCraw at the Harvard Business School has tallied the wave of consolidation during the laissez-faire era. Between 1897 and 1904, some 4,227 companies had been merged into 257. By 1904, only 318 firms controlled 40 percent of the nation's manufacturing assets.[7] Compare that to today when no one firm, or group of companies, controls a percentage of manufacturing assets as large. Then antitrust was in its infancy. The Sherman Anti-Trust Act of 1890, considered ineffectual, was followed by the Clayton and FTC Acts of 1914, which targeted anticompetitive practices. For the most part this wave of corporate consolidation proceeded amid government indifference, receding only when the pressure of a furious political backlash forced the breakup of "trusts."

Compare the situation today. By the late 1970s, the federal government not only began dismantling economic regulations, which had actually served as protections for established companies, and enforced antitrust more vigorously, its role was far from passive or indifferent as it had been in the early twentieth century, before the Progressive movement altered public policy. On the contrary, the contemporary policy climate is one committed to actively promoting competitive forces. With its support for free trade (compared with the protectionism of industrial-era America) the federal government cannot be relied on (other than intermittently) to shield established companies or entire industries from foreign competition as it had done in the past. Moreover, through its vigorous support for the entrepreneurial sector via a range of public policies providing incentives to young technology and biotechnology companies, the federal government has served as a catalyst for the subsequent explosion in the number of innovative competitors entering the economy. In addition, as the private sector, by the mid-1990s, found the confidence to fund new entrants on its own, the marketplace evolved rapidly into a ferocious free-fire zone completely unlike that of any previous era.

As the effects of entrepreneurial capitalism began to be felt, the private sector found itself forced to adapt and restructure. To accommodate the much more demanding environment it now faced, a number of compensatory strategies evolved. From this perspective, mergers, regarded by some as an indicator of a less competitive contemporary environment, must be reconsidered in a new light. Mergers are only one of a variety of strategies—and one not always successfully implemented—employed by corporate America struggling to cope with the frenetic environment of entrepreneurial capitalism. Indeed, the skepticism of investors has often pounded the stock prices of acquiring companies. For example, when AOL proudly announced its merger with Time Warner in January 2000, its stock price promptly plummeted by more than 45 percent.

The chief point is that mega mergers may not succeed in creating dominant market share and shielding large companies from brutal competition. This was brought into sharp focus by the surprising results of a study by Pankaj Ghemawat of the Harvard Business School and Fariborz Ghadar of Pennsylvania State University, published by the *Harvard Review of Business* in July 2000. The authors, who had begun the study intending to prove the theory that megamergers led to success in international markets, studied over forty years of market-share data for companies in twenty industries. They were surprised to conclude the opposite—namely, that market share ultimately decreased for giant globals in all sectors other than the semiconductor industry. Some reasons why, the authors speculated, included the rapid entry of smaller competitors fueled by advances in technology, lowcost producers, and niche marketers.[8]

External strategies aside, corporations have also had to restructure and reengineer their internal operations, as well as redefine their corporate missions. Before we can evaluate these internal and external corporate responses to their new, more challenging environment, however, we must return to our initial task: defining entrepreneurial capitalism.

Defining Entrepreneurial Capitalism and Evaluating its Consequences

I should clarify at the outset that entrepreneurial capitalism, with its acceleration of entrepreneurial innovation, emphatically does not mean the return to a nineteenth century precapitalist economy of "mom and pop" businesses struggling to survive! It is not synonymous with small! By the late 1990s, ready access to equity capital meant that ever-younger companies were being taken public, rapidly acquiring market valuations in excess of one billion dollars (the cut off for being considered a "small-cap" stock). Even the "generals" of the stock market were being challenged, often eclipsed, in terms of market capitalization by young entrepreneurial upstarts. For example, in early December 1999, Yahoo, upon its inclusion in the Standard & Poors 500 Index, acquired a market capitalization double that of General Motors, albeit briefly. A day later it was reported that GM's chairman of the board took the company to task for having a market share no bigger than the one it had in 1920. And for several months of that year the entrepreneurially founded Microsoft had a market capitalization at times bigger than 100-year-old General Electric, the only original member of the Dow Jones Industrial Average (DJIA) in 1896. By the start of 2000, Microsoft, struggling under the weight of its antitrust troubles and competitive threats, was itself eclipsed by Cisco Systems, which briefly overtook General Electric. Other "generals" of long standing, like Woolworth or original Dow member Westinghouse, found themselves de-listed, the latter taking on the CBS label, eventually swallowed by Sumner Redstone's upstart Viacom. Dow stalwarts Sears, Goodyear, and Union Carbide found themselves unceremoniously dumped, to be replaced by Intel, Microsoft, and Home Depot, all entrepreneurially founded companies.

In fact by the end of the twentieth century, the market capitalizations of younger, entrepreneurially founded and managed companies surpassed that of several more established competitors, even if only briefly: AOL's premerger market value at one time exceeded not only IBM's, but that of Disney, CBS, and Viacom combined, while Charles Schwab's briefly exceeded that of Merrill Lynch, forcing Merrill to revamp its business model entirely. Even less well known entrants like 1 2 Technologies, a company producing supply chain management software, had, by March 2000, a market valuation larger than venerable S&P member Dow Chemical.

What entrepreneurial capitalism does mean is that much smaller new entrants have accelerated the pace of change and compounded already fierce competitive pressures. Consequently, no monopoly is permanent, nor is any proprietary advantage ever secure. Barriers to entry, especially with ready access to equity capital, have fallen, introducing new competitors into the marketplace overnight. New technologies, new products, and new business platforms and practices have made monopoly—a key feature of laissez-faire capitalism—a thing of the past. Thus, Edward Luttwak's claim that monopoly is the defining characteristic of "turbo-capitalism" is not supported by the facts.[9]

Sten Thore in his 1995 book, *The Diversity, Complexity and Evolution of High-Tech Capitalism*, emphasized the disruptive effects of this new environment: "Monopoly profits and cartels are becoming rare as fierce international competition and the proliferating technical possibilities to develop alternative manufacturing processes make it difficult for any one producer to protect exclusive information or exclusive designs."[10]

Thore's insight has been confirmed by several other academic observers. Business economists Carl Shapiro and Hal Varian in *Information Rules: A Strategic Guide to the Network Economy* contrasted the "industrial" with the "information" economy:

The industrial economy was populated with oligopolies . . . In contrast, the information economy is populated by temporary monopolies. Hardware and software firms vie for dominance, knowing that today's leading technology or architecture will, more likely than not, be toppled in short order by an upstart with superior technology.[11]

Similarly, Kevin Kelly's *New Rules for the New Economy* predicted that the new economy may lead to monopoly-like concentrations of power, but they would be temporary, quickly overthrown by new concentrations.[12] The brutal realities of entrepreneurial capitalism even surfaced at the level of the popular business press and were frankly and widely discussed. Robert Baldock's *The Last Days of the Giants: A Route Map for Big Business Survival* claimed to offer readers a "highly innovative look at a major concern for large corporations in the new millennium—the threat of smaller, quicker, more flexible competitors."[13] Even advertising copy took note of the critical features of this "new business paradigm:"

It's the Age of ALL—But can You handle it?

All the rules keep Changing . . .

Yesterday's collaborators? Today's Competitors.

The company you want to buy Now Wants to Buy you!![14]

Corporate CEOs have frankly confirmed that with rapidly evolving markets and products, no one company could be secure in its present market position. The title of a book by Intel's chairman and cofounder, Andy Grove, *Only the Paranoid Survive,* was oddly revealing of the market insecurity this engendered, especially among entrepreneurs themselves. Grove doubtless had in mind his own company's adjustment to the speed of technological innovation, which has made product life cycles short and company dominance "ephemeral." It was one of the factors affecting his company's profitability. By the end of the 1990s, Intel realized that the normal eighteen-month product cycle was not enough to earn back its massive R&D expenses at the same time it faced competition not only from low-cost, sub-PC models but also from the move to non-PC-based applications. Intel's response (like many other of its high-technology counterparts) was to diversify into the computer networking business and into providing chips for a variety of applications. This was accomplished by buying out other companies and making investments in others, a set of survival strategies to be examined at length later in the chapter.

Echoing the siege mentality expressed by Grove, Jeff Bezos, Amazon.com founder and CEO, confessed in a television interview that he came to work "terrified" every morning and advised his employees to do the same. Hyperbole, no doubt, but equally revealing all the same. Emphasizing the pace and unpredictability of change, John Chambers, president and CEO of Cisco Systems, during an appearance at a televised "Internet Summit" at Stanford University on February 27, 2000, looked across the podium at the other companies present (which included Microsoft, Yahoo, eBay, Amazon.com, AOL, and Intel) and predicted that in ten years half the companies on the podium probably would not be in existence. When Chambers made that prediction no one in the audience could have even remotely imagined that market darling Cisco itself might be in jeopardy. Yet by spring 2001 the company had lost billions in market capitalization as its stock price plunged, while technology experts such as Brett Swanson of the Gilder Technology Report predicted technological obsolescence for the company unless it changed its focus. Its products, developed to overcome bandwidth scarcity, were becoming irrelevant as bandwidth abundance was being rapidly created by younger, technologically innovative optical networking companies such as Avanex.[15]

The acceleration of new entrants has meant that companies have had to constantly transform themselves to have any hope of survival, making speed, agility, and adaptability critical. New companies are required to enter the marketplace prepared to modify their business models and adapt to this hypercompetitive environment. Agilent Technologies, spun off from its corporate parent Hewlett Packard in November 1999, even incorporated agility into its name and made the necessity of adapting to speed part of its core mission statement in its 1999 Annual Report:

Success demands that we "pick up the pace" in everything from decision-making to product development to responding to customers. Greater speed has to be coupled with agility—the agility to be nimble, well co-ordinated and mentally resourceful. Our name is based on the word "agile" and reminds us of this value.[16]

Responding and adapting to constant change has forced established corporations to reengineer both their internal organizations and redefine their corporate missions.

Restructuring the Organization

It is important to recognize that corporate America has transformed itself in ways John D. Rockefeller, Sr. would not even remotely recognize. In assembling the companies that became Standard Oil and in eliminating and merging several of the companies he acquired, Rockefeller had sought to impose centralized management and create a hierarchical organization under his sole control. In sharp contrast, today's CEO must process, evaluate, and respond to crushing amounts of information faster and faster. This need for organizational speed and agility prompted Bill Gates, co-founder and chairman of Microsoft, to suggest in *Business @ The Speed of Thought* that corporate America urgently needed to develop "digital nervous systems" in order to circulate information more efficiently throughout their companies.

To speed up response time, the new corporate organizational model incorporates decentralization, flattened hierarchies, and "bottom-up" learning, quite different from the "top-down" command and control model of the industrial era. Consider General Electric, pioneer of "reverse mentoring"—in which senior executives increase their knowledge of the Internet and e-commerce by meeting weekly with a younger person on their staff who is an expert on the subject.[17] In introducing "reverse mentoring" into GE's U.S divisions, then Chairman and CEO Jack Welch, Jr. observed: "E-business knowledge is generally inversely proportional to both age and and the height of the organization ... I find this to be a wonderful tool, among many others, to change that equilibrium."[18] The advertising world, quick to spot new trends, took a humorous shot at this practice through its series of Ameritrade ads, in which a young punk working the copying machine was summoned to teach the CEO how to trade online.

General Electric also pioneered practices such as "boundaryless selling," in which managers from one part of the company were expected to help colleagues in other divisions market different products and services. Lateral or horizontal connections thus joined the "bottom-up" connections to reengineer the organization.[19] Similarly in the quest for speed and agility Jorma Ollila, CEO of Finland's Nokia, deliberately built chaos and uncertainty into his company by introducing the practice of job switching among executives. His goal was to encourage new ideas and discourage status quo thinking. As Ollila explained: "We want to build a certain amount of chaos and a sense of urgency. Switching also helps people learn from one another."[20]

The Internet, more than any other new technology, destabilized the business models of established companies, rapidly rendering their existing models obsolete. While General Electric's former CEO Jack Welch exulted that it had the potential to make "old companies young again,"[21] it also enabled startups to create new "spaces," rapidly amass huge market share, and become fierce competitors. For example, the book business was revolutionized in less than two years by Amazon.com, forcing market leader Barnes and Noble to respond, belatedly, with its own web-based model. High-flying Borders was altogether too late with its own Internet strategy and by early 2000 was up for sale, surviving by the skin of its teeth.

With the transparency of pricing information and ease of online access, entire industries, ranging from the brokerage industry to the travel industry, have been changed, forcing them to reinvent themselves in order to survive. For example, faced with low-cost air travel posted on the Internet, corporate travel specialist Rosenbluth Travel had to alter its business model from one based on receiving commissions from airlines for corporate bookings—once its core business—to one based on getting paid by corporations to act as "travel specialists" in arranging the cheapest form of corporate communication, which may or may not include traveling, substituting teleconferencing in certain situations.

The whirlwind change at "Internet speed" forced almost minute-to-minute reevaluations of even the most successful business models as new challenges and opportunities presented themselves. For example, the business models of Internet service providers, particularly market leader America Online, was threatened by free Internet access from competitors AltaVista, NetZero, and Juno. Since AOL relied on subscriber fees for the major portion of its revenues, this threat put pressure on the company to upgrade its future services to include premium access channels by developing broadband capability. To help implement its strategy of "AOL Everywhere" the company responded in Europe by starting up a free Internet service in the United Kingdom called Netscape Online.[22] In the United States it responded by announcing a merger with Time Warner in January 2000, thereby gaining proprietary broadband access (and 20 million new customers) via Time Warner's cable division as well as proprietary content from all Time Warner's media properties. A survival strategy indeed, but one not apparent to investors who subjected AOL's stock to a body-slamming decline.

Computer-box makers, even newly established companies like Gateway and Dell, found themselves having to adapt their business platforms to accommodate a shift to non-PC applications, as well as to the challenge of low-cost PCs. One alternative was to offer free internet access to customers as an inducement to purchase a computer. For example, in 1999 Dell launched DellNet in Europe, making it the first major computer manufacturer in Europe to offer free Internet access, a strategy it was slow to begin in the United States. Its rival, Gateway, under CEO Jeffrey Weitzen, adapted its business model, leveraging its existing platform with its "Beyond the Box" strategy. Its success was underscored by the fact that by 1999, 40 percent of Gateway's revenues came from non-PC business applications.[23] Compaq, which once had a leading share of the market, was slow to respond to the Internet and adapt its business model accordingly. In consequence, it found its profitability erode and its share price plummet in 1999, at which time the company was forced to begin the painful process of transforming its business model to include the Internet and to add services to augment its hardware product line.

The list of potential challenges to existing business models in the new era of entrepreneurial capitalism remains endless requiring established corporations to recognize the mandates it has imposed: adapt by becoming agile and flexible or face extinction. Hence, mature companies have been forced to become as entrepreneurially minded as the innovative entrepreneurs they now faced in the marketplace. By the mid- to late 1990s, examples of established corporations undergoing transformations abounded. Stodgy AT&T, faced with a stagnant long-distance business being daily undermined by upstarts to whom it was required to lease its lines, future competition from the Baby Bells, as well as by the growing threat of cheap Internet telephony, began the process of metamorphosis under CEO Michael Armstrong in 1998. Adding to its wireless division, it found novel sources of transmission via cable, seeking to become a high-speed voice, data, and video provider through its purchases of TCI, Liberty Media, and Media One. AT&T turned itself into an integrated telecommunications provider, hoping to position itself to compete more effectively with entrepreneurial rivals such as MCI WorldCom and Global Crossing. By fall 2000 even that strategy had fallen apart as consumers resisted purchasing "bundled" services from a single provider and AT&T announced a restructuring into four parts.

New entrants have, from the start, recognized the importance of utilizing an adaptable business platform capable of morphing into many uses. Consider, again, Amazon.com, which entered the Internet space as a bookseller. Rapidly acquiring a market capitalization whose justification would have required it to sell every book in the universe, founder and CEO Jeff Bezos used the advantage of being first in the "Internet retailing space" to adapt his business platform to accommodate an increasing variety of products and services ranging from drugs to hardware to running an auction site, including a short-lived joint venture with venerable Sotheby's.

Paradoxically, if corporate structures themselves have changed to accommodate change, focus has been one key to staying alive, leading to an explosion of "outsourcing," which allows companies, especially technology companies, to concentrate on their core competencies. Even Microsoft contracted out its customer service functions to subcontractors such as Zomax. This strategy was made more feasible with the advent of electronic business through the Internet, which made it possible for corporations to more easily outsource functions such as accounting, link management teams in different locations, allow sales forces to communicate more effectively, and easily locate lowest cost suppliers in order to manage supply chains more efficiently.[24] Under entrepreneurial capitalism, temporary agencies like Robert Half International have flourished because they provide corporations with a flexible labor force.[25]

Perhaps the most extreme organizational strategy of all has been the emergence of "virtual corporations," which focus on a core function and outsource everything else to an ever-changing array of subcontractors to preserve maximum flexibility. The movie industry was one of the first to embrace the "virtual corporation." It is an industry that not only faces fickle and unpredictable consumers but since the breakup of the studio system has also had to cope with competition from independent producers, free-agent movie stars, and myriad other forces of change. Intense pressures such as these have led to the emergence of "virtual studios" such as Dreamworks that do not employ writers, directors, or movie stars permanently but work with a variety of people and companies on a project-to-project basic as independent contractors, thereby conserving fixed overhead costs and maximizing flexibility.

Business strategist Geoffrey Moore goes a step further in suggesting that all corporations should make this their modus operandi in order to compete in the New Economy. In *Living on the Fault Line: Managing for Shareholder Value in the Age of the Internet* Moore suggests that companies identify a "core" function, one that gives them a competitive advantage. Company resources should be targeted exclusively at "core" functions. All other functions, such as accounting, he views as "context," functions which should be outsourced or even eliminated. In an era of rapid change, the "core-to context" ratio must be constantly monitored and if the competition has caught up new "cores" identified.[26]

Inside the Corporation: Redefining the Mission

Reengineering the organization, however, has not been sufficiently transformative in the age of entrepreneurial capitalism. Corporations have also been required to redefine their missions and reexamine their identifications with specific products or services. Technology companies have had to cope with product cycles so short they are unable to earn back R&D costs. Consumer companies have had to adapt to the challenge of fickle customers who, newly armed with the advantage of price transparency because of the Internet, are more knowledgeable than ever before.

Market information, combined with technology, has made it more feasible, as well as profitable, to "demassify" and exploit niche markets, a trend first noted by the Tofflers in *Creating a New Civilization: The Politics of the Third Wave*. Established companies slow to respond, like Sears, found market share and profitability eroded by specialty retailers such as the Gap or low-end ones like Old Navy or Target. In the computing industry, the trend moved to mass customization, much as the Tofflers had predicted. Both Dell and Gateway offered to build to customer specifications, leading to lower inventory costs, as well as healthy cash flow for them and better service for their customers. Even cars could be customized and ordered on the Internet. Technology consultants such as the Gartner Group predicted that mass portal sites on the Internet, like Yahoo or Excite, could eventually face competition from "niche-interest portals" targeting specialized markets such as finance or medicine in the near future.[27]

The corporate business model in the age of entrepreneurial capitalism is, therefore, very different from the corporate model prevailing during the laissez-faire/industrial capitalist era. Then, unlike now, large companies with mass production for mass markets became the standard for profitability, with Henry Ford proclaiming that his customers could have any color as long as it was black! Today, information technology has altered and made obsolete the textbook concept of "economies of scale" that once gave large companies a competitive edge over smaller ones. It has been replaced by what the Tofflers have called "economies of speed" because "since markets change constantly, position is less important than flexibility and maneuverability."[28] The advantage under entrepreneurial capitalism has shifted to the smaller, innovative new entrant.

In an era of demassification and niche markets, pleasing consumers has become critically important to profitability, and forging deep relationships with customers has become critical to success. This explains the market's receptivity to companies such as Broadvision, which realized early on that the Internet was not simply a broadcast mechanism but also a potential customer-relationship mechanism. Its software enabled companies to tap and keep track of customer purchases to better build those relationships. Internet technology generally made "data mining" techniques more sophisticated,[29] making it possible for companies such as Siebel Systems, Blue Martini Software, and Engage Technologies to provide software to draw profiles of net users and build new types of customer relationships. Other entrepreneurs have spotted opportunities to create software that has enabled suppliers to forge deep relationships with "hyperaffiliated" customers (participate.com) or to glean market research from customers who complained (feedback.com).

Corporations have had to reexamine and redefine their missions in other important ways in an era of entrepreneurial capitalism. Ironically, the value of global consumer product brands so entrenched in consumers' minds that that they constituted an insurmountable advantage may have lessened, causing companies to reevaluate the value of global branding.[30] Business journalist Richard Tompkins offered an intriguing explanation of why this has occurred. Product-based brands, he speculated, have become obsolete in a global and highly competitive economy precisely because they can fall prey to rapidly changing fashions and to alternative products from competitors. He offered examples of three former consumer giants: Levi Strauss, Kellogg, and Woolworth. In 1997, Interbrand, a global consulting firm, placed Levi Strauss as the world's eighth greatest brand, but two years later, Levi's abruptly announced closures of half its U.S. manufacturing capacity after sales fell 13 percent—which was in addition to the closure of thirteen U.S. plants and four European plants a year before. CEO Robert Haas, in a comment which revealed the company's late recognition of the demanding environment of "entrepreneurial capitalism," belatedly acknowledged, "Consumer trends move not just locally or regionally now, but globally, and with breathtaking speed."[31] Kellogg cereals, in sixteenth place in the Interbrand study in 1997, had weak earnings by 1999 caused by changing consumer breakfast preferences and low-cost unbranded competitors, while venerable Woolworth had actually ceased to exist, closing all its U.S. stores and turning itself into a sportswear retailer, Venator. Tompkins regretfully commented: "These days it seems a history spanning generations and a high ranking position in the list of the world's best-known names is just not enough to cut it in the world's marketplace."[32]

In the era of "entrepreneurial capitalism," with its imposition of speed and agility, informed observers of the consumer marketplace recognize a new phenomenon—the "philosophy brand"—which is elastic enough to provide companies with infinite flexibility: "Philosophy brands express a certain attitude towards life . . . the brand can export that attitude and that philosophy and stretch it into a variety of different areas."[33]

Chris Cleaver, director of brand development at Interbrand, added:

Markets are changing dynamically and the brand that is too closely associated with any particular product format or physical manifestation, and which doesn't use the power of that relationship to extend and evolve into new formats and markets, is probably destined to curl up and drop off the perch.[34]

Exemplifying this new model of the versatile and elastic brand is United Kingdom-based Virgin, with interests in a wide range of products and services from railways and airlines to vodka, while in the U.S. Ralph Lauren and Martha Stewart exemplify "position brands" organized around the theme of "lifestyle" rather than being tied to specific products. Thus, they have retained the advantage of flexibility: "The brands that have prospered are those that retained the core of what they were but reinterpreted themselves every now and again to make themselves relevant."[35]

When Coca-Cola, which had focused on expanding global distribution during the 1980s and early 1990s, found itself struggling with plunging profits by 1999 it announced that it, too, was launching a line of clothing, belatedly adapting to the concept of "philosophy branding." Perhaps General Electric was being prescient in the 1950s when it chose "Progress is our most important product" as its advertising slogan on General Electric Theater, emphasizing its corporate philosophy!

CORPORATE SURVIVAL STRATEGIES

Adapting to the External Environment

By the end of the twentieth century the vertically integrated corporate model with centralized management operating in a stable, government-protected environment had vanished. Hypercompetition and kaleidoscopic change introduced by new entrants into the economy arrived to take its place. Having reorganized their internal operations and redefined their company missions, corporate America was simultaneously forced to turn its attention to strategies for surviving the much more demanding external environment of entrepreneurial capitalism. As we shall soon see, no one strategy guaranteed success.

Survival Strategy Number One: Mergers

Mergers have been, without question, one survival strategy to cope with conditions of extreme competition and constant change. On closer examination, however, this has been the strategy of choice mainly in certain heavily fragmented but fast growing sectors such as banking, telecommunications, or pharmaceuticals, where achieving global scale is critical and where having less than 10 percent of global market share is considered undesirable. In addition, mergers have also been a trend in beleaguered industries such as oil that are unable to generate "top-line" growth because of overcapacity and long-term changes in demand. In this case, the justification for mergers has been that companies can improve their balance sheets through cost cutting.

Banking in the late 1990s underwent a spate of mergers, the largest of which in America was undoubtedly the marriage of insurance conglomerate Travelers with Citibank to form Citigroup in 1998. In the United States, banks experimented with ways to stave off domestic forces that have been making them less important as sources of capital and advice. They no longer had a monopoly on money and information. In today's deregulated financial markets institutional investors, like mutual funds, can supply capital while companies such as General Motors or G.E. Capital float their own bonds. Since information can be transmitted electronically, smaller rivals gained equal advantages. In addition, the banking industry increasingly faced competition from European banks whose "universal banking" model allowed them to underwrite securities and engage in consumer banking and a range of activities which, until 1999, were disallowed U.S. banks under the 1933 Glass–Steagall Act. Its repeal will no doubt lead to an acceleration of merger activity in the banking sector along the lines of the Citibank model.

Still it should be emphasized that size alone may not save banks from the unrelenting forces of global competition. Japanese banks, among the world's largest during the mid-1980s, stumbled under a load of bad debt in the 1990s. Business practices unique to Japan, such as consensus decision making by centralized boards, deepened the problems because it made responsibility shared and blame difficult to assign.[36] In the United States, a study of 661 bank holding companies between 1991 and 1997 on behalf of the Conference Board in New York by economist Kevin Stiroh came to the conclusion that despite a wave of mergers that created megabanks, there was little evidence that bigger banks were more efficient, productive, or profitable than smaller banks. Stiroh suggested that technology may be a cost leveler for smaller banks.[37]

Oil has been another industry where consolidation appeared to be the preferred form of adaption to global competition and technological innovation. In 1998, British Petroleum and Amoco merged, followed by Total and Petrofina in France and Exxon and Mobil in the United States. However, the circumstances at the end of the twentieth century were far different from those prevailing at its beginning. Protectionist trade policies and underdeveloped foreign competitors created a stable business environment in which John D. Rockefeller was free to buy up, then close down thirty-two of fifty-two smaller companies, consolidating his grip on Standard Oil through vertical integration and centralized management. Today oil giants face a range of competitive threats, not the least of which have been periods of global recession and price collapse. Even under conditions of robust demand and price recovery, other long-term factors depressing demand remain. Mark P. Mills, a research fellow at the Competitive Enterprise Institute,[38] pointed out that oil, while still the dominant transportation fuel, has been replaced by electricity as the fuel for the new information economy because information technology equipment runs on electricity. Moreover, electricity generation uses a variety of energy sources including coal (52 percent), gas (15 percent), nuclear reactors (19 percent), and hydroelectric power (10 percent). Factor in the new fuels such as solar and wind power, and new technologies such as lead acid batteries to power vehicles and hydrogen-powered fuel cell electricity, and the pressures on oil companies become abundantly clear.[39]

Despite short-term spikes in oil prices (as during 2000–2001), other long-term factors could depress demand and increase supply potential. On the one hand, cars are more fuel efficient than they were twenty years ago, while, on the other, new technologies, such as remote imaging and supercomputers, have lowered the costs of exploration per barrel of oil by 75 percent. These same technologies have simultaneously increased oil recovery from wells thought unproductive or from terrain thought too difficult, increasing supply pressures. In 1999, for instance, smaller, more nimble companies such as Triton Energy of Dallas rapidly developed a field off the coast of Guinea, West Africa, in fourteen months; by 2001 projected output climbed from 4,500 barrels daily in late 2000 to 80,000 barrels daily by the end of 2001. In Australia, Apache Corporation of Houston accurately projected offshore production to zoom from 25,000 barrels per day in 1999 to 100,000 a few years later, so was ready to meet the demand.[40]

Mergers of giants must, therefore, be viewed as one response to a difficult environment in which it may be impossible to achieve "top-line growth," that is, to grow assets and revenues. Some believe that the best that can be expected from the oil giants are cost cuts and synergy savings, or "bottom-line" shrinkage. This brings us back to the Exxon–Mobil merger. It was reported that almost as soon as the merger was approved, Mr. Raymond, chairman and CEO of Exxon, announced initial job cuts of 9,000 or about 7 percent of the combined work force. The company projected costs savings of $2.8 billion annually from those redundancies alone. It was also suggested that savings could be far bigger once Exxon's efficiencies were applied to Mobil.[41] After an aborted attempt to merge with Texaco, Chevron, a competitor, announced that it would go it alone, but industry analysts greeted this decision, and Chevron's claim that it could achieve future "top-line" growth, with skepticism.[42] Texaco, meanwhile, announced its own go-it-alone survival strategy: It would pursue diversification by increasing spending on power generation and on a proprietary "gasification" technology which could power gas turbines. As Peter Bijur, former chairman and CEO, explained: "If we are going to be an energy supplier, it might as well be electricity as oil and gas."[43] Still, conditions in the oil industry changed so rapidly that a year later Texaco reversed course and agreed to merge with Chevron!

Critics who fear that the trend towards global consolidation will have dangerously anticompetitive effects express particular concerns about the car industry. To be sure, 1999 saw several cross-national mergers—Daimler with Chrysler and Ford with Volvo, among others—with the former chairman of Ford, Alex Trotman, forecasting that there would ultimately be only five car producers left in the world. These trends appear, at first glance, to argue strongly against our hypothesis of the fragmenting impact of entrepreneurial capitalism as new competitors enter the marketplace.

However, a strong counterargument against the prospects for increased consolidation has been presented by John Kay, Peter Moores director of the Said Business School at Oxford University. He was highly skeptical of concerns about consolidation, stating that "it would be a dramatic reversal of the historic trend," which has been leading to less, not more, concentration in the car industry, despite globalization. Chart 2.2 supports his argument:

Chart 2.2
Consolidation Myth: Changing Structure of World Car Business[44]

	1969	1996
Share of largest three producers	51%	36%
Share of largest three producers in 1969	51%	33%
Number of producers of over 1M vehicles	9%	14%
Number of companies with 1% market share	15%	17%

Kay pointed out that in 1969 the three largest U.S. auto producers—GM, Ford, and Chrysler—made one out of every two cars. By 1996, this ratio had fallen to one out of three. In 1969 there had been nine mega producers but by 1996 there were fourteen. And whereas the share of the original nine producers in 1969 was 84 percent by 1996 the share of the new top nine producers had fallen to 66 percent, with sales of the original 1969 leaders down further, and some of them out of existence altogether.

The fundamental reason Kay gave for the countertrend towards less, not more, consolidation is reminiscent of the Tofflers' argument that the "Third Wave" favors "demassification." Consequently, he argued that: "The era of immensely long runs of the same car—which began with Ford's Model T and reached its climax with the Beetle and Mini—probably ended with the Toyota Corolla."[45]

Thus, in an era of fragmented, niche markets Kay suggested:

The fundamental economics of the industry may be changing but they are probably moving in directions that will make size less important as manufacturing processes become more flexible and consumers more willing to pay a premium for differentiated products.[46]

Paradoxically, mergers of larger, more established companies may actually help smaller rivals and hence increase competition. The federal government often requires divestiture of ancillary companies by merging mega partners, creating opportunities for smaller competitors, who are now free to acquire the divested assets and become stronger competitors themselves. For example, gaining Federal Trade Commission approval of the Mobil–Exxon merger required the combined companies to spin off 2,431 gas stations on the eastern seaboard, with Robert Pitovsky, FTC chairman, announcing a search for one or two rivals who could acquire them in order to preserve competition. By March 6, 2000, it was reported that 1,740 stations in the Northeast and mid-Atlantic states had been sold to Tosco for $860 million in December 1999, with the remaining 350 gas stations plus a refinery sold in March to Valero Energy for $895 million.

Strategy Number Two: De-Mergers

While mergers have been receiving a lot of attention from those who argue that twenty-first century America is becoming dangerously like early twentieth century America, far less attention is given the fact that many much heralded unions are disgorged, often at "fire sale" prices. While a simple explanation might be that managements make expensive mistakes, it is equally the case that constant market shifts caused by new entrants, as well as by rapid changes in consumer preferences for new products, have introduced an element of risk that did not exist in the past. Thus, the best companies have had no alternative but to keep reassessing their strategies to accommodate changes in the marketplace.

Ironically "de-mergers" have become yet another strategic response by corporations to the competitive pressures of entrepreneurial capitalism, including pressures from shareholders to unlock shareholder value, exemplified by a series of high-profile de-mergers in the 1990s. Sometimes the same company was both merging and de-merging almost simultaneously. AT&T was a case in point. Under CEO Robert Allen, AT&T had acquired NCR for $7 billion in stock in May 1994, yet sold it at a loss in May 1995 for $3.4 billion when new CEO Michael Armstrong took over. Whereas Allen had confidently predicted that "together AT&T and NCR will achieve a level of growth and success that we could not achieve separately. Ours will be a future of promises fulfilled," his successor expressed the sobering view that "the complexity of trying to manage these different businesses began to overwhelm the advantages of integration." Armstrong instead embarked on a new strategy of delivering a bundle of telecommunications services using both wireless and cable broadband access, acquiring cable giants TCI, Liberty Media, and Media

One in order to begin delivering on its promises to investors of enhanced top-line growth. A year later, Armstrong was forced to concede that the strategy had failed, but not before spending over $100 billion on the effort!

In the pharmaceuticals sector, SmithKline Beecham bought Diversified Pharmaceutical Services in May 1994 for $2.3 billion. It was subsequently sold at a loss to Express Scripts for $700 million and $300 million in tax benefits. Upon the acquisition, its CEO said: "Over the past year we have conducted an exhaustive analysis . . . and concluded that the unique alliance announced today positions us to win." Upon its sale, however, he said: "I am confident that we will deliver accelerated financial performance with a sharper focus."

Even in the somewhat more staid consumer nondurables sector, Quaker Oats paid $1.7 billion for Snapple in November 1994 yet sold it to Triarc in May 1997 for only $300 million, a fraction of its purchase price. Triarc, in turn, sold Snapple to Cadbury Schweppes in 2000 for over $1 billion. At the time of its original purchase, Quaker's CEO had confidently said: "Snapple has tremendous growth potential through increased penetration, broader distribution and international expansion." Upon its sale, he expressed a more sober view: "After reviewing all possible options, we decided it was in the interests of the shareholders to remove the financial binders and risks Snapple brought to the portfolio and better focus on our value-driving business."[47]

It is equally true that mergers can either add value or create problems for the acquirer in the unstable environment of entrepreneurial capitalism. Recognizing these risks, investors today have tended to bid down the shares of an acquirer's stock. It was reported that by 1999 the average acquirer's stock price fell 0.25 percent on average, whereas in 1994 it had risen 1.6 percent. James Gipson, manager of the $ 1.2 billion Clipper Fund, explained the often dramatic drop in share prices that accompanies a merger announcement: "It's a risky business to acquire another company, and there's now more investor experience with acquisitions that have disappointed."[48]

Survival Strategy Number 3: Spinoffs

Linked to de-mergers is the strategy of "spinoffs," justified by the belief that once businesses are freed from central management control they can act more entrepreneurially.[49] Hewlett Packard's spinoff of Agilent in November 1999 was based on this justification. However, the parent company benefits from its offspring's vigor by retaining majority ownership because, in most cases, market valuations of spinoffs have been higher. This was the supposed strategic advantage for 3Com, which spun off its popular Palm division in March 2000 but retained a 95 percent ownership stake. Reversing course, however, 3Com subsequently divested that as well! Corporate spinoffs had taken off by the mid-1990s when AT&T spun off its equipment and research arm as Lucent Technologies, as well as its computer division NCR in 1996; Sears spun off Allstate and sold off Dean Witter and Discover; while 3M spun off Imation. Adding to the spinoff frenzy, General Motors spun off its Delphi Auto Parts unit in 1999 and Dupont sold off its Conoco Unit in 1998—and these were only a few of the larger name divestitures! By 2000, Lucent itself announced its own spinoff of three underperforming units. The Tofflers had predicted this strategic development much earlier when they wrote: "Big businesses are getting smaller, small businesses are multiplying. IBM with 370,000 employees is being picked to death by small manufacturers around the world. To survive it lays off many workers and splits itself into thirteen different companies—smaller business units."[50]

IBM, of course, survived and prospered under the leadership of CEO Lou Gerstner, who changed the focus of the company to become more service oriented, introducing Internet-based "ebusiness solutions." In 1999, RJR Nabisco announced that it had sold off its international tobacco unit to Japan Tobacco and would separate its tobacco and food units, hoping to unlock value and protect some assets from tobacco litigation and obligations to the state governments. While corporate spinoffs did not always succeed, especially when weaker units were de-coupled from the parent company (like Imation, a spinoff from 3M), there were several successes. For example, the Agilent spinoff from Hewlett Packard, the Williams Communication spinoff from Williams companies, or the GM Hughes Electronics Division spinoff were all, until the savage 2000–2001 bear market, awarded rich market valuations that initially unlocked hidden shareholder value, setting the companies free to pursue more entrepreneurial paths.[51]

Survival Strategy Number Four: Acquisitions

Whereas mergers have been a strategic choice in sectors that are either fragmented (like banking) or beleaguered (like oil), the strategy of acquisitions has been preferred in sectors like technology, where marketplace demands and technological innovations occur rapidly and where new "spaces" are defined almost overnight, outpacing even the most robust in-house R&D efforts. Cisco Systems pioneered the strategy of acquiring young technology startups as part of its growth strategy—acquiring Vinod Khosla's Cerent, for example, for over $7 billion in 1999, a year in which Cisco eventually acquired a total of twenty other companies; this brought the total number of acquisitions since it began this strategy to an astonishing fifty-one. More established technology companies, including General Electric, have also followed this strategy of acquiring smaller companies. Similarly Intel, faced with the rapidly evolving market for non-PC-based applications, began a rapid program of acquisitions in areas outside its traditional expertise—semiconductor chips. Thus, in the fourteen months preceding February 2000, the company made thirteen acquisitions including Dialogic in 1999 and Voice Tech Group in February 2000.[52] Even Lucent, which had originally preferred a strategy of internal innovation, found itself left behind in the shift to optical networking equipment and was forced to change course. Oracle, which also had preferred internal innovation, found itself outmaneuvered in early 2000 by upstart I 2 Technologies which acquired the technologies it need via strategic acquisitions.

Survival Strategy Number 5: Strategic Alliances, Partnerships, and Joint Ventures

Another popular strategy to cope with the environment of entrepreneurial capitalism has been the formation of strategic alliances between large companies, as well as between more established companies and smaller entrepreneurial ones. Several partnering alliances between competitors were forged early in 2000: GM, Ford, and Daimler Chrysler partnered with Commerce One and Oracle to establish a web-based auto parts procurement site; Boeing and three competitors joined forces with Commerce One for an aircraft parts procurement site; and IBM and Quest Communications announced a partnership to develop web-hosting services.

J. W. Botkin and J. B. Matthew presciently identified the trend to select young companies as partners in their 1992 book *Winning Combinations: The Coming Wave of Entrepreneurial Partnerships Between Large and Small Companies*. The authors noted that large companies had advantages of marketing, distribution, global reach, and access to capital but lacked the flexibility to innovate rapidly. Entrepreneurial startups, on the other hand, had a high failure rate because they often lacked crucial money, marketing and management skills, although they were able to respond to the demands of the marketplace more quickly. In the book, written before the trend had picked up steam, they also noted the difficulties that large companies might have with what they called the "NIH or Not Invented Here Syndrome." An example was a brochure from 3M called "About Your Idea": "We understand you have an idea you think may be of interest to 3M. We should say at the outset that only rarely does 3M use an idea submitted by a person outside of the company. Our general practice is to rely on 3M's own technical and scientific resources for new ideas."[53]

In an era of pressures from swifter, more entrepreneurial competitors, the standard corporate response to new ideas changed dramatically. By the end of the 1990s, partnering with smaller startups became the strategy of choice for several industries, especially high technology. Microsoft selected this option as it struggled to respond to the movement towards non-PC applications. So, too, did IBM, forming a Global Business Partners Group which worked with 45,000 IBM business partners in areas such as hardware resales, web integration, and ebusiness solutions. Instead of IBM relying solely on its in-house sales force, partners accounted for 80 percent of total sales of AS/400 midrange servers in 1999, up from 21 percent in 1995. By 1999 it was reported that these partners had generated one-third of IBM's revenue of $87 billion—a big jump from 1996, when partners contributed only 10 percent of IBM sales.[54] Foreign high-tech companies in particular, lacking both the management and marketing skills to grow into global companies, were actively sought out as partners, or even bought out; for example, in 1999 BMC Software of Houston bought out New Dimension Software of Tel Aviv.

Similar partnering arrangements between large and small companies occurred in the pharmaceutical industry, where it became commonplace for large, integrated companies to subcontract R&D or clinical trials to smaller biotechnology companies such as Quintiles Transnational or Sepracor, to whom Eli Lilly subcontracted formulation of its patent extension of Prozac in 1999.[55] No doubt smaller biotech companies in the future will actively be sought as partners by the established giants of the pharmaceutical industry.

Survival Strategy Number 6: Mature Companies Establish Venture Capital Units

Yet another strategy has emerged, one in which established companies, faced with acute competitive pressures and rapid change, particularly in the technology and bio technology sectors, have been establishing their own in-house venture capital units to fund early stage startups in order to buy a strategic head start. While critics contend that this may merely be a strategy to artificially boost reported revenues when these young companies go public, corporations themselves have insisted that it is a way for them to keep abreast of rapid technological innovation and pioneering developments coming from hundreds of high-tech upstarts from which they would otherwise be excluded.

According to the National Venture Capital Association, venture capital investments made by established companies made up as much as 16.3 percent of the $43 billion (later revised to over $54 billion) funneled into venture capital in 1999, compared with 7.5 percent of the $20 billion invested in 1998.[56] Microsoft led the corporate venture capital wave with investments worth $19.8 billion in startups, while Intel followed with a portfolio of 350 companies valued at $8.2 billion in emerging company investments that it claimed "provide strategic benefits such as accelerating a new technology or creating a new market." This stood in stark contrast to just fifty companies in its portfolio valued at $500 million in

1997, indicating how novel this strategy was. In 1999 alone, Intel invested $1.2 billion in its Capital Portfolio, which selected 245 startups, having turned down 4,750 other opportunities. The *Wall Street Journal* assessed this strategy: "Mr. Vadasz and Intel represent the new breed of venture investor: the successful multinational, often in the technology business itself, that views investing in startups as a strategic mission with an added fillip—the prospect of staggering profits."[57]

Initially, Intel invested in companies like chip makers with technological ingredients that could return direct benefits to Intel. Marking the maturation of this strategy, Intel began investing in companies that complemented and expanded Intel's markets by creating new uses and new users for the personal computer. For example, Intel invested in companies creating 3D graphic chips, which led to an explosion in the market for 3D games on PCs.

Nortel Networks forcefully articulated the risks of not investing seed money in entrepreneurial startups. First, new, highly focused companies could emerge to develop and then capture the lead in new "market spaces"—or mature rival technology companies could acquire them. In an interview with *Financial Times* columnist Scott Morrison, George Cooney, Nortel's vice-president of corporate business development, said that its strategic relationships with venture capital funds gave it "prioritized introduction" to the newest technology and "early engagement" with entrepreneurs. Without this strategy, Nortel would have an "unfocused, sporadic awareness of new developments in the industry."[58] If an emerging technology appeared to be vital, Nortel did not hesitate to buy the upstart company as it did when it acquired Shasta Networks founded by former Cisco employees.

By no means have high technology companies been the only ones making corporate venture capital investments. By the end of the 1990s, companies from various sectors of the economy—including General Electric, Chase Manhattan (Chase Capital Partners), SmithKline Beecham, and even old-economy companies such as Eastman Chemical—had become venture investors!

Survival Strategy Number 7: Established Companies Start Their Own Startups

At the cutting edge of strategic responses to innovative new entrants who can put more established companies out of business, is the strategy whereby established companies themselves start new entrepreneurial companies that may be expected to eventually use the parent company's own products and services. Thus, in early 2000, UPS announced the creation of its eVentures Unit to test and launch new businesses aimed at boosting the company's presence in e-commerce, while a few months later, Eastman Chemical created its own dot.com unit, ShipChem.com, to help other chemical companies, even competitors, with logistics issues.[59] Other companies will doubtless explore this strategic option if it succeeds.

Conclusion

The challenging, even frenetic, economic environment described in this chapter did not occur by accident. The federal government played a catalytic role in its emergence. Structural changes at the political level catapulted the American economy from the predictability of regulatory capitalism into the vortex of entrepreneurial capitalism. The next three chapters take a closer look at why the federal government decided to play such a transformative role and examine exactly what it did to facilitate the emergence of entrepreneurial capitalism.

CHAPTER 3

The Genesis of
Entrepreneurial Capitalism

LOOKING INTO THE ABYSS: AMERICA FACES
ECONOMIC DECLINE

To more clearly understand the reasons why federal policy makers were impelled to set in motion the forces of entrepreneurial capitalism, we must return to the America of the late 1970s and early 1980s. It was a time when corporate America was being bested by rivals in Japan and Germany and the American economy was sliding into what many informed observers feared would be an irreversible decline. Alarm bells were being sounded all over Washington as the realization dawned that having created the global economy and championed the cause of free trade America had failed to prepare for the consequences.

Spearheading the growing sense of alarm within the academic community, the Harvard Business School convened a colloquium of economists and the other experts in 1984 to explore the subject of declining U.S. competitiveness. In 1985 a collection of papers from the conference was published. Summarizing the basic findings of the colloquium, Bruce R. Scott and George C. Lodge, editors of the conference proceedings, unequivocally stated: "For some fifteen years the United States has been losing its capacity to compete in the world economy . . . declining U.S. competitiveness is evident in the performance pattern of several measures."[1] They were equally blunt in their assessment of what needed to happen:

We must recognize that the U.S. economy can no longer be counted on to deliver the performance level required to meet the nation's goals and commitments. Either the goals need to be changed reflecting more modest prospects for the American economy, or the strategy needs to be changed to increase the prospects for more robust performance in the future.[2]

Throughout the 1980s many in the academic community voiced similar concerns about declining U.S. competitiveness. Martin K. Starr, for instance, brought together a group of distinguished economists, including Laura Tyson, to contribute to a volume titled *Global Competitiveness: Getting the U.S. Back on Track*,[3] with Richard D. Lamm, then governor of Colorado, joining the discussion.

By the mid-1980s, Yale historian Paul Kennedy brought this debate to a broader audience in his book *The Rise and Fall of the Great Powers*, the most widely disseminated and influential work of 1987. Kennedy not only echoed the concerns voiced by the Harvard conferees but went one important step further. His book focused the general concern over declining competitiveness into a more alarming concern over national security. Kennedy was one of the first to suggest that America may have already joined a long list of "declining hegemons." He offered persuasive evidence of the loss of global military power that occurred when nations overstretched their economic resources, "especially when new technologies and new centers of production shifted economic power away from established Great Powers—hence the rise and fall of nations."[4]

Kennedy's book chronicled the economic shift that had already taken place since the end of the Second World War. Europe, he suggested, had recovered sufficiently by the 1950s so that a period of sustained economic growth meant that many countries were back to their prewar levels of production and some were ahead, notably Germany and France. By the 1960s and 1970s the CIA had compiled figures showing that the European Economic Community possessed a larger share of gross world product than the United States, and that it was twice as large as that of the Soviet Union."[5] Indeed, economic growth in Europe was so vigorous that, according to Paul Kennedy, "In one generation after 1950, per capita income increased as much as it had during a century and a half before that date."[6] Looking at the European Economic Community as a whole, in comparison with the American market, Kennedy went on to say that

the sheer economic size of the EEC meant that the international landscape was significantly different from that of 1945 or 1984. The EEC was by far the largest importer and exporter of the world's goods . . . and it contained, by 1983, by far the largest international currency and gold reserves; it manufactured more automobiles (34 percent) than either Japan (24 percent) or the United States (23 percent) and more cement than anyone else, and its crude steel production was second only to that of the USSR.[7]

Even so, Europe's economic challenge dwarfed the one now presented by Japan. To put Japan's resurgence in perspective, Kennedy offered this comparison: "When the Allied Occupation ended in 1952, Japan's GNP was ⅓ that of France's or the UK's . . . By the late 1970s, the Japanese GNP was as large as the UK's and France's combined and half that of America's."[8]

Between 1950 and 1973, Japanese GNP had grown at an stunning average annual rate of 10.5 percent and, even after the 1973 oil crisis had dealt the American economy a nasty blow, Japan's growth rates remained twice as large as that of its major competitors. Japan had achieved parity, if not dominance, with America in a number of traditional industries such as cameras, shipbuilding, cars and steel, while moving rapidly into high-tech areas such as computers, aerospace, robotics, and biotechnology.[9] Books such as Ezra Vogel's *Japan as Number One: Lessons for America,* published in 1980; Chalmers Johnson's *MITI and the Japanese Miracle,* published in 1982; and even Martin Fransman's *Japan's Computer Communications Industry: The Evolution of Industrial Giants and Global Competitiveness,* published in the mid-1990s before Japan's economic decline became truly evident, admiringly analyzed the political strategies and public policies that undergirded the Japanese economic miracle. In a gargantuan irony, given Japan's subsequent economic stagnation throughout the 1990s, Paul Kennedy had made a confident prediction in 1987 about its future, even if he qualified it initially:

(while) there is no guarantee that . . . Japan's impressive economic expansion over the past four decades will continue during the next two . . . If it did happen that Japan stagnated . . . between now and the early twenty first century, then that could only come about from changes in circumstances and policies far more drastic than it is reasonable to assume from the available evidence.[10]

Under these circumstances, Kennedy worried whether the United States could "preserve the technological and economic base of its power from relative erosion in the face of the ever shifting patterns of global production,"[11] particularly since "global production balances . . . have already begun to tilt in certain directions: away from Russia and the United States, away also from the EEC, to Japan and China."[12] Citing a weakening capacity to bear the burdens of defense, he colorfully remarked that the pattern of history suggested that "Rome fell, Babylon fell, Scarsdale's turn will come!"[13]

For many in the academic community Great Britain's rapid economic and international decline between the two world wars offered a frightening parallel and one to be avoided at all costs. Paul Kennedy merely articulated the growing sense of dismay when he wrote:

Here again it is instructive to note the uncanny similarities between the growing mood of anxiety among thoughtful circles in the United States today and that which pervaded all political parties in Edwardian Britain and led to what has been termed the "national efficiency movement": that is, a broad based debate within the nation's decision making, business and educational elites over the various measures which could reverse what was seen as a growing uncompetitiveness as compared with other advanced nations . . . Then the "number one" power of 1900 seemed to be losing its position with dire implications for the country's long term strategic position, hence the calls for "renewal" and "reorganization" from the Right as from the Left.[14]

Earlier, Bruce Scott, one of the Harvard conferees and coeditor of the proceedings, had voiced a similar concern:

starkly put, the question is whether the United States is in the early stages of a decline similar to the United Kingdom's which, over the last century, led ultimately to a reduction in its political and military role and more recently to a loss of capacity to achieve a rising standard of living.[15]

Not long after, this issue reached the level of popular concern as magazines including *Business Week* began running urgent headlines such as "Is the U.S. Going the Way of Britain?" and "Can America Compete?," predicting a lasting decline if productivity levels were not raised.[16]

Under the circumstances, some argued there was only one thing America could do and that was to adjust gracefully to its altered and diminished circumstances. Paul Kennedy cautioned that "the only serious threat to the real interests of the United States can come from *failure to adjust sensibly to the new world order*"[17] (emphasis added)! His dismal conclusion was that "there is a need to" manage "affairs so that the relative erosion of the United States takes place slowly and smoothly."[18] Even as late as the early 1990s, Henry Nau, scholar and former State Department bureaucrat, was reiterating these depressing concerns. He, however, offered some soothing reassurances about America's global position, even as he appeared to accept that it had, indeed, declined:

America's purposes are more widely shared in the world today than they were in 1947 or even 1967. Accordingly, to influence this world, America does not need as much power as it did twenty or forty years ago. *It can maintain its leadership by being more of a global pope than a global power*[19] (emphasis added).

Why did America find itself in this woeful condition scarcely thirty-five years after it had been the only country to emerge economically stronger after the Second World War?

America Failed to Adjust to Global Competition

Having assumed the mantle of postwar global leadership from an exhausted Great Britain facing "financial Dunkirk," the United States had confidently championed the cause of trade liberalization and global economic development. In doing so, Washington could scarcely have imagined that, as a consequence, America itself might be unprepared to face serious global competition and that its own economic dominance might wane.

At that time Roosevelt's Secretary of State Cordell Hull and Treasury's Harry Dexter White were actively pushing the cause of free trade—along with the institutions to support it, such as the International Monetary Fund and World Bank—because they were determined to avoid the ruinous consequences of trade protectionism that had brought global trade to a halt and worsened the Great Depression, creating the unstable economic conditions that led ultimately to the Second World War.

Thus, their new postwar economic order was to be based on a different principle than the old one had been. If the old order had been based on exclusive trading blocs such as Japan's Greater East Asia Co-Prosperity Sphere, or even Great Britain's Empire, the new one was to be based on the principle of inclusiveness, as international affairs scholar John Ruggie pointed out in *Winning the Peace: America and World Order in the New Era*.[20] The principle of inclusiveness and the emphasis on economic growth for the postwar global economy were meant to reduce economic conflicts and prevent war. But they also made the international economic playing field more competitive as, for example, manufacturing capabilities spread worldwide, intensifying pressures on corporate America to adapt.

In the late 1940s, however, the possibility of relative economic decline or any loss of American economic dominance as a consequence of these policies seemed remote. As Paul Kennedy pointed out, America had been the only country made stronger by the war and Pax America was based on that one simple fact: "Among the Great Powers, the United States was the only country which became richer—in fact much richer—because of the war."[21]

During the war the size of productive plants within this country grew in real terms by nearly 50 percent and the physical output of goods by more than 50 percent. U.S. gross national product grew by 50 percent. By comparison, Europe's GNP (minus the Soviet Union) had fallen by about 25 percent. Paul Kennedy had taken note of the scope of Europe's economic devastation:

Europe's share of total world manufacturing output was lower than at any time since the early nineteenth century; even by 1953, when most of the war damage had been repaired, it possessed only 26 percent of the whole (compared with the

United States' 44.7 percent). Even by 1950, its per capita GNP was half that of the United States.[22]

Postwar, only the Soviet Union counted in economic terms. But Kennedy dismissed this possibility by stating that of the two, the American "superpower" was vastly superior. With Britain out of the picture, France similarly exhausted and impoverished, and Germany, Japan, and Italy all vanquished and defeated, Washington had no reason whatsoever to assume it would be ceding economic dominance in the near future—or that it needed to put in place public policies to address this possibility.

The private sector, moreover, had applauded America's postwar shift towards a global economy. Export-oriented corporations in particular had been enthusiastic supporters of Washington's postwar trade liberalization policies, foreseeing the opening of lucrative markets abroad for the first time. According to Paul Kennedy, they also feared a "post-war slump might follow the decline in U.S. government spending unless new overseas markets were opened up."[23] Corporate America simply failed to recognize that global trade would not always be a one-way street and was woefully unprepared to face the possibility that U.S. industry, never before exposed to foreign competition, might find itself unable to compete.

Since independence, after all, America had followed a policy of trade protectionism, not free trade. American industry had never been exposed to the full force of global competition but had grown strong, sheltered behind a wall of protective tariffs. Summing up America's historically protectionist trade policy, business historian Thomas McCraw noted that:

there can be no question that the United States protected its home market, just as Germany did during the key period of its economic growth (1879–1914), and as Japan did during and after its own "miracle" growth era (1951–1973). The wisdom and efficacy of these policies is open to question; but their systematic implementation is a settled historical fact. In America throughout the nineteenth century, the law was on the side of producers who were protected, not consumers who paid higher prices as a result.[24]

Labor leader Gus Tyler succinctly summed up this reality: "American manufacture was reared behind a protectionist fence almost from the day of the nation's birth."[25] He traced the historical roots of protectionism back to the 1816 "Tariff of Abominations" (as it seemed to the southern states that relied on imports), which raised tariffs 42 percent after the War of 1812. He dispelled the myth that the century prior to World War I was an era of U.S. free trade, pointing to: the 1890 McKinley Tariff that raised duties on manufactured goods more than ever before and was followed by a series of hikes in the period leading up to the Great

Crash, beginning with the Dingley Act, which restored the 1890 schedule; the Payne–Aldrich Tariff Act of 1909; the Underwood–Simmons Act under Woodrow Wilson, which lowered tariffs a scant 10 percent; the Emergency Act of 1921 and the Fordney–McCumber Act of 1922, which lifted tariffs to their highest levels ever. The Smoot–Hawley Tariff Act, enacted in 1930 after the economy had already weakened though popularly remembered as a defining symbol of trade protectionism, was actually its last gasp.

This history of trade protectionism was reversed so abruptly after the Second World War that by the late 1950s corporate America found itself facing international competition on a scale it had never done before. Private industry simply could not compete, and private sector productivity growth lagged woefully behind Europe and Japan. In the period between 1977 and 1982, it had fallen to 0.2 percent from 2.4 percent in the period 1965–1972. Moreover, the economies of other nations revived more quickly than anticipated and the mighty American economy began to lose ground, particularly to the "miracle" economies of Japan and Germany.

While the consequences of globalization for world economic revival may have been profound, Washington failed to recognize how those same pressures would impact America's competitive position. It took twenty-five years before the full implications of America's push for globalization became uncomfortably clear. As the industrial economies recovered from World War II and new rivals in Asia emerged, taking advantage of free trade to export to the newly opened American market, America found itself for the first time facing relative economic decline. Ironically, having been the architect of globalization, this nation had failed to prepare for its consequences. Secure in the belief that "economically, the world was its oyster" America had diverted its attention to achieving military, rather than economic, leadership.

Why America Failed to Prepare for Global Competition

During the 1950s and 1960s Washington decision makers became preoccupied with the Cold War, expanding the nation's commitments overseas. Paul Kennedy explained how preoccupying this could become:

Like the British after 1815, the Americans . . . found their informal influence in various lands hardening into something more formal—and more entangling; like the British, too, they found "new frontiers of insecurity" whenever they wanted to draw the line. The Pax Americana had come of age.[26]

A foreign policy based on containment of the Soviets and on the "domino theory" inevitably led America into an expansive and expensive move to prop up South Vietnam, viewed at the time as the ultimate "falling domino" and one to be protected at all costs. This led to an involvement that escalated through several administrations, culminating in the Johnson-era debacle, when spending on the war abroad and a war on poverty at home severely overstretched America's resources and set the nation on the slippery path of relative economic decline.

By then several other factors had begun to force the federal government to reexamine its global competitive position and its technological status. In 1958 the Soviets launched "Sputnik," causing the United States to accelerate science and technology education and spending, leading to a race for the moon that was ultimately won by the United States in 1969. Though reluctant to cede military and technological superiority to the Soviet Union, the United States from the late 1960s on found itself in the uncomfortable position of confronting economic decline in relation to its Cold War partners. The 1960s and 1970s were the heyday of the German and Japanese economic "miracles" and by then even France and Italy were gaining speed. Added to these pressures were several other problems of the 1960s and 1970s—civil rights unrest and the oil crisis of 1973, among them. The overall decline in national confidence (President Jimmy Carter had referred to it as a "national malaise") coincided with America's economic decline and led to a profound soul searching by the academic community into its causes. This alarm spread to Washington by the late 1970s, forcing policy makers into action to reverse this crisis of confidence, setting in motion the forces leading to entrepreneurial capitalism and the ultimate resurgence of the American economy.

THE ACADEMIC COMMUNITY EVALUATES THE CAUSES OF AMERICA'S ECONOMIC DECLINE AND WORKS TO ALTER THE POLICY CLIMATE

While the experts ruminated, there was no academic consensus on what had caused the decline or on what the policy solutions might be. Some observers, like Mancur Olson, blamed systemic failures that could not easily be remedied. In *The Rise and Decline of Nations*, published in 1982, Olson had suggested that, over time and in the absence of war or upheaval, nations became ossified as special interests came to dominate policy making, making those societies less efficient and dynamic. Conversely, he suggested, societies in which narrow interest groups had been destroyed—by war or revolution, for example—enjoyed the greatest gains in growth. Accordingly:

Since it achieved its independence, the United States has never been occupied by a foreign power. It has lived under the same democratic constitution for nearly 200 years. Its special interest organizations, moreover, are possibly less encompassing in relation to the economy as a whole than those in any other country. The United States has also been since World War Two one of the slowest growing of the developed democracies.[27]

Clearly, Olson's analysis seemed to imply that there was very little a stable society such as the United States could do, short of revolution or war, to reverse its ossification. Fortunately, the explanations and policy proposals suggested by other experts were slightly more sanguine. Several observers, for example, suggested that America's postwar preeminence was artificial, hence temporary, a by-product of the devastation of other industrialized nations that had had comparable educational levels and industrial capacity before the war. Paul Kennedy was one who made this point:

As argued above, the United States' favorable economic position at that point in history was both unprecedented and artificial. It was on top of the world partly because of its own production spurt, but also because of the temporary weakness of other nations. . . . [28]

Kennedy concluded that what we were witnessing was simply the ebbing away from an extraordinarily high figure to a more "natural" share. That decline was being masked by the country's enormous military capabilities at that juncture, and also by its success in "internationalizing American capitalism and culture." He then focused on a much more pressing concern:

The real question was not "Did the United States have to decline relatively?" but "Did it have to decline so *fast*?" For the fact was that even in the heyday of the Pax Americana, its competitive position was already being eroded by a disturbingly low average rate of growth of output per capita, especially as compared with previous decades.[29]

Others had come to very similar conclusions. Bruce Scott and George Lodge fretfully commented that

many experts seem to deny the competitiveness problem rather than confront the issue. Some correctly claim, for instance, that the U.S. is not "deindustrializing" in absolute terms overall, and therefore, that there is no cause for alarm. But U.S. goals and commitments surely require much better performance than the mere avoidance of decline.[30]

Still other experts looked to quite different causes. Many suggested that the main factor contributing to economic decline was that the United States had embarked on a voracious consumption binge. Consumers spent more than they earned, corporate America voraciously consumed global capital even while the nation had a low and declining level of capital formation, and government implemented public policies that were redistributive and stimulated growth solely by promoting domestic demand rather than by addressing the deeper problems of declining productivity,[31] which had fallen from 2.4 percent in the 1960s—to as low as 0.2 percent by 1977–1982. American government was borrowing from abroad to finance spending at home, and by 1985 we had become the world's largest debtor nation. Bruce Scott and George Lodge, summarizing the Harvard Colloquium's dismal conclusions, made oblique reference to yet another concern—namely the deleterious effects of the welfare state:

(U.S policy) gives low priority to competitiveness and long-term development and high priority to short-term distributional equity through a centralized system of income distribution, entitlements, regulations, and subsidies for consumer goods from credit card purchases to housing.[32]

On the other hand, The Council of Economic Advisors, in its 1983 Economic Report to the President, focused more narrowly on declining levels of public investment relative to our competitors:

The share of U.S. gross domestic output (GDP) devoted to net fixed investment during the last decade was only 34 percent of the comparable share in Japan and 56 percent of the comparable share in Germany. No other major industrial nation devotes as small a fraction of total output to new investment as does the United States.[33]

However, there was also a consensus among the experts that a major factor in America's relative economic decline was that our European and Japanese competitors permitted their governments a greater role in guiding the private sector, even altering market outcomes, although it was universally acknowledged that "industrial policy" would likely never be implemented in the United States. Nevertheless, there was widespread admiration within the academic community for the favorable economic consequences of "managed capitalism." The Harvard Colloquium had concluded at its conference that the competitive thrust of new challenges did not come from natural resources but from "coherent national strategies through which each country mobilizes and shapes its productive capabilities to achieve economic growth and global competitiveness" and warned that future competitiveness hinged on the creation of new technologies but that "the educational system, grants for research and incentives to take risks all play a role in stimulating creativity and are primarily shaped by government." Thus, they concluded that "one cannot evaluate future U.S. competitiveness without also considering the impact of government policies and institutions since these shape the business environment more than natural resources do."[34]

It may seem remarkable today, but in the near panic of the 1980s many of the Harvard conferees actually had doubts about the free market approach. Bruce Scott had introduced the conference findings with this comment: "Perhaps the most basic premise is that the market system, guided by the invisible hand, gives the highest level of economic performance obtainable, consistent with a democratic society . . . The following chapters question the validity of that premise."[35]

His statement reflected the contemporary lack of confidence among many in the academic community about whether free market principles worked, as well as the belief that perhaps rival nations had a better way:

Traditionally committed to the principles of free trade and the free market, both for ideological reasons and because of a long-standing belief that American interests are promoted by such principles, the United States finds itself facing a new type of competition in which business and government work together to achieve what might be called "managed competition."[36]

Managed competition, they explained, required government to play a role in mediating decisions about who would give up what and contrasted sharply with American practice, which had always assumed that maximum competition was best. Perhaps, it was suggested, it was time to consider an alternative.

The Harvard Group gave serious consideration to the concept of a "national strategy," suggesting that "The critical element in this new competition is the effective participation of national governments in shaping the business environment."[37] William Firin and Annette M. La Mond, narrowing down the discussion to microelectronics, explained why the Japanese approach of greater government involvement worked better:

The problem, quite simply, is that the Japanese government has a coherent strategic orientation towards its industry and the U.S. government does not . . . This is not a question of picking winners and losers. It recognizes that governments can influence market structure and firm behavior in ways that can have detrimental consequences for the United States.[38]

Harvey Brooks in "Technology as a Factor in U.S. Competitiveness" echoed the same theme: "In Japan the selective use of all available policy instruments towards the single, overriding objective of international competitiveness has become an important ingredient of success completely lacking in the United States."[39]

Clyde Prestowitz, a former U.S. trade negotiator and president of the Economic Strategy Institute, argued in favor of a strong industrial policy for the United States in his 1988 book *Trading Places*, a view he subsequently disavowed in the 1990s. Even Paul Kennedy had written admiringly of Japan's Ministry of International Trade and Industry:

there seems little doubt that the broad direction (MITI) gives to Japanese economic development by arranging research and funding for growth industries and a gentle euthanasia for declining ones has worked better to date than the uncoordinated laissez-faire approach of the United States.[40]

While Japan was the focus of much of the academic admiration for industrial policy, European governments, even that of pre-Thatcher England, also guided their economies during the period from 1950 until the 1970s. As Paul Kennedy observed of their postwar efforts: "There was broad determination to 'build anew' . . . and a willingness to learn from the follies of the 1930s. State planning, whether of the Keynesian or socialistic variety, gave a concentrated thrust to the desire for social and economic improvement."[41]

Even more remarkable, at one point the U.S. Office of Technology Assessment issued a report arguing the case in favor of a more frank industrial policy! In 1983 it stated:

People can, and will argue endlessly about the successes and failures of industrial policies in other countries, but the primary lesson to be drawn from foreign experience is simply this: industrial policymaking is a continuing activity of governments everywhere. In the United States industrial policy has been left mostly to the random play of events. Improvement is clearly possible . . . Until the nation begins this task, American firms will continue to find themselves at a disadvantage when facing rivals based in countries that have turned to industrial policies as a means of enhancing their own competitiveness.[42]

The Policy Response: Defining An American Path

The warnings of the academic community were taken to heart in Washington. Having created the "problem" for the private sector by backing free trade, which unleashed ferocious foreign competition onto a corporate America unprepared for its onslaught, forces in Congress and the Executive branch came together and stepped into the breach to fix it. Fixing America's competitive position thus became part of the "low visibility agenda" of the late 1970s and 1980s. Decision makers were well aware—academic alarmists like Paul Kennedy had made certain of that—that if they did not act, unchecked economic decline would ultimately undermine national security and American global leadership. Fixing the problem meant one thing and one thing only—determining what steps the federal government should take to make the private sector more competitive.

While the experts had galvanized Washington into action, they were generally of little help when it came to actually providing policy solutions. The majority of their recommendations went unheeded because for political or ideological reasons they could not be implemented. For example, despite the support of some Democrats, an industrial policy was never seriously considered as a remedy even though many academics had called for one to be implemented. Consumer spending, moreover, was never curbed; indeed, by the late 1990s American consumers had become the world's consumers of last resort, actually spending more than they earned. Business continued to rely on net inflows of foreign capital while the trade deficit waxed and waned, becoming increasingly large by the end of the 1990s. The only area where the United States made any headway with respect to addressing the concerns of the academic community was that the national budget came into balance, with a surplus projected for the early part of the twenty-first century.

Summing up the three major factors thus far identified by the experts as contributing to the declining American economy: the first, the circumstances surrounding America's artificial dominance, could not be changed; the second, over-consumption by consumers and capital markets, did not change; the third, government planning via an industrial policy, was never implemented.

Steps Toward A Policy Response

Acknowledging the Link Between Technology and Economic Growth

Buried in the academic hand wringing over America's future was a crucial insight which ultimately did lead to a reversal of economic fortune. Academia discussed it, Congressional studies took note of it, and Congress and the President ultimately addressed it. Injecting more growth into the U.S. economy and making it more globally competitive required investments in technology. As Paul Kennedy had noted: "Technological and organizational breakthroughs, bring greater advantage to one society than another,"[43] and it was widely agreed that the United States lagged its rivals badly in this area. As far back as 1982, Edwin Mansfield and others had identified and explored the link between technological change and its effects on productivity and hence economic growth and expressed concern over the decline in U.S. productivity.[44] In February 1985 a Conference on Technology and Economic Policy was held in Washington D.C., focusing on "the contribution of technology to economic growth and the impact of public policies on technology."[45]

Members of Congress were educated on the relationship between technology and economic growth by a series of "Issue Briefs" prepared by Wendy Schacht and others in the Congressional Research Service.[46] Government support for technological innovation, which would bolster productivity, could have a sizable impact on economic growth rates and competitiveness.

Commercialization Was Key

Having singled out technology as the key to improving productivity and increasing economic growth, the academic community pointedly noted that both Europe and Japan had spent the postwar years focusing their investments on commercially viable technology. In contrast, the United States had not concerned itself with commercialization but had focused exclusively on military applications. Harvey Brooks, one of the Harvard Business School conferees, had warned: "It is in the ability to commercialize or operationalize new ideas before its competitors that America is losing its lead, even while it leads in the origination of new ideas."[47]

In fact, the United States had squandered its technological lead since the Second World War in breakthrough technologies such as computers, communication, and aerospace technologies. Brooks was especially critical of the "general rule . . . that civilian spinoff is not considered seriously in the planning of defense R&D."[48] Unfavorable comparisons with the Japanese were being made during this entire period. Robert Reich, in an article titled "The Rise of Techno-Nationalism," published in *Atlantic Monthly* in May 1987, suggested that the problem was not that the Japanese were exploiting American discoveries, but that "we can't turn basic inventions into new products nearly as fast as they can."[49] Writing in *Science*, John A. Young made a similar argument a year later. In an article titled "Technology and Competitiveness: A Key to the Economic Future of the United States," Young claimed that the "United States still is a leader in technology and innovation, but American industry has been slow to translate that advantage into commercial success."[50]

The federal government had still not addressed this issue. Since the 1950s and 1960s, Cold War-related R&D spending had continued to eat away at our competitive position by diverting resources from commercial applications. By the 1980s, Paul Kennedy noted an acceleration of that trend when he wrote that "today's armaments industry is becoming increasingly divergent from commercial free-market manufacturing." Daniel S. Greenberg, writing in *Discover* in 1987, cautioned that the Pentagon was sapping R&D resources, hindering our ability to compete in international trade, and warned that the United States could no longer splurge on military research and still prosper on the civilian front.[51]

However, Cold War concerns were not the sole reason for lack of government support for the commercialization of technology. There were ideological reasons as well, and they could be traced to a lack of political support for more activist government and a preference for private sector solutions in matters relating to commercialization. In fact, the lag in government support for commercialization of defense-related technologies emerging from World War II could be traced back to the late 1940s. Policy makers then had debated whether the federal government should limit its support to basic research or extend it to applied research with commercial applications. This debate surfaced with particular intensity during discussions over the formation of a National Science Foundation. When the NSF was finally created in 1950 it was under a governmentally imposed mandate to promote science development by funding only basic research, a mandate subsequently extended to other government research agencies. A Congressional Research Service study prepared for Congress in 1988 by William C. Boesman traced the roots of the National Science Foundation back to Senator Harley Kilgore's Senate Committee on Military Affairs in 1945 and its consensus that there was a need "to create a central scientific agency within the Federal Government." Kilgore spearheaded the view that a national research agency should develop research for broad societal purposes. However, a second camp had coalesced around Vannevar Bush, head of the wartime Office of Scientific Research and Development and Truman's unofficial science advisor who argued in the "Bush Report" that government should limit itself only to basic research. Bush's more limited vision prevailed and the NSF (along with NASA and the USDA) became an institution focused upon basic research disconnected from any practical or commercial value.[52] Parallel developments took place in medical research. In 1950, soon after the NSF act was passed, Congress passed the Omnibus Medical Research Act, which authorized the Surgeon General to establish a number of new institutes (such as the National Cancer Institute, made a part of the National Institutes on Health) and to conduct and support research and training related to various diseases. Supporting commercialization efforts, however, was still a long way off.

By the mid-1980s, however, it was becoming increasingly evident that this exclusive governmental emphasis on basic research was impeding commercialization of new technologies, especially those that had emerged as a by-product of military spending and that this, in turn, was impeding productivity gains and dampening economic growth. For commercialization to occur, public policy would have to be modified to support applied research, particularly in areas which the private sector deemed too risky or where the payoffs were far in the future. High technology and biotechnology were two areas that fit this profile and eventually became specific targets of government attention.

Thus, warnings by the scholarly community on the necessity of technology transfer eventually began to be taken seriously in Washington. The National Science Foundation itself took up the issue of transforming basic research into new products and services by commissioning a joint study on the subject of technology transfer and the relationship between R&D and U.S. competitiveness. It was undertaken by the Center for Policy Research and Analysis, the Conference Board, and the National Governor's Association and reported in 1987.[53] By 1988 a full series of studies prepared by the Congressional Research Service had crystallized the problem for policy makers. In one study, Wendy Schacht prepared legislators for the task they faced:

Many observers feel that the United States lags behind its foreign competitors in transferring new technologies from the laboratory to the marketplace. At issue is what role, if any, the Federal Government should play in helping the private sector develop and use new products and processes.

The United States is the only industrialized country without a coordinated national policy for industrial innovation. Current policy is to fund basic research, while removing barriers to technology development in the private sector, thereby permitting market forces to operate more efficiently.[54]

Schacht's study continued to identify—and challenge—the ideological basis of U.S policy with respect to commercialization of technology:

The basic tenant [sic] is that the commercialization of technology is the responsibility of the private sector. Yet, since the Federal Government influences the environment in which private sector decisions are made, questions remain as to the proper role of the Government in promoting innovation and technological advancement.[55]

The report then went on to point out that

there appear to be several general trends related to technological development which have contributed to the current difficulties many domestic industries are facing. Foremost among these is the fact that Governments in most other industrialized countries actively promote commercial technological advancement and application as a component of economic growth activities.[56]

Noting the often adversarial relationship between government and business in the United States in comparison with other industrialized countries, the Congressional study went on to point out a more pressing concern:

In the United States, the Government funds almost half the national R&D endeavor: over 70 percent of this support is for defense. Thus, a large portion of the spending decisions reflect Government, rather than commercial market demand. The technological requirements of the Government generally do not co-incide with those of the private sector and the commercial marketplace.[57]

Evidence of serious Congressional concern and attention to these is-sues was reflected in the focus of several Congressional Committee and Subcommittee hearings during the mid-1980s. Beginning in 1985, for in-stance, the House Subcommittee on Economic Stabilization held hearings on the "Report of the President's Commission on Industrial Compet-itiveness." Investigations continued through 1988, with hearings on economic development and technology transfer before the House Com-mittee on "Science, Space and Technology." By 1988, there was ample evidence that the federal government was making serious efforts to ac-tively promote the use of federal R&D dollars for commercial innovation. Studies emerged analyzing this new focus. Department of Energy Lab-oratories, for example, formerly engaged exclusively in defense R&D, expanded their missions to include nurturing technological innovation in the civilian sector, with the aim of increasing U.S. competitiveness.

Conclusion

Expanding federal defense R&D to include a new mission of civilian commercial technological innovation through technology transfer be-came the fulcrum around which incremental structural changes were made. These changes, however, which aimed at reviving economic growth by increasing competitiveness, did not proceed along the path of industrial policy as the academic community had begun to hint was nec-essary. Instead they headed off into an entirely new direction, relying on an invigorated entrepreneurial sector, protected by public policy, to spearhead technological innovation.

It was this distinctive path taken by the federal government to com-mercialize defense-related technologies that set the United States apart from its foreign rivals, who had also aggressively used public investment in the private sector to boost competitiveness. They, however, had cho-sen to do so through industrial policies. Government bureaucrats in Eu-rope and Japan selected and supported "winners" in the race to develop commercially viable new technologies throughout the 1960s, the 1970s, and the 1980s. In the absence of any political consensus in Washington for similar industrial policies, policy makers not only went in the op-posite direction but ventured where they had never gone before. Instead of selecting and supporting a few established large companies to develop commercial applications of technologies derived from military spending, they decided to provide a variety of incentives, and even to underwrite multiple new small entrants in the marketplace. Policy makers simulta-neously used antitrust policy not only to prevent monopoly power, but also to ensure that major technological innovators adopted liberal licensing policies to disseminate the new technologies widely. Moreover, they put in place tax incentives, such as the still-temporary R&D investment tax credit, to boost innovation through private sector R&D.

The move toward federal support for commercially viable research differed from Europe and Japan in another crucial respect: whereas government initiatives in those countries were consolidated and centralized under one, perhaps two, major government agencies, in the United States several agencies were involved in disbursing funds to new entrants. While the pluralism of public policy made it difficult to track what was going on, it also insulated the agencies involved from pork barrel pressures (as we shall see in subsequent chapters).

Before policies supportive of new entrants could be developed, however, the chokehold of regulatory protections needed to be dismantled. As regulatory capitalism slowly receded, entire sectors of the economy began to be exposed to market forces for the first time. Unwittingly perhaps, the United States began implementing policies that resulted in "maximum competition" in response to its foreign competitors' policies of "managed competition." These policy changes, incrementally implemented and with bipartisan support, ultimately served as a catalyst for the creation of a new economic environment: entrepreneurial capitalism. It is to a detailed examination and evaluation of these transformative public policies that we now turn in chapters 4 and 5.

CHAPTER 4

Legislating Entrepreneurial Capitalism

OVERVIEW

If the challenge for the federal government by the late 1970s was to prepare the U.S economy for global competition by stimulating commercially viable technological innovation, relying especially on entrepreneurial innovators, the road taken was uniquely American. In crafting public policies to meet its objectives, Washington acted incrementally, in bipartisan fashion, never fully articulating the direction taken in any single document or national plan that would certainly have invited intense opposition. In the now familiar words of Charles Lindblom, policy makers quite simply "muddled through." Both Congress and successive presidents resolutely resisted pressures from many in the academic community to emulate the managed, planned economies of Europe and Japan—unlike Great Britain where policy makers were briefly, if disastrously, mesmerized by their "miracle economies" until Margaret Thatcher reversed direction in 1979.

Instead, the United States informally chose the path of increased domestic competition, altering the mandates of public policy to support new entrepreneurial entrants while simultaneously dismantling regulatory protections for larger, more established companies and more vigorous antitrust enforcement. In consequence, the private sector was exposed for the first time ever to intensely competitive forces both at home and abroad. Europe and Japan, meanwhile, had gone in the opposite direction. To compete globally, their governments had opted for

more state guidance in the economy, along with support for a few selected "national champions" who were protected from domestic competition.

Only with the benefit of hindsight is it possible to assess the impact
and consequences of the policy choices made by America in the 1980s
and 1990s. At the time, especially given the ad hoc, piecemeal nature of
the policy response, it may not have been clear—even to the participants
involved in crafting public policy—which of several policy decisions
over a twenty-year period were the most crucial in transforming the
American economy from one strangled by "regulatory capitalism" into
one energized by the ferocious competition of "entrepreneurial capitalism."

Thus, it has been left to academic observers like myself to piece together the jigsaw puzzle of federal action from the "clues" that are available: congressional research reports, governmental commissions, and the
public policies themselves. It cannot be emphasized often enough that
radical change—a metamorphosis of the American economy—was never
the intended consequence. It occurred, nevertheless, because of the syn-
ergies created by the public policies adopted, however fragmented. By
dismantling regulation, as well as by passing a series of public polices
whose combined effects created an economy in which innovative new
entrants were admitted at a hitherto unprecedented and accelerated rate,
the American economy was in fact transformed. Entrepreneurial capitalism was born!

Out with the Old: Dismantling Regulation

The next two chapters identify the core political decisions that pushed
the U.S. economy from an era of regulatory capitalism spanning some
thirty years—beginning in the 1930s and ending in the early 1970s—into
a new era of entrepreneurial capitalism that began in the late 1970s,
gaining momentum in the 1980s and early 1990s, an era that precipitated
massive adjustments and restructurings in the private sector and even
within government itself.

The primary policy objective—to stimulate commercially viable,
market-driven technological innovation—was accomplished by means of
tactics that reversed the thrust of regulatory era legislation, substituting
competition for regulatory protection. Trade policy, since the end of
World War II, had exposed the economy to foreign competition. Now
regulatory policy, so the thinking went, was holding the economy back,
preventing it from facing the challenges trade liberalization had imposed.

By the late 1970s, economic arguments critical of regulation had
reached a critical mass, "a tipping point." The assumptions underlying

the regulatory era, which had itself undermined laissez-faire capitalism, began to be challenged not only intellectually but in practical terms, by technological advances, as well. The regulatory regime had begun when the free-wheeling laissez-faire era of industrial capitalism generated an intense political backlash, resulting in the Sherman Anti-Trust Act of 1890 and the Clayton and Federal Trade Commission Acts of 1914, enacted to curb the market power of monopolistic trusts. Subsequently, ideas supporting more active federal regulation of economic activity gained momentum, beginning with the Depression of the 1930s when statist ideologies of socialism, communism, and national socialism appeared to be more successful, while capitalism itself appeared near collapse.

Economic regulation, which persisted and intensified until the 1960s and early 1970s, was supported by a variety of arguments. These arguments only began to be seriously challenged in the late 1970s, when America's lack of global competitiveness became crystal clear to observers both inside and outside government. In some industries, it had been assumed that regulation was necessary to save business from "wasteful duplication" and "ruinous competition." Financial services in the 1930s were a case in point and the Roosevelt administration's goal became price stabilization. Indeed, it was not until 1975 that the Securities and Exchange Commission (SEC) eliminated fixed commission rates for securities brokers that had been set in the 1930s, with the new objective of moving from price stabilization to achieving a greater degree of competition in the securities industry. Competitive forces continued to blast the securities industry with the entry of discount brokers and then web-based deep discount brokers. By the end of the 1990s, stock exchanges themselves were swept by the forces of ECNs (Electronic Communications Networks), which permitted after-hours electronic trading of stocks. Although initially they attracted little volume and generated little revenue, their entry threatened to revolutionize the trading monopolies of the major stock exchanges. The New York Stock Exchange, the oldest, faced the possibility that the Securities and Exchange Commission would sweep away the last barriers protecting it from competition. These initiatives would make it easier for regional stock exchanges, non-member dealers and eventually ECNs to trade Big Board stocks. The SEC hoped that increased competition would spur increased competition and lead to lower costs for investors: "The expected moves reflect the SEC's stepped up efforts to come to terms with the rapid and sometimes chaotic changes in markets spurred by advancing technology and its own pro competition stance."[1]

Also in the 1930s, the collapse of many depository financial institutions resulted in the imposition of more direct federal controls that set interest rate ceilings and limited the geographic areas where banks could offer their services and the types of financial products they could offer con-sumers.[2] Fifty years were to pass before these Depression-era restrictions were repealed by two pieces of legislation: the Depository Institutions Deregulation and Monetary Control Act of 1980 (which phased out interest-rate ceilings imposed on savings instruments offered by all de-pository institutions, thus helping to avert the disintermediation that arose when interest rates rose) and the Garn–St. Germain Depository Institutions Act of 1982 (which provided flexibility and protection to fi-nancial institutions in financial difficulty, broadened the power of thrift institutions to increase loans and accept deposits from commercial cus-tomers, and allowed all depository institutions to establish a new type of account to compete with money market mutual funds). The upshot of these changes was to offer consumers a wider range of savings options and to permit depository institutions more flexibility so that they could compete with newer types of financial products offered by other financial institutions such as mutual funds.[3] Some thrift institutions subsequently made disastrous investment choices, leading to a $500 billion bailout under the direction of the Resolution Trust Corporation and the reim-position of some controls.

Finally, in November 1999, The Glass–Steagall Act of 1933, another Depression-era remnant that had separated investment from commercial banking and had forbidden banks to own insurance companies, was re-pealed. While repeal was expected to spur consolidation, the force mo-tivating Congress' decision in 1999 was the threat of global competition from fully integrated financial firms abroad and the marketplace realities of the Travelers/Citicorp merger earlier that year.

Other regulatory rationales protected other industries. For instance, it was assumed that industries such as power generation, transportation, or telecommunications, where barriers to entry were high, were "natural monopolies." Whereas in the rest of the industrialized world these in-dustries were nationalized and placed under direct public ownership, America concocted a unique hybrid of privately owned but publicly reg-ulated companies. In certain instances, the government even helped set up these monopolies. For example, when a General Electric engineer filed a patent for the "Alexanderson Alternator," the government considered this new radio technology used for trans-Atlantic communications so vital to national security that it was loathe to see it move into foreign hands. Thus, when the British Marconi Company offered to purchase it in 1919, the federal government made a counterproposal to GE: the al-ternator would be placed with a newly created subsidiary of GE called Radio Corporation of America (RCA). The subsidiary would operate the U.S. end of international wireless circuits for both governmental and commercial traffic. According to journalist Jeff Kisselhoff, "as a fur-ther inducement, the Navy offered to turn over wireless patents it had received through wartime research. *The government, in effect, was handing GE a private mint, its own monopoly instituted and supported by the United States. Of course GE accepted*"[4] (emphasis added).

AT&T was probably the most widely known private company enjoying government protection of its monopoly status in exchange for regulation. Theodore Vail, the organizational patriarch of AT&T, had enthusiastically embraced regulation as a substitute for competition in order to permit the orderly development of an efficient nationwide communications system. In 1910, in AT&T's annual report, Vail had carefully laid out his strategy for establishing a universal and extensive telecommunications system. He wrote that universal service could not be accomplished "by separately controlled or distinct systems nor . . . can there be competition in the accepted sense of competition,"[5] and he called for a private monopoly subject to government regulation. By 1924, an AT&T executive described the Bell system as "really a new sort of thing—a privately owned, publicly managed institution."[6] Another observer assessed the validity of other arguments in favor of a "natural monopoly" in telecommunications, particularly those of efficiencies of scale:

The high cost of fixed plant, the steadily declining average cost of service and the need for all customers to interconnect with one another made monopoly seem inevitable. The broadcast industry was viewed as a natural monopoly. It depended on inherently "scarce" airwaves and was therefore populated by a small, government appointed elite.[7]

Consequently, by the time The Communications Act of 1934 was enacted, it was widely accepted by regulators, consumers, and the industry itself that telephone service was a "natural monopoly." Hence AT&T was able to survive prior to government antitrust actions in 1913 and 1956 and was maintained as a regulated monopoly until the government signaled its intention to permit the entry of market forces into the telecommunications industry with the 1974 filing of the Justice Department's antitrust suit, which ended with the Consent Decree leading to the breakup of "Ma Bell" in 1982.

A third argument supporting regulation was the assumption that "scarcity" prevailed in certain areas such as, for instance, "radio spectrum." Thus, allotments of spectrum for both wired and wireless communications, rather than being owned privately, had to be made by a government agency—the Federal Communications Commission—whose role it would be to ration the scarcity to certain entrants by granting licenses, while policing and constraining their activities. Peter Huber, looking back at the original assumptions supporting regulation, acknowledged that in 1887 the airwaves must have seemed small and crowded, a place of scarcity. It was a natural place for cartel and monopoly, requiring strict rationing and central control.[8]

Yet slowly and inexorably the arguments supporting regulatory capitalism began to be undermined and a new era began to emerge, one in which the public interest was to be protected by commercial competition rather than by regulatory defense.[9] By 1987, Robert W. Crandall of the Brookings Brooking Institution expressed a fresh conventional wisdom essential to the emergence of entrepreneurial capitalism. He suggested that once industry and its regulators completed their adjustment to new competitive realities "consumers (would) find that they benefit substantially from a system driven by market forces instead of negotiations between a monopolist and and its state and federal regulators."[10] Thus, deregulation would benefit consumers (whose protection had always been a focus for antitrust regulators), and they would come to demand the benefits of increased choice, later if not sooner.

By the late 1970s, a critical discussion emerged both inside and outside government, concerning not so much the practicality of federal regulation of economic activity but its costs. Parenthetically, it should be emphasized that social regulation, even during the present era of entrepreneurial capitalism, has not abated. There continues to be strong public support for worker health and safety, civil rights, and environmental protection, as one congressional study duly noted.[11] In fact, especially during the Clinton Administration, social regulation increased.

That federal regulation imposed costs and burdens had already begun to be recognized as far back as the 1960s. During the Kennedy Administration an Office for the Oversight of Regulatory Agencies had been proposed, while Lyndon B. Johnson had established the Administrative Conference of the United States in 1964 as a permanent government agency to reform the regulatory process. Subsequently, Nixon's Task Force on Productivity and Competition, headed by George Stigler, criticized the regulatory process as rigid, overly concerned with trivial details, and unable to achieve results. It urged the President to work towards freer entry into regulated markets and to abandon minimum rate controls. With Nixon's tenure in office shortened by his resignation, Gerald Ford was left to continue the work on regulatory reform, which he did with zeal, his initial impetus being to reduce inflation.[12] In his first major economic address to Congress in October 1974, he outlined a four-point program on regulation and asked Congress to establish a National Commission on Regulatory Reform to report within one year on unnecessary and costly rules and practices of ten independent regulatory agencies. By July 1975, Ford had met with the heads of those agencies and called for steps to improve the effectiveness of their regulatory activities through the use of cost–benefit analysis. Thus, the executive branch broached the controversial issue of regulatory reform earlier than

Congress, even though two simultaneous investigations—one in the executive branch, the other in the legislative branch—eventually precipitated action. In October 1976, the Committee on Interstate and Foreign Commerce–Sub Committee on Oversight and Investigations issued a report titled "Federal Regulation and Regulatory Reform," followed in January 1977 by the Domestic Council's Review Group on Regulatory Reform report titled "The Challenge of Regulatory Reform."

The Carter Administration, with many proponents of deregulation such as Alfred Kahn among its members, extended the work of the Ford Administration. The most far reaching reform was the Regulatory Reform Act of 1977, which Carter followed with Executive Order 12044, "Improving Government Regulations," in March 1978, designed to make federal regulations clearer, less burdensome, and more cost effective.

A special series of congressional studies clarified for members of Congress the arguments now swirling about the subject of the costs versus the benefits of economic regulation. These studies identified three types of costs: administrative costs for government itself; compliance costs for industry; and, crucially, previously ignored social costs, which it was now believed served to limit economic growth and competitiveness, issues of vital importance to policy makers anxious to reverse America's relative economic decline.

Thus, even as the regulatory responsibilities of the federal government increased in the 1970s "with little sign of abatement," the first of several studies prepared for Congress, published in 1978, informed and alerted policy makers to the increasing concerns of many economists about the costs of regulation in relation to its benefits: "These costs and benefits have included not just the direct costs to those immediately affected by regulation, but to an increasing degree upon the economy generally and wider segments of the Nation's society."[13]

Administrative Costs of Regulation for Government and Industry

Since 1970 several attempts had been made to estimate the aggregate costs of federal regulations, and by 1974 the Office of Management and Budget estimated them at $130 billion.[14] In 1975, the Economic Report of the President[15] estimated total regulatory costs at 1 percent of GNP. By 1977, private economists at the Center for the Study of American Business at Washington University in St. Louis estimated administrative costs to government in policing sectors of the economy at $3.2 billion.[16] For fiscal year 1999, the Center estimated that costs to the government had ballooned to $17.9 billion.[17]

Added to costs imposed upon government were compliance costs for industry—including costs to capture bureaucrats. A study by Roland N. McKean paid particular attention to the costs of avoiding regulation, which he called "bargaining costs," incurred in efforts to "capture" the regulatory agency.[18] Conversely, there were also costs to consumers, which one study prepared for members of Congress called "static efficiency costs"; these resulted from private enterprises engaging in less efficient use of resources that they would without regulation. Julius Allen, the author of the congressional study, went on to add:

In some areas, restriction of entry and regulating prices and rates of return prevent the price and product rivalry which would be economically more efficient. Specifically, regulation often permits setting of rates above competitive levels and protects both the inefficient producer and the firm earning excess profits.[19]

Costs to industry included more subtle costs such as transfer of income to workers in regulated industries: "Thus regulations sometimes make it possible for unions, such as those of truckers and airline pilots, to negotiate higher wage contracts than they could in more competitive markets."[20]

The Center of the Study of American Business had in 1976 estimated the costs to business at $66.1 billion and in 1979 at $102.7 billion.[21] At the same rate, we can estimate those costs by 1999 at approximately $500 billion dollars, even after economic deregulation. Paul McAvoy, an economist at Yale University, had estimated that those costs alone sliced 1.5 percent off economic growth.[22]

Given the climate of deep and growing concern over America's lagging global competitiveness, Congress was especially receptive to the costs of regulation, particularly the stultifying effects it had on technological innovation, managerial incentives, and the introduction of new products. A congressional study prepared in 1978 restated this effect several times in a detailed critique:

where regulatory agencies set limits on profits, the incentive to engage in technological advances that would bring about, even for a limited period supranormal profits is removed. . . . Since rates permitted by regulatory agencies are based substantially on capital costs, firms considering alternative innovations have often opted for the more capital intensive approach even though an alternative approach would have been less costly. The delays in approval of new products or techniques by a regulatory agency has been a disincentive to technological advance in several cases. Similarly, regulatory resistance to rate changes has slowed innovations . . . There is also reason to believe that the umbrella which a regulatory agency holds over a regulated company where it restricts entry and allows a fair rate of return can lead a company to be less dynamic in undertaking technological and managerial innovations than it would be under the spur of competition.[23]

At the time, however, it was far from certain that economic deregulation was the answer. In 1978, the author of the same congressional study warned policy makers about its possible adverse effects on consumers:

Much of the attack on Government regulation has been based essentially on strictly and sometimes narrowly defined economic considerations . . . One of the basic assumptions of many advocates of deregulation is that in the absence of regulation, competitive market conditions could prevail, and that the market mechanism would do a better job of meeting the legitimate needs of the consuming public than regulation does. But to what extent deregulation would in fact bring about effective market competition remains conjectural.[24]

However, by the 1980s and under the Reagan presidency, deregulation gained momentum, acquiring a degree of bipartisan legitimacy it had never had before. One of Reagan's first official acts was to impose a moratorium on further government regulation and to require that new rules go through the Office of Management and Budget, which would impose a "cost–benefit" yardstick before they took effect. For example, in the drug regulation area, emerging studies suggested that the costs of keeping beneficial drugs off the market as a result of prolonged testing and other regulatory requirements were exceeding the benefits of keeping harmful drugs from consumers.[25]

Adding to the momentum for regulatory change, the New Right by the 1980s had perfected new computerized fund-raising methods that enabled it to raise the money required to hire economists and other academics who produced a host of studies hostile to most regulated activity and which challenged the assumptions of natural monopolies. A host of new "think tanks" such as the Heritage Foundation, the American Enterprise Institute, the Hoover Institution, and Georgetown University's Center for Strategic and International Studies targeted the media with "remedial information," balancing what was assumed to be its "leftist" bias. Business also became more organized in the 1980s and more apt to express its frustrations with regulation.

Ultimately, however, despite an evolving political climate hostile to regulation—encompassing Democrats, Republicans, the courts, and the regulatory agencies themselves—policy makers were pushed into the uncharted waters of economic deregulation by marketplace developments that challenged the assumptions of regulatory capitalism. Emerging technologies now undermined the regulatory era assumptions of "scarcity" and "natural monopoly." In the communications industry, for example, the emergence of microwave technology pioneered by MCI presented an alternative means of communication to phone line technology. Thus, as early as 1971, the Federal Communications Commission announced a new policy favoring the entry of new firms in the private-line market after it recognized that new microwave technology had eroded the "natural monopoly" position that had been the basis for its earlier regulatory rationale. Subsequently, The Communications Act of 1978 stated in its preamble that regulation should be necessary only "to the extent marketplace forces are deficient."[26] These developments were acknowledged by Judge Greene in the AT&T antitrust trial in 1982 as undermining the old argument for "natural monopolies."[27] Moreover, the more recent emergence of "broadband" technology has permanently removed "scarcity" as an argument for any future communications regulation. As Peter Huber points out, glass and silicon have amplified our power to communicate: "Engineers double the capacity of the wires and radio about every two years, again, and again and again. New technology has replaced scarcity with abundance and cartels with competition."[28]

The implications of this new era were monumental:

The electronic web of connection that is now being woven among us all is a catalyst for change more powerful than Gutenberg's press . . . Every constraint of the old order is crumbling. The limitless, anarchic possibilities . . . contrast sharply with the limits to growth we now encounter at every turn in the physical world.[29]

If, as one observer pointed out, bottlenecks of monopoly still existed, the preferred solution for removing them now became more competition instead of regulation.[30] In any event, competitive access to the Internet became a prime example of this new orthodoxy of more competition in lieu of regulation. For example, by 1999 AT&T had acquired a commanding presence in cable broadband access via a series of acquisitions of cable companies, costing the company over $140 billion. When the city of Portland, attempting to ensure "open access," challenged AT&T's right to proprietary use of cable access in that city, the FCC stepped in with a friend-of-the-court brief in the Ninth Circuit Court, arguing that only the FCC had nationwide authority over broadband providers, not localities. Yet the FCC at that time also declined to regulate the cable platform to ensure "open access." This apparently paradoxical stance appearing to sanction AT&T's cable monopoly was defended by William Kennard, then chairman of the FCC, in a *Wall Street Journal* Op/Ed column. Instead of regulating cable access, enhancing competition in alternative technologies of broadband access—wireless, digital subscriber lines, and satellite—in addition to cable was now the FCC's preferred policy. As Kennard explained:

We believe that by giving all competitors the tools to compete, we can create a robust broadband marketplace in which the American consumer will have many different options at competitive prices. . . . Internet users want and expect choice, and they will not be satisfied until they get it. A national policy of openness and competition has brought it to them so far; it should be our policy for the future as well.[31]

By 2001 the FCC, now faced with the looming threat that all cable broadband assets would be owned by two giants, AT&T and the merged AOL Time Warner, now switched positions to mandate "open access" to competitors on AOL Time Warner's cable lines. This led technology experts such as George Gilder and Brett Swanson to forcefully argue against FCC policies, claiming that this cable "open access" rule amounted to a "forced sharing of entrepreneurial assets and profits." Clearly, regulatory policy is still in a state of flux.

On the other hand, there began to be increasing recognition that regulation had been constraining technological innovation. For example, prior to 1982 regulators had permitted AT&T to prohibit customers from connecting any device to its lines if it was not furnished by the phone company, even a device as innocuous as the Hush-A-Phone, added to the receiver to muffle noise! In that case the FCC sided with AT&T— and it was not until 1968 in the Carterphone case that the FCC reversed itself and concluded that AT&T's prohibition of the use of the Carterphone was "unreasonable and unlawful."[32]

Ultimately, AT&T itself recognized that it was being constrained by regulation, even while it was being protected from competition. For example, new technology emerging out of its own Bell Labs division had obliterated the line between communications and data processing but AT&T, saddled by its 1956 Consent Decree with antitrust regulators, which allowed the company to keep Western Electric, had agreed to confine its business to regulated voice telecommunications only and to refrain from entering data communications, even as customer needs, changed by the emergence of computers and other technological developments, made it possible. One reason why AT&T agreed to enter into its 1982 Consent Decree with the government was that in return for divesting the twenty-two regional phone companies the company was released from the technological straitjacket of its prior 1956 agreement. AT&T would now be permitted to capitalize on market opportunities and use its own technological innovations to the fullest in any markets it chose.[33] Alongside AT&T, America made a transition from "a long period of regulated monopoly and limited competition when one firm dominated all aspects of the telephone business to an environment marked by open entry, rapid technological change and a proliferation of new entrants."[34]

Furthermore, technology was also converging in a way that made it impossible for regulators to keep the emerging computer industry and

the telecommunications industry separated. Telephone networks required sophisticated computer switching systems while, as Richard
Wiley noted, "in the process of developing the telecommunications applications for computers, large numbers of firms outside the traditional
telephone and telegraph industry acquired technical expertise that was
directly transferable to communications. Telecommunications companies
were also developing computer processing expertise."[35] A consensus was
quietly emerging that the electronic revolution made many former regulatory boundaries irrelevant. As Jeremy Tunstall observed:

In 1950 electronic communications and mass media were all still quite neatly
confined behind their regulatory fences. But in each case there were new technologies which, as they emerged in the third quarter of the century, began to
make the regulatory fencing look arbitrary and irrelevant.[36]

Under the circumstances a new approach was needed, and it became
obvious what it should be: the fences had to removed and technological
convergence accepted, even encouraged. Thus:

Under deregulation, new services, new technologies are encouraged; the general
approach is to get new technologies out of the marketplace as fast as possible
... New technologies in private hands are to be encouraged and regarded as
innocent until proven guilty; old, more cautious regulatory attitudes—with
prime attention devoted to protecting existing services and technologies—have
been rejected.[37]

The free marketplace approach extended to not specifying official standards for new technologies, especially if regulators thought that standards would impede market forces. This created a certain amount of
incompatibility and confusion. For example, there are no cellular standards in the United States—AT&T'S TDMA standards compete with
Sprint's CDMA standards, while Europe uses GSM technology currently
not in wide use here. And new standards are still coming onstream.

Consumer demands were also becoming more complex, and it was
increasingly apparent to regulators and academic observers alike that the
resources of one or two publicly regulated private companies were in-
adequate to satisfy the array of new products and services the public
interest required, even demanded. Jeremy Tunstall noted the critical role
government now played in helping provide resources to competitors:

Whereas before 1940 high tech research and development was largely confined
to a few dominant firms which could afford massive outlays, such as AT&T and
RCA, *after 1940 the federal government funded research on a scale that even AT&T
could not match* ... research and development became much more widely prac-
ticed in a whole range of fast growing new and related industries. In consequence

there came to be many other companies . . . which introduced their own technologies and began to stake commercial and regulatory claims . . . And these new industries led to new generations of technology and new market entrants coming onto the scene more quickly and unpredictably.[38]

The basis for entrepreneurial capitalism was thus established, with government as the catalyst both as funder and chief consumer of technology, a role to be discussed at length in chapter five. Initially, federal research was confined to defense products, with commercial innovation emerging as a new direction only after America's global economic decline became clearly apparent in the 1980s. As the effect of government support for technology broadened into private sector support for innovation in the 1990s, the product cycle speeded up and "the whole advent of new technologies seem(ed) to be shifting from the measured tread of the old AT&T elephant to the pace of small computer companies with twenty-five year old chief executives working 24 hours a day searching for a market niche."[39]

By the end of the 1990s, new areas of monopoly once thought to be "natural" were being investigated, and many were forced to open themselves to competition. They included areas as diverse as domestic satellite communications networks and even space satellite delivery systems, once under the exclusive control of NASA and now opened to new entrants such as Orbital Sciences, formed in the 1980s to take advantage of this new deregulated environment. Power generation was opened to competition in 1996 (albeit disastrously in some states), as was local phone service in an extension of telecommunications deregulation. Cable deregulation completed the range of communications deregulation with the passage of the Cable Policy Acts of 1984 and 1992.

Moreover, the new technology of the Internet was undermining remaining areas of monopoly, exposing the entire American economy to price transparencies of a kind never before experienced, contributing to lower inflation despite strong growth. The ideological journey from regulatory to entrepreneurial capitalism is best exemplified by the hands-off governmental policy with respect to the Internet, compared with earlier, more direct regulatory approaches towards telecommunications. This sea change fueled by the Internet, opened to commercial competition in 1992, was summed up by telecommunication expert, Peter Huber:

The Web is probably the best model at hand for the broadband architecture of the future. It is already the world's largest communications system. It spans the national, and regional and local communications networks used by commercial, government and educational organizations nationwide. It is also, at the same time, an array of independently owned and managed networks, separately funded, separately developed and separately maintained, with no single entity or agency in charge of managing everything. It is, in short, the model of the future. A broadband Web will offer decentralized and non-hierarchical connectivity, but not simplicity or uniformity.

(Once) all broadcasting happened to be under the control of governments or great monopoly companies. No more. The "telescom" [sic] is being transformed into a network of networks . . . (with) no single dominant center.[40]

The new political mandate was made crystal clear in the Senate preamble to the Telecommunication Act of 1996, which described it as "a bill to promote competition and reduce regulation in order to promote lower prices and higher quality services for American telecom consumers and encourage the deployment of new telecom technologies."[41]

In With the New: A Change in the Direction of Public Policy

Prior to the 1980s, agencies of the federal government had been going in opposite directions in economic policy: antitrust enforcement mandated competition, but regulatory policy effectively protected monopolies. Now for the first time, antitrust and regulatory agencies were both going in the same direction—one of encouraging competition and allowing market forces to prevail. Indeed, as part of the move to encourage new entrants into the marketplace and speed technological innovation through rapid dissemination of information, government agencies urged, even mandated, liberal licensing policies upon large companies with innovative technologies. For example, according to the terms of the 1956 AT&T Consent Decree, Bell Labs and Western Electric were required by antitrust enforcement to cross-license all existing patents royalty free to domestic firms and to provide future licenses at reasonable rates.[42] As a result of government pressure, by 1956 Bell Labs no longer dominated communications technology and companies such as Texas Instruments learned to build transistors.

Going one step further, national security considerations led the Department of Defense to fund research that helped non-Bell competitors such as Hughes, IBM, and Motorola build extensive technical capabilities in technologies key to the development of modern communications systems.[43] By the 1970s, the Department of Defense, concerned at obtaining all its "chip" needs from a sole source supplier, Intel, acted again to inject competition. It required the company to cross-license its chip-making technology with competitors such as Advanced Micro Devices.

Another market-dominant company, IBM, underwent a series of antitrust investigations that resulted in opening up several key areas of the company's operations to competition from smaller companies. In the 1930s and again in the 1950s, the Justice Department objected to IBM's practice of selling its parts and services as an integrated system. As a result of the subsequent 1956 settlement, IBM was required to lease its computers and to sell its data processing and servicing separately, leading to the creation of a vibrant market of new competitors in the leasing and servicing businesses. IBM was the target of yet another antitrust action but in this case, six months after the filing of a Justice Department lawsuit in 1969, IBM abandoned the practice of "bundling" its services. The company had argued helped it served its customers better by offering service packages with hardware purchases, but Justice saw this as a "restraint of trade." Rowina Oligario noted the consequences of this apparently arcane ruling for entrepreneurial competitors:

In forcing IBM to abandon its bundling practice, the federal government opened the way for numerous companies to enter the software and computer services markets. Thereafter, IBM machines would function as a platform for a diverse array of software application, generated by a collection of highly competitive small firms.[44]

IBM was sued soon after for anticompetitive practices by Control Data, an upstart company, forcing the Justice Department to join the case, which was not settled until 1972 when IBM settled the case out of court and agreed to sell Control Data its Service Bureau Corporation subsidiary and gave it a package of cash and contracts worth $101 million.

But it was not antitrust action alone that challenged IBM's dominance so much as technological change. New industry dynamics and the rise in the 1970s of faster, cheaper semiconductor technology undercut IBM's main product: the large mainframe computer. Mini- and microcomputers now gained market share.

The new semiconductor technology broke IBM's hold on the industry for several reasons. For one thing, the semiconductors were standardized, a circumstance that allowed independent suppliers to provide parts to a host of new computer markers. Barriers to entry fell, and competition proliferated . . . Product cycles shortened. Young entrepreneurs, unhindered by bureaucratic corporate structures, exploited the new growth segments and brought their products to market with a speed IBM could not match.[45]

During this period, many foreign computer competitors such as Fujitsu and Hitachi, underwritten by supportive policies of the Japanese government, were encouraged by IBM's troubles to enter the market. Then IBM, possibly distracted by its antitrust troubles, allowed an upstart, Microsoft, to develop a PC operating system which, together with Intel semiconductor chips, created a new WINTEL monopoly. By the late 1990s, Microsoft itself had become the target of federal antitrust regulators, Intel having settled antitrust allegations earlier.

By now the marketplace, even without government prodding, had embraced open-source codes, and liberal licensing practices had now become the industry standard, with the marketplace rewarding dissemination. Companies such as Apple, which had chosen not to license till 1994, were punished in the marketplace and saw market share shrink, while open-source, licensed JAVA and LINUX networking operating system gained customers. In the new Personal Digital Assistant (PDA) space, Palm chose to license its Palm OS system to competitors such as Handspring. Thus, it was in this new open environment that Microsoft's PC operating system monopoly, particularly after it bundled its "Internet Explorer" in its Windows operating system, was challenged and the company vilified as a "predatory monopolist" by Judge Thomas Penfield Jackson at the conclusion of its antitrust trial. One section of the Judge's antitrust ruling was for Microsoft to open "relevant and necessary portions" of its source code (its "crown jewels") to representatives of third-party software and hardware developers, a remedy reminiscent of that in the earlier IBM case and in keeping with the federal government's goal of disseminating technological innovation more widely in order to increase competition.[46]

Technology Innovation Legislation Encourages New Entrants

While less regulatory intrusion and more vigorous antitrust enforcement resulted in major structural changes to the economy, they were nevertheless in keeping with the orthodoxy that the primary job of American government was to act indirectly and not pursue any conscious development strategy, leaving investment and product development decisions to the private sector.

Under pressure to make America more competitive, the federal government took on a much bolder role, one that many informed observers have not publicly acknowledged and which Peter Eisinger's ground breaking book, *The Rise of the Entrepreneurial State*, published in 1988, did not consider relevant at the national level, because it had not yet fully emerged—namely, the government's transformation into an entrepreneurial catalyst. By the mid-1980s, having accepted that national economic security had become as important a goal as national security, Congress now stood ready to do what several states, such as Massachusetts, had already done with respect to economic development policy—namely "identify, evaluate, anticipate, even help develop and create . . . markets (and products) for private producers to exploit aided, if necessary, by government as subsidizer or co-investor."[47] Eisinger had gone on to elaborate the reasons why the states had decided to undertake this novel role, reasons which applied with increasingly urgency to the federal government by the mid- to late 1980s:

International competition in the marketplace, a phenomenon that began to take serious shape in the 1970s, put a premium on product innovation and technological pioneering . . . The entrepreneurial state is a response to increasing technological complexity and to great international economic forces whose mastery eludes the capacity and resources of most individual private entrepreneurs.[48]

Thus, as the 1980s progressed, the federal government made the decision to become a facilitator and participant in the market economy to a degree unaccustomed in America and inexplicable in conventional ideological terms. That it occurred at all, and began to accelerate under a Republican president, Ronald Reagan, reveals the extent to which Congress had become alarmed by America's global economic underperformance and was now ready to accept the academic arguments that fundamental policy changes were necessary on grounds of national security, a goal restated as national economic security. This rationale was, and remains, the only one that could have attracted bipartisan, particularly Republican, support. Lacking a consensus for a coordinated industrial policy, however, these "back door" policy changes were made piecemeal and over a long period of time, some enacted much earlier and well before this rationale had emerged and been fully articulated as it was, for example, in Section 2a of The Small Business Act of 1997 (Public Law 85–536): "The essence of the American economic system of private enterprise is free competition. . . . The preservation and expansion of such competition is basic not only to the economic well-being, *but to the security of this Nation*" (emphasis added).[49]

Thus, in addition to public policies that removed the federal government as an impediment to innovation and competitiveness, policy makers took steps to place the federal government at the epicenter of change as enabler and catalyst. Entrepreneurial capitalism, defined by an unprecedented and accelerated rate of technological innovation, was a consequence of strategic changes in policy priorities, enhanced by a variety of incentives for multiple new entrants to develop and disseminate new technologies with commercial applications.

Federal support of technology innovation had begun as far back as 1950 with the National Science Foundation's mandate to fund basic research. The need for federal support became more urgent when the Eisenhower Administration, frightened by the launch of Sputnik, struggled to respond to the Soviet's lead in technology. It led to the creation, in 1958, of the Advanced Research Projects Agency in the Department of Defense (DARPA) as well as the establishment of NASA. However, it was not until the late 1970s that America's lack of global competitiveness in technological innovation came to be of such serious concern that Congress responded with the first of many initiatives designed to remedy the situation: The National Science and Technology Policy, Organization and Priorities Act of 1976. This act mandated that the federal government promote those R&D programs that contribute to the long-term health of science and technology.

In the decades since, two related policy directions can be identified. First, commercialization of technology became key to encouraging economic growth and to making America more globally competitive. Federal support moved away from funding basic research with purely military applications and towards the direction of commercially viable applied research. It was a controversial policy direction and one not taken in the 1950s when the National Science Foundation was founded. Federal support for applied, rather than basic, research was always controversial and by 1997, as private sector R&D accelerated, the National Research Investment Act reversed this direction. It doubled the annual authorized funding for basic science and medical research but prohibited these funds from being used for commercial purposes, permitting them to be used only for "precompetitive research and development of technology."[50]

Second, as federal technology innovation policy developed throughout the 1980s and 1990s, we witnessed the evolution and strengthening of the political commitment to include new entrants in the process. It was that commitment—specified in public policy—that definitively shifted the American economy towards entrepreneurial capitalism, leading to an explosion of high-risk technology and biotechnology innovation by a multitude of entrepreneurial startups that the private sector initially had neither the resources nor the will to fund on its own.

At the core of federal technology legislation that supported innovation through competition to stimulate economic growth was the commercialization of federally sponsored R&D through cooperation between federal laboratories, the academic research community, industry, and state and local government, a process known as technology transfer. The Stevenson–Wydler Technology Innovation Act of 1980 laid the basis for federal technology law. It focused broadly on the dissemination of technology information by requiring agencies to establish Offices of Research and Technology Applications and to devote a portion of their budgets to technology transfer. The act also established a Center for the Utilization of Federal Technology. It initiated legislation making it easier for federal laboratories to transfer their technologies to state and local government, as well as to the private sector, via what came to be known as CRADAs or Co-operative Research and Development Agreements (precursors were early executive orders, the 21954 Atomic Energy Act, and the 1958 Space Act). Other initiatives modified the earlier legislation specifically to include support for new entrants, making fairness of access to federal technology and openness to competition a basis for all transfer policies.[51]

The most significant amendment to the Stevenson–Wydler legislation was the Federal Technology Transfer Act of 1986. Its goal was to improve the flow of technologies with potential commercial applications to the private sector. The Federal Technology Transfer Act of 1986 made technology transfer a responsibility of all federal laboratory scientists and engineers and legislated a charter for a Federal Laboratory Consortium for Technology Transfer. It also allowed the directors of federal laboratories to make advance agreements with large and small companies on title and licensing to inventions resulting from cooperative R&D agreements with government laboratories. The National Institutes for Health, for example, established an NIH Office for Technology Transfer to promote and license biotechnology developed in its government-funded laboratories. It also created a charter for a Federal Laboratory Consortium for Technology Transfer, comprised of over 700 research and development federal laboratories, from seventeen federal agencies and departments to coordinate and develop strategies for linking government technology with the needs of the marketplace. So eager were policy makers to energize entrepreneurial innovation that a provision of the act even directed agencies to allow employees to patent inventions when the agencies themselves did not patent or otherwise promote commercialization.[52]

While several pieces of legislation were passed relating to technology transfer, there were some that had particular significance for small business. A milestone piece of legislation marking the shift to strong support for smaller entrepreneurial businesses was the passage of the Small Business Innovation Development Act of 1982. That seminal act mandated "set-asides" specifically for entrepreneurial companies, requiring agencies to provide special funds for small business R&D connected with the agencies' missions. DARPA was given the task of coordinating and enforcing this mandate. It marked a sea change in the allocation of federal grants and subsidies, which had previously been given exclusively to established companies.

Another key piece of legislation with several provisions that had profound implications for entrepreneurially generated technological innovation was the Omnibus Trade and Competitiveness Act of 1988. It redesignated the National Bureau of Standards as the National Institute of Standards and Technology (NIST) and added new responsibilities to its mandate, charging it with assisting the commercialization of technology. It was directed to provide for the creation and support of Regional Centers for the Transfer of Manufacturing Technology with one very specific goal in mind: "These Centers are to transfer the knowledge and technologies developed under NIST programs to small and mid-sized manufacturing firms."[53]

The emphasis on supporting innovation through the entrepreneurial sector continued into the 1990s. The Defense Authorization Act for FY

1991 established model programs for national defense laboratories to demonstrate successful relationships between federal, state, and local governments and small business. The Small Business Technology Transfer Act of 1992 established a three-year pilot program, the Small Business Technology Transfer Program (STTR) at several government departments and agencies including DOD, DOE, HHS, NASA, and NSF. It also directed the SBA to oversee and coordinate implementation of the STTR program. Moreover, it required each of the five agencies to fund cooperative R&D projects involving a small company and research at a university, federally funded R&D center, or nonprofit research institution.

The Clinton Administration continued the policy momentum favoring smaller, younger companies with the passage of the National Department of Defense Authorization Act for 1993, which further facilitated and encouraged technology transfer to small businesses. As the decade progressed, the 1995 National Technology Transfer and Advancement Act created significant incentives for prompt commercialization of new technologies developed under a CRADA, while the Technology Transfer Commercialization Act of 1998 enacted with the aim of improving the ability of Federal agencies to license federally owned inventions, included a provision of crucial importance to small business:

Section C: SMALL BUSINESS—First preference for the granting of any exclusive licenses in this section shall be given to small business firms having equal or greater likelihood as other applicants to bring the invention to practical application within a reasonable time.[54]

Technology transfer policies were augmented by important changes in patent policy which overhauled intellectual property rights, providing protections that were specially important to entrepreneurial innovators. The Bayh–Dole Patents and Trademarks Amendment Act of 1980 was seminal because it was based on the explicit belief that private entities would do a better job of commercializing inventions than federal agencies. It was noteworthy, however, because it specifically included small business, as well as universities and nonprofits, and gave them permission to obtain title to inventions developed with government support. This move was opposed by some in Congress as granting public monies for private profit, but was overridden by the urgency to advance economic growth through commercialization of technological innovation—and by the new consensus that the way to do that was to permit young companies to enter the fray. Following on the heels of Bayh–Dole, The Trademark Clarification Act of 1984 included a provision permitting private companies "regardless of size" to obtain exclusive licenses and attempted to stimulate innovation by permitting laboratories run by universities and nonprofits to retain title to inventions without limitations. For those needing proof that these new policies actually increased the rate of innovation, several studies have credited the Bayh–Dole Act with creating the U.S. biotechnology industry. They have shown that university R&D is responsible for developing 44 percent of all new U.S. drugs and 37 percent of all new pharmacological processes; in addition, the act protected and enhanced the possibility of commercialization of academic intellectual property. Moreover, the number of patents (a proxy for innovation) produced by U.S. universities exploded by 500 percent after Bayh–Dole from under 250 annually before 1980 to over 1,500 afterward.[55] By the late 1990s, so many technology and biotechnology companies had been launched taking advantage of taxpayer-funded research money, particularly in the pharmaceutical sector, that debate resurfaced among lawmakers on the question of whether private companies making profits using government-funded research should be required to pay a "return on investment fee," or lower the drug prices to consumers, through contributions to the Medicare Trust Fund.[56]

Technological innovation through the entry of small business was also advanced through radical and pioneering changes in government procurement practices. Well before the private sector enthusiastically embraced web-based "business to business" procurement, the federal government had experimented with it, intending to use the Internet to provide access to government business for entrepreneurial vendors and contractors, thereby lessening its own dependence on sole-source suppliers in order to decrease its costs and increase efficiency.

The Department of Defense, since it had the largest procurement budget, had initially funded Procurement Technical Assistance Centers and then seventeen Electronic Commerce Resource Centers (ECRCs) in the early 1990s. In 1994, the Federal Acquisitions Streamlining Act mandated that the government use e-commerce as its main method of procurement to increase efficiency. A provision of that act specified a mandate to be fair and to support small business. ECRCs were given the task of training and helping small and medium-sized businesses participate in the government supply chain, either as suppliers of prime contractors or as direct suppliers to the government.[57]

In sum, the federal government committed itself, albeit incrementally, to overhauling public policy in order revitalize the American economy. The next chapter, Financing Entrepreneurial Capitalism, examines in more detail the support, both direct and indirect, the government provided at every stage of the financial life cycle of entrepreneurial companies: from funding R&D, to providing seed and early-stage venture capital, as well as overseeing the evolution of open and diversified equity markets capable of supporting young companies.

CHAPTER 5

Financing Entrepreneurial Capitalism

Having begun the process of dismantling regulatory protections, substituting public policies to encourage competition, the federal government turned its attention to expanding its role from facilitator and catalyst of entrepreneurial innovation to financier and underwriter.

This expanded role began at a time when the private sector had neither the will nor the resources to support new entrants. It is important to recognize that in the late 1970s and early 1980s capital to finance entrepreneurial innovation was anemic at best. In contrast, by 1999 private sector investment was flourishing. Not only was private sector R&D spending robust, but private venture capital flowed freely, reaching over $58 billion by some estimates,[1] compared with only $5.8 billion four years earlier[2]; a record 3,619 young companies received venture funds[2], while 613 new companies went public that year.[3] Private investors, perhaps "irrationally exuberant," seemed willing to finance companies at much earlier stages than ever before, including some without any profits or even earnings.

The confidence of the private markets by the late 1990s must, however, be traced to the foundations laid by the federal government twenty years earlier. Then private sector R&D was declining, private venture capital was practically nonexistent, lending by risk-averse depository institutions exceeded capital raised by securities markets by a margin of 60 percent (versus 30 percent by 1999),[4] and the Nasdaq stock market, less than decade old, was unable to support a large number of new entrants, especially after the nasty 1973–1974 bear market.

It was during this period of private sector malaise that the federal government undertook the responsibility of jump starting critical investments in young companies engaged in high-risk technological innovation. It subsequently entered every stage of the financial life cycle of young companies from funding their R&D to providing and organizing seed capital for early stage startups, as well as making later stage public venture capital investments. At the same time, it facilitated the development of diversified private capital markets. A strong case can be made that without federal financial support and the expenditure of public funds at that critical juncture, it is unlikely the technological revolution of the late twentieth century would have developed so rapidly, despite federal attempts to legislate innovation.

This argument will doubtless raise objections that should be acknowledged and quickly dispatched at the outset. Why, for example, did such a bold new role for the federal government not attract media and public attention, becoming a contentious partisan issue? And why, as is usually the case, did these initiatives not become subverted by "pork barrel" pressures or political interference?

Frankly, several factors insulated the public financing of entrepreneurial capitalism despite the political pressures that could have overwhelmed this new direction in public policy. First, policies underwriting innovation did not attract public scrutiny because of the complex nature of the issue itself, which prevented it from becoming a visible "red-flag" issue like abortion or the death penalty. Relegated to the realm of the technical, it became a low-visibility issue, a part of what one observer terms the "hidden agenda." And once part of the hidden agenda, only the relevant interest groups became involved. Generally, as John W. Kingdon suggests "the lower the partisanship, ideological cast and campaign viability of the issue in a policy domain, the greater the importance of interest groups."[5]

It is interesting that Peter Eisinger in *The Rise of the Entrepreneurial State* had come to a strikingly similar conclusion as to why equally significant critical changes in the roles of many state governments had gone unnoticed:

The advent of the entrepreneurial state has curiously gone almost unnoticed among the public. But this is perhaps not surprising: the initiatives that define this new intervention are small, technically complex and difficult to evaluate . . . Furthermore, the problems of the entrepreneurial state are not the products of mass political demands or the subjects of extended media debate or party platform planks. They appear instead to be technocratic experiments, emerging from the nexus of research institute, academic and bureaucratic connections to achieve highly general and almost universally popular employment goals articulated most often by chief executives.[6]

Moreover, the rationale of national security and the involvement of the Defense Department provided a convenient method of extracting agreement from Republicans who would otherwise have been reluctant to support any intervention in the operations of the free market and the investment choices it might make. Without a doubt, had the issue been presented to Congress in terms of an "industrial policy" rather than as one of national economic security, it might have become embroiled in a bitter and partisan public debate that might well have spilled over into the public arena with a far different outcome.

On the other hand, why did these initiatives not attract pork barrel pressures? And how did government avoid the political interference that other kinds of federal spending inevitably attracted? To be sure, there are those who would disagree that the federal government's public venture investments were free of pork barrel pressures. Linda Cohen and Roger Noll in *The Technology Pork Barrel* leveled this criticism as far back as 1991, providing such well publicized and expensive failures as the breeder reactor and synthetic fuels as prime examples of why government–business partnerships did not work. They were joined in the late 1990s by some established high-technology companies, who began lobbying Washington to stop funding applied research leading to commercially viable innovation and return to funding only basic research. In 1998 T. J. Rodgers, chief executive of Cypress Semiconductor Corporation, attacked public venture capital programs as "techno-pork" and, along with seventy-eight other Silicon Valley business leaders, signed a "Declaration of Independence" requesting Congress to appoint a panel to mark for extinction programs they called "corporate welfare."[7] Opposing this initiative were high-technology industry groups, which argued that federal programs provided a crucial launching pad, an incubator for risky technologies with potential, but distant payoffs for the economy, giving young companies a chance to survive in a highly competitive sector.[8] Josh Lerner, in an article titled "The Government as Venture Capitalist: The Long-Run Impact of the SBIR program," reported that many dynamic high-tech giants of the late 1990s received support through federal programs when they were still startup private entities, which gave them the credibility to attract later stage private venture capital. He included Intel, Apple Computer, Compaq, and Federal Express among that group. He did note, however, that having received spectacular commercial benefits from the SBIR program, their CEOs became reluctant to publicize the federal support they had initially received. He speculated that the reason may have been to avoid unwelcome scrutiny from reporters and politicians and, I might add, from competitors.

There is, on the contrary, a strong case to be made that federal initiatives to fund entrepreneurial high-technology companies did not attract interference by congressmen seeking to bring home the "pork" for local businesses. Josh Lerner made this case with respect to the Small Business Innovation Research program "although he found that Congressional officials did pressure program managers to make geographically diverse awards."[9]

He continued:

Conversations with federal program managers, as well as assessments by evaluators (US GAO, 1985, 1987b, 1995), suggest the program is . . . insulated from many of the political pressures to make awards to particular firms that are encountered in other programs.[10]

To explain this unexpected outcome, Lerner suggested that the government grants involved were far too small (not exceeding $750,000) to attract official interest and political pressure, that they required the approval of hundreds of mid-level officials rather than a single committee, and that perhaps bureaucrats had acquired the skills necessary to select promising companies with viable technologies because a formal scoring process was used to rank applicants on the technological merits of their proposals; "This may leave evaluators with less discretion to choose well-connected applicants."[11]

Another of Lerner's arguments accounting for the lack of political interference with respect to the SBIR program was that there was no single federal source of R&D funding but rather a pluralistic organizational structure. In fact, administrative pluralism was applied to the entire federal effort to finance young companies. Historically, while there had been several attempts to reorganize and consolidate the Federal science and technology establishment, all of them failed to achieve that goal. Several pesidents and successive congresses had chosen to defend fragmentation, fending off pressures to form any single government agency to oversee and disburse federal technology expenditures. In one Congressional Research Service study, authors William C. Boesman and Michael E. Davey pointed out that since the 1960s several proposals to establish a single Department of Science and Technology had all failed. The Reagan Administration, at one point supporting consolidation, had proposed transferring the Department of Energy laboratories to the Department of Commerce to create a unified "Energy Research and Technology Administration" and had also proposed the transfer of the National Bureau of Standards to the National Science Foundation as part of a plan to establish a "Department of Science and Industry." In the 98th Congress there had even been a proposal to establish a National Technology Foundation, to be comprised of the National Bureau of Standards within the Department of Commerce and parts of the National Science Foundation.[12]

By the end of the 1990s, however, the pluralistic organizational structure of the federal R&D mission had been recognized as a strength rather than a weakness, not least because it made it difficult to "capture" the effort for purposes of political interference. As William Boesman noted:

The U.S. R&D structure is a complex of federal and non-federal organizations which fund and conduct basic and applied research and development and train future scientists and engineers for a broad range of federal defense and civilian R&D in furtherance of national S&T policy goals. . . . *This pluralistic national system, involving as it does a number of federal R&D mission agencies . . . is generally considered by science policy makers to be one of the world's most productive R&D systems, if not its most productive, in part because of its pluralistic nature* (emphasis added).[13]

We are now in a position to return to a detailed examination of the role of the federal government in the financing life cycle of smaller, innovative younger companies.

THE FINANCING LIFE CYCLE AND THE ROLE OF THE FEDERAL GOVERNMENT

Federal Direct and Indirect R&D Expenditures

By the 1980s, policy makers had begun to recognize that there had been a decline in private sector R&D spending and took steps to increase R&D tax credits to boost private sector R&D investment. However, in keeping with the piecemeal nature of government action, the credit was extended nine times but not made permanent. By the early twenty-first century, estimates of what it would cost to make credits permanent kept climbing into the billions, and it has remained a tax break that Congress has been reluctant to enact. But much more had to be done—and quickly—if the government's goal of generating commercially viable technological innovation was to be met.

The federal government itself would have to provide the boost in R&D funding. Federal expenditures for defense-related R&D had long been substantial, spurred by the Cold War. As liberal economist Robert Kuttner noted in his book, *Everything For Sale*, federal R&D spending during the entire Cold War period exceeded the combined expenditures of all other advanced industrial nations. It also far outstripped private sector R&D expenditures. The federal government's responsibilities with respect to R&D were formalized in 1976 when Congress passed the National Science and Technology Policy Organization and Priorities Act, which mandated that the federal government promote R&D programs that contributed to the long-term health of science and technology. To be sure, roles came to be reversed by the late 1990s. By then the federal share of national R&D expenditures vis-à-vis the private sector had dropped from about 50 percent in 1980 to 33 percent in 1996.[14] Indeed, the private sector now outspent the federal government in R&D, its $120 billion exceeding the federal government's R&D spending of about $75 billion in fiscal year 1998.[15] Thus, as the 1990s came to a close, critics claimed that government R&D spending was unnecessary. However, it must be emphasized that up until the mid-1980s, government investment matched that of the private sector and was as important a source of R&D funding as that provided by the private sector. Moreover, where the federal government spent its R&D dollars was as important as how much it spent.

Prior to the 1980s, 70 percent of federal dollars had been spent on defense R&D, but by the 1980s a dramatic shift in the policy debate surrounding the issue of economic security and competitiveness crystallized and had massive implications for America's transformation from regulatory to entrepreneurial capitalism. Congress began to awaken to the fact the United States now had to face a fresh challenge: techno-economic competition from friendly governments. A position paper prepared for Congress in 1988 put the issue bluntly:

Technological advancement contributes substantially to economic growth through the commercialization or enhancements of products and processes and their use. The United States has been a leader in science, but this does not necessarily insure leadership in the development of technology. Many observers feel that the United States lags behind its foreign competitors in transferring new technologies from the laboratory to the marketplace. At issue is what role, if any, the Federal Government should play in helping the private sector develop and use new products and processes.[16]

The paper noted that the U.S. Government did not have a formally delineated national policy for innovation or for the development of technology and that it was the only major industrialized country without one.

Congress, as we have already noted, began to recognize that the heavy focus on defense rather than civilian R&D put the nation at a disadvantage in terms of the new debate on national economic security. This policy change, as it developed, paralleled the gradual shift in thinking about national security in solely military terms to thinking about America's national security in economic terms as well. Another Congressional Research Service study made this point unequivocally: "The balance between military security narrowly defined and 'national security' broadly defined to include economic well being, is an important political issue that bears upon the balance between U.S. defense and civilian R&D funding."[17] There came to be a recognition that "R&D, particularly civilian R&D, contribute significantly to a nation's wealth."

As far back as the early 1980s Congress had come to recognize that the nation's global competitive position was being compromised by the fact that its support for R&D since the end of the Carter Administration had become overly defense-oriented. Although the United States still spent more for civilian R&D than other nations, Japan and West Germany had increased their civilian R&D expenditures vis-à-vis the United States, indicating an increasing commitment by those nations to enhance their competitive positions. A Congressional Research Report in 1984 had warned:

The international competition in science and technology between the U.S. and other nations likely will increase in the years ahead. Japan for example, is moving rapidly into space science and technology, an area of U.S. dominance since the Space Age began. It may even be questioned whether the U.S. will be able to improve, or even maintain, its competitive position in international science and technology over the long term if its funding of civilian research and development vis-à-vis its major international competitors (mainly Japan and the countries of Western Europe) continues to decline.[18]

The Reagan Administration between 1981 and 1985 wanted to stimulate private sector R&D as part of its policy to stimulate the nation's economy and had called for cuts in federal civilian R&D spending. But the Congressional research study warned legislators against relying too heavily on defense related R&D to pick up the slack: "some may consider it unsound to rely (in fact if not exclusively) on the D.O.D to be a major federal supporter of science and technology with high civilian payoffs since D.O.D's principal mission is national defense, not international techno-economic competition with friendly nations."[19]

By the mid-1980s these warnings had begun to be taken seriously and the federal government began a shift in R&D priorities to favor civilian R&D over defense and applied research over basic. The shift became clearly apparent by the 1990s. Thus, between 1990 and 1994, in constant 1987 dollars, federal defense R&D decreased about 15.5 percent while civilian R&D increased about 15 percent.[20] Looking at a slightly different time period, 1992–1997, in real 1987 dollars, defense R&D fell by 13.3 percent while nondefense R&D grew by 6.9 percent.[21] For fiscal year 1998 defense R&D remained flat at $40.48 billion while civilian R&D increased by 4 percent to $34.9 billion. In keeping with these new policy priorities, the emphasis also shifted from basic to applied research. One study noted that while the federal government was still the largest source of funds for basic research, as a percentage its share decreased from 65 percent in 1985 to 58 percent in 1994.[22] Moreover, after 1993, basic research experienced a 20 percent decline in funding.[23]

Behind these dry statistics lay the recognition that to compete effectively in the global marketplace the United States had to commercialize more rapidly. But since, as one Congressional Research Service study suggested, "defense technology is becoming increasing complex and specialized and probably less easy to transfer to the civilian sector and translate into innovations in the marketplace,"[24] government had to make the decision to play a more proactive role in helping private industry translate innovation into marketable products.

Having decided to do more to stimulate innovation and technological advancement in the private sector, two major federal policy thrusts emerged which involved removing barriers to technology development in the private sector thereby permitting market forces to operate and providing incentives to encourage private sector innovation-related activities.[25]

It was partly as a result of this more proactive focus that the federal government decided to allocate some funds to entrepreneurial companies with early stage technologies deemed too risky and long term to attract private venture capital and mandate that these technologies have commercial applications.

Thus, the federal government moved from funding basic military research, with military contracts given exclusively to large, established defense contractors such as Lockheed, Martin Marietta, and McDonnell Douglas to funding applied civilian research with federal contracts now going to a variety of younger, smaller companies. The focus on funding commercially viable technologies came to benefit previously excluded entrepreneurial companies whose more rapid research innovations would result in products that could be sold in the marketplace.

The importance of this new emphasis cannot be overestimated in explaining America's subsequent global technological dominance and economic ascendancy. In comparison, the former U.S.S.R. made enormous public investments in basic R&D but did not focus attention on its commercial potential as much as on the military power and prestige it conferred. Japan meanwhile (and Europe to a lesser extent) also made huge investments in R&D, but, despite its commercial focus, these state-directed investments were given to a few large, established companies, not a variety of entrepreneurial ones. And in both Japanese and European capitalist models the government's goal was protection from domestic and international competition. Japan, in particular, placed restrictions on the import of semiconductor chips and on foreign direct investment in this sector starting in the 1960s and 1970s.[26]

The federal government's goal, in contrast, was to make the private sector more competitive in the global marketplace by removing regulatory protections and by choosing not to shelter it from competition. On the contrary, it increased competition by investing in a variety of technology startups, exposing older, established companies to these innovative new entrants. If accomplishing the goal of increased competitiveness through marketplace competition, rather than state-sponsored protection, seems obvious today it was far from obvious in the 1960s, 1970s, and 1980s.

At center stage of this policy shift was the 1982 Small Business Innovation Development Act passed almost unanimously by Congress. The stated purpose of the 1982 act was to stimulate technological innovation by using small business to meet federal R&D needs and to increase private commercial innovations derived from federal R&D projects. As suggested earlier, the mandate to fund new and innovative technologies actually favored smaller, entrepreneurial companies over established contractors, particularly in the defense and aerospace sectors, but with the passage of the Small, Business Innovation Development Act, this thrust was codified into policy.

The act—modeled after a 1977 initiative of the National Science Foundation and requiring a joint effort by almost all departments and agencies—created Small Business Innovation Research Programs (SBIRs) and made it mandatory for agencies with budgets over $100 million to set aside part of their research outlays, initially 1.25 percent, for small bidders. The Small Business Administration was charged with monitoring compliance with the law, making the federal government, in effect, a public "small-cap," high-tech venture capitalist. In 1992, when the program was reauthorized by Congress, the set-aside was increased and in 1997 reached its new level of 2.5 percent, representing annual funding of about $1.1 billion. The Department of Defense estimated that since the program's inception, the SBIR program has provided over $7 billion to more than 40,000 small high-technology firms.[27] The Defense Department now hosts an annual SBIR Conference in Washington to make entrepreneurs aware of the one billion dollars in funds available for technological innovation. Moreover, Josh Lerner's research demonstrated that SBIR awardees, which include Intel and Apple Computer among its alumni, grew significantly faster than a matched set of firms over a ten-year-period.

As we enter the twenty-first century, government's goal of establishing American technological dominance appears to have been accomplished. A Congressional Research Service study published in 1997 confidently concluded:

In terms of many science and technology indicators, the U.S. ranks at the top of the world's research and structure . . . the U.S. funds about 38 percent of the world's research and development. It also, according to one source, ranks first in a composite measure of world competitiveness and in overall national science and technology capabilities.[28]

However, with deficit reduction a top governmental priority by the end of the 1990s, and with private sector confidence growing, private sector funding began to exceed federal funding. By 1995, the last year in which industry statistics were available, the technology sector invested some $40 billion on R&D, with the top ten companies alone contribution $12.9 billion.[29] Although private sector R&D investments eventually dwarfed the expenditures earmarked by government agencies specifically as seed money for entrepreneurs (plus the billion dollar SBIR program), it must be emphasized that federal funding was aimed at funding early-stage startups which do not normally attract venture capital. In this way, the federal government ensured the creation of the competition necessary for entrepreneurial capitalism. A sector shift became evident by the late 1990s. Federal R&D support had moved from high technology to biotechnology and the life sciences, with the Human Genome Project a centerpiece of this new direction.

	1970	1997[30]
Life Sciences	29.4%	43.1%
Math and Computer	1.9%	5.7%

The Role of the Federal Government in Cooperative R&D

Funding the competition, however, has only been part of the story. The federal government, again, responding in the mid-1980s to America's competitive malaise, undertook an even more controversial role: funding cooperation between federal agencies and industry groups and between government, industry, and universities, a role much more in keeping with European style "cooperative capitalism" and one requiring revisions of antitrust laws. While the notion of cooperation remains a contentious one, the rationale was to maintain and enhance American competitiveness vis-à-vis other countries and to encourage investments in technologies too risky for individual companies to undertake on their own, but which could ultimately produce commercially viable products. Again, the focus on technology benefited primarily young entrepreneurial companies rather than established ones.

The first cooperative venture or consortium was Sematech in 1987, which brought together leading semiconductor companies and the Pentagon in order to overcome a perceived Japanese superiority in this field.

It was funded on a 40–60 basis by the Pentagon and participating semi-conductor manufacturers, respectively. A Congressional Research Service study, authored by economist Gary L. Guenther in 1988, noted the ironic shift in policy direction: "What is most striking about the Federal role in Sematech is that *D.O.D dollars* will help finance efforts that are intended to bolster the ability of U.S. chip makers to compete in *commercial* markets" (emphasis added).[31]

Why did Congress, in addition to making the crucial shift from funding defense-oriented, basic research to funding commercially oriented applied research, decide to take the extra step of facilitating cooperative R&D? Clearly, legislators had become alarmed at the competitive decline and erosion of market share of U.S. chip makers and the increase in market share by the Japanese. As Guenther states: "Between 1980 and 1987, the U.S. share dropped by 21.9 percentage points, while Japan's share rose by 22.2 percentage points."[32] Thus, Congress was ready to accept two new arguments. The first, as Guenther suggests, was that the semiconductor industry played such an important role in industrial competitiveness, as well as national security, that the U.S. government should do whatever necessary to ensure that chip makers retained their global dominance. To do less might mean a loss of technological leadership that would be difficult to reverse and which could inflict lasting damage on many important industries that relied on chips. The second argument was the realization that one of the principal factors accounting for the rapid rise in Japan's competitive position was the Japanese government's willingness to organize and fund cooperative R&D projects. Proponents arguing for a similar effort in the United States maintained that a massive pooling of resources from the public and private sectors was needed to overcome the Japanese competitive challenge.

Thus, by 1987 Congress stood ready to invest in cooperative R&D, at least on a temporary basis. In fiscal year 1988, $100 million was allocated to the Department of Defense (DARPA) to conduct joint research projects through Sematech. Its mission was not only to develop, test, and demonstrate new generations of computer chips but also to promote the diffusion of these techniques among a number of U.S. suppliers.[33] By 1996 federal support ended and Sematech became fully funded by the private sector amid heated Congressional discussion over whether cooperative ventures served the overall goal of a competitive economy. Moreover, a new concern was whether the government should be involved in any ventures that involved commercialization. We can speculate that many technology companies, having once been recipients of federal funds themselves, had by now become alarmed that the federal government continued to underwrite potential competitors, exacerbating an already competitive sector, and organized themselves politically to lobby Congress to redirect government funding primarily to basic research.

In any event, by the late 1990s the United States had regained its global competitive edge. Indeed, as early as 1992, a Very Large Scale Integration Systems (VLSI) Research report found that in 1991, U.S. semiconductor equipment companies made a 2.8 percent gain in the global market over the prior year, capturing 46.7 percent of the global market versus 44.9 percent for Japanese firms. A Congressional Research Service study prepared by Glenn J. McLoughlin in 1996 concluded: "This is considered important to Sematech because the data demonstrate that the U.S. semiconductor industry has made significant progress against foreign competition."[34]

It is important to note that of the eleven companies that comprised the Sematech consortium, most of the merchant chip producers (as opposed to captive producers like AT&T and IBM, which produced chips for their own use) were entrepreneurial companies. Indeed, the project was headed in 1988 by Dr. Robert Noyce, vice-chairman of Intel (one of America's premier high-technology entrepreneurial companies) who became CEO of Sematech.

The Clinton Administration expressed strong support for federal programs to provide funding for a variety of newer technologies in the form of cooperative programs and consortia modeled after Sematech.[35] In 1993, The National Cooperative Production Amendments Act amended and extended the prior National Cooperative Research Act to include joint ventures between manufacturers. The latter act, in keeping with Congress' desire to encourage companies to undertake joint research in long-term, high-risk areas deemed too expensive for one company to finance alone, clarified antitrust laws requiring that the "rule of reason" be applied in determining violations of these laws and that cooperative research ventures not be judged illegal per se.[36] In keeping with the Clinton Administration's support for stimulating technological advancement in the private sector, several other consortia—including NAVLAB, the Lead Acid Battery Consortium, and most recently the Electric Battery Consortium—were formed. NAVLAB's primary mission was to produce automated cars and other technologies that could reduce pollution and congestion and reduce accidents. In 1994 NAVLAB, a nine-member consortium that included General Motors, Toyota, and Honda plus suppliers, universities, and mass transit systems received a $160 million federal grant, matched by $40 million from its members.[37] That this type of collaborative government initiative is now the norm is reflected by a recent report in the *Times* of London that the U.S. government had set up an Advanced Battery Consortium to develop new (non-lead acid) batteries for cars, following the success of the Advanced Lead Acid Battery Consortium, which had increased lead-acid battery life by 40 percent. Individual government departments also took the lead in funding cooperative initiatives. For example, in 1997 NASA funded studies in

Solar Powered Satellites, organizing a series of conferences to bring together scientists and utility company executives, while the Department of Energy funded electrical techniques for cleaning contaminated land through the Pacific North West.

At this time it is impossible to gauge whether political pressure and hubris will alter the role that the federal government has thus far played as a catalyst for entrepreneurial competition by sponsoring collaborative efforts. By the late 1990s one observer noted that in Congress "a number of Members continued to oppose federally funded university and/or industry co-operative initiatives aimed at developing civilian technology, seeing it as "corporate welfare"[38] (subsidized commercial research that should be privately funded).

One initiative in the direction of limiting federal support for applied civilian research was a section of the National Research Investment Act in 1997, which doubled the annual authorized funding for basic science and medical research but prohibited these funds being used for commercial purposes, permitting them to be used only for "precompetitive research and development of technology."[39] Wendy Schacht with the Congressional Research Service, however, in a 1997 report to Congress, repeated a warning she had made a decade earlier—namely, that commercialization of technology was a critical factor in maintaining U.S. global competitive advantages:

Economic benefits accrue only when a technology or technique is brought to the marketplace where it can be sold to generate income and/or applied to increase productivity. . . . In recent years it has become increasingly common to find that foreign companies are commercializing the results of U.S. funded research at a faster pace than American firms. In a rapidly changing technological environment, the speed at which a product process or service is brought to the marketplace is often a crucial factor in its competitiveness.[40]

Seed Capital and the Federal Government

By the 1990s the federal government stepped up efforts to facilitate the raising of private capital and to ensure its allocation to even smaller entrepreneurial companies, an effort which gained momentum under the Clinton Administration. The primary reason for doing this was that high-risk, early-stage startups needing relatively modest amounts of venture capital remained unattractive to private venture capital. This argument was underscored by a series of focus groups convened by the Small Business Administration's Office of Advocacy between September 1995 and March 1996 after the 1995 White House Conference on Small Business had identified a lack of equity capital as a major problem for startup entrepreneurs. These focus groups confirmed that there was a significant

gap in the ability to raise patient, long-term, third-party seed capital for
rapidly growing firms needing between $500,000 and $5 million:

The popular fable is that the organized venture capital industry has plenty of
capital to meet the needs of "worthy" high potential small businesses. It is often
stated that there is not a shortage of capital, just a shortage of "good deals."
Unfortunately the popularity of this myth is exceeded only by its inappropriate-
ness. The organized venture capital market has always been a very narrow and
limited market. The number of deals consummated in a year is on the order of
1,000 and of these, fewer than 100 are start-up or seed deals.[41]

Moreover, since it takes almost the same time to perform due diligence
on a small company as on a larger one, it is more efficient for institutional
venture capitalists to fund larger entrepreneurial companies. Hence, the
National Association of Venture Capitalists estimated the average deal
at over $6.8 million, more than smaller startup entrepreneurs were ready
to borrow.

Additionally, focus groups at the 1995 White House Conference on
Small Business had identified geographic concentration as a major problem for raising capital, since most venture capitalists were located in
California's Silicon Valley and on Route 128 outside Boston, Massachusetts. Thus, closing the gap between the number of potential capital investors and small businesses and dispersing the capital available rapidly
became goals of the Clinton Administration.

Indeed, the federal government itself sought to guarantee a source of
capital for startup entrepreneurial business during the Clinton years. An
earlier law, Title 111 Section 301 of the Small Business Investment Act
of 1958, had authorized the organization and licensing, by the SBA, of
Small Business Investment Companies (SBICs), privately managed investment firms using their own capital as well as funds borrowed at
favorable rates through the federal government. The licensing of SBICs
by the SBA accelerated in the first two years of the Clinton Administration so that more SBICs were licensed than in the prior fifteen years.
According to an SBA report in June 1996, in the federal government fiscal
year ended 1995, SBICs provided capital to to 1,068 businesses totaling
$1.1 billion. If Specialized Small Business Corporations (SSBICs), which
specifically target socially disadvantaged entrepreneurs, are included an
additional $154 million was financed with federal assistance.[42]

In the mid-1990s the federal government moved to organize a hidden
but more important source of private capital that provided an estimated
$20 billion dollars annually to entrepreneurial innovators—a far larger
pool of money than SBICs or even institutional venture capitalists combined. Small private investors with high net worth have long been willing to invest in young companies, to participate in their growth, and to

wait five, even ten years, for their investments to mature, unlike organized venture capitalists who have much shorter time horizons and require larger payoffs. Such individual investors, popularly known as
"financial angels" (but officially as accredited investors meeting federal
and state securities regulations) found it difficult to identify entrepreneurs who required the kind of funding and hands-on advice they provided.

Informal attempts to bring some organization to the "angel" networking process had started in the 1980s when regional "angel" capital networks, associated with universities, came into being. One of the earliest
was the SEC-sanctioned Technology Capital Network, originally located
at the University of New Hampshire, then at MIT. Seeking to make the
process more efficient, the SBA's Office of Advocacy, working with the
University of New Hampshire, developed the Angel Capital Electronic
Network (ACE-Net) in 1996. Sponsored by the Office of Advocacy of the
Small Business Administration and working in consultation with the
SEC, state regulators and the North American Securities Administrator's
Association (NASAA), ACE-Net was a nationwide Internet-based listing
service bringing together well-heeled individual investors with smaller
amounts to invest, and dynamic, growing startup companies seeking
$250,000 to $5 million in equity financing. This created the nation's first
organized, systematic method for "angels" and small companies to get
together no matter in which state they were located, providing a solution
to both the problems raised at the 1995 White House Conference on
Small Business.

ACE-Net's Internet Home Page and central computer system is maintained by the Center for Venture Research at the University of New
Hampshire's Whittemore School of Business, while MIT's Technology
Capital Network and the University of Texas' Capital Network at Austin
operate ACE-Net. While initial listings on ACE-Net were funded by the
Department of Defense's Small Business Innovation Research Office,
which prepaid listings for 200 DOD SBIR awardees interested in raising
equity capital, ACE-Net has become self-supporting from subscription
fees.

The importance of "angels" as a source of equity financing and advice
for startup entrepreneurs should not be underestimated. "Angel" venture capital equals or exceeds more established venture capital sources.
In 1996, an analysis of the angel marketplace prepared for the SBA's
Office of Advocacy by the Center for Venture Research estimated that
the $10 billion raised by larger institutional venture capitalists was ex-
ceeded by the estimated $20 billion raised by some 250,000 "financial
angels" for over 30,000 ventures.[43] Clearly, a centralized, nationwide Internet listing service solves a very basic problem of bringing entrepreneurs and investors together, and it could play a key role in multiplying

the financing available, by some estimates fivefold to tenfold. The same study estimated that more than 300,000 growing companies and about 50,000 startups need equity capital each year. The total funding needed was projected to be $60 billion and the number of potential angels at 1.5 to 2.5 million. By regularizing procedures, ACE-Net could help bridge the gap in capital needed and capital available. Moreover, the problem of geographic concentration has been alleviated by the fact that "angel" investors tend to be dispersed across America and can if they choose invest in companies closer to home.

A second problem weighing heavily on entrepreneurs was the complex Securities and Exchange Commission registration process that raised costs for startup companies. As a result of the first White House Conference on Small Business held in 1980, the SEC had been directed to host an annual forum on capital formation specifically for small business. A direct consequence of the Forum's recommendations for government to cut red tape and allow more latitude in the registration process for new companies wanting to list their stock was that the Securities and Exchange Commission (SEC) introduced two registration categories: Regulation A for companies with equity requirements of up to $5 million, which can now raise up to five million dollars in a year through exempt public sales of securities using unaudited financial statements, thus reducing the costs of filing; and Regulation D, Rule 504 for companies wanting to raise up to $1 million, who can now do so with no federal requirements. The SEC also raised the threshold from $5 to $10 million in assets before a company is required to report under the federal securities laws.

In addition, the SEC also introduced a "test the waters" provision to let companies gauge the extent of investor interest in purchasing their stock before incurring the expense of a formal SEC registration process. Three states—Massachusetts, Texas, and Pennsylvania—have already established a securities registration exemption for companies listed on ACE-Net. The modified registration was intended to save time and money and efficiently streamline the process using less voluminous standardized forms. Prospectuses can now be downloaded online, bypassing the expensive prospectus filing process. A standardized form, the Small Corporate Offering Registration (SCOR) or form U7, is now accepted as the primary disclosure form in forty-three states. A draft model "terms and agreement" form developed by ACE-Net will reduce transaction costs.[44]

The bottom line is that these government-directed initiatives setting up institutions for the generation of private capital have played a part in America having 75 percent of the world's entrepreneurs, who have generated more companies than all the European Union countries and Japan combined! Arthur Levitt, then chairman of the Securities and

Exchange Commission, speaking before a Small Business town meeting in 1996, acknowledged the importance of the entrepreneurial sector. Referring to an article in *INC.* magazine, he stated that: "Most of the 20 million new jobs created during the past fifteen years came not from established giants but from the independent entrepreneurial sector. That is one of the most impressive and important statistics I've ever heard."[45] Moreover, young entrepreneurial companies do not merely create jobs, they also innovate at a faster rate than larger, more established companies. According to studies sponsored by the National Science Foundation and others, small technology companies, in particular, created nearly 2.5 times as many innovations per employee as large companies.[46]

Creating the institutions that raise capital has been only one aspect of government support for entrepreneurs. As we are about to see, the federal government undertook a much more active role, in the process becoming the single largest source of early-stage technology financing in the United States. By 1995 President Clinton, in an address at the National Medal of Technology Ceremony, summed up this new role when he stated: "We are in a way, a whole Nation of investors and explorers . . . We believe in technology and we are determined to pursue it in all its manifestations."[47]

The Federal Government as Later Stage "Public Venture Capitalist"

Though seed capital has never been plentiful, in the late 1970s private sector venture capital, even for later stage companies, was also in short supply, particularly for companies in high-risk sectors. An increasingly alarmed Congress therefore took steps on two fronts. First, it acted indirectly to alter the tax code to provide inducements to boost the availability of private sector venture capital. Peter Eisenger noted that whereas in 1970 a paltry $97 million in new private capital was committed to venture capital firms, by 1975 that had fallen to an even more meager $10 million. He also noted that although the industry seemed to recover the following year with commitments of $50 million, the pool of venture capital fell the following year to $39 million. Congress immediately took action, lowering the capital gains tax rate from 49 percent to 28 percent through the Steiger Amendment to the 1978 Tax Act. That one move increased the pool of venture capital to $600 million; a further reduction in the capital gains rate to 20 percent by the 1981 Economic Recovery Act boosted the amount still more to $1.3 billion in 1981, rising to $4.2 billion in 1984. In 1986, however, under a tax simplification plan, the capital gains rate was raised to 28 percent, leading many to claim that the venture capital pool was underfunded. In 1997, a new 18-month holding period was introduced with a lowering of the rate to 20 percent, with further reductions in the holding period and rate under review. Thus, the venture capital pool by the 1990s had stabilized at $10 billion annually, peaking at over $46 billion in 1999 by the government's own estimates.[48]

Second, the federal government moved to directly fund new entrants via changes in public policy. The effort to fund early-stage, high-risk companies was led by the Department of Defense through its Defense Advanced Research Projects Agency (DARPA), which played a key role in implementing provisions of the 1982 SBIR program by subsidizing emerging technologies and supporting entrepreneurial companies deemed too risky for the private capital markets.

Companies developing space telecommunications, for example, were prime beneficiaries of DARPA funding under the SBIR program. In an interview, David Thompson, founder and CEO of Orbital Sciences, which today launches private telecommunications satellites, confirmed that the commercially driven New Space Age was born in 1982 after the Reagan Administration announced a space policy encouraging entrepreneurial companies to enter space development and satellite delivery. He acknowledged that 80 percent of the company's early revenues came from DARPA and other government agencies that had developed an ability to pick promising technologies to back early on in their development cycles and were willing to take a little extra risk to reap the benefits. Unlike the raison d'etre of the first Space Age, the driving forces of this New Space Age were the markets for industrial and consumer products (such as messaging, navigational/tracking systems, and television). It was public money that underwrote some of their initial development costs at a time when private venture capital was unwilling to undertake such a risky venture with a long-term payoff.[49]

DARPA, as is now widely recognized, also played a key role in the creation of what later became the Internet, a platform for the explosive growth of high-technology companies. Initially the result of a defense-related need to link army bases to create an information "daisy chain" that could not be breached by war, the Internet was funded by DARPA in conjunction with the National Science Foundation. In the 1970s universities were permitted to become a part of the network administering Network Access Sites, and by 1995 private corporations were permitted to take control. As recently as 1990, 94 percent of Internet traffic was funded by universities and government agencies, with only 3 percent of commercial origin. By 1997, 97 percent of Internet traffic was commercial, creating an entire new field of IT (information technology) and Internet-related startup companies with rapidly expanding stock market capitalizations and a host of new technology products.

Thus, if the intent of the SBIR program, in addition to funding small companies, was to ensure commercialization, in this respect, too, the SBIR program proved successful. The Small Business Administration, which oversees the administration of the program across the federal agency participants, estimated that over 24 percent of SBIR activities resulted in commercially marketed technology products. It concluded that this rate was comparable to success rates for other high-risk technology ventures and underscored the "significant contribution the SBIR makes to national technology advancement and small business development."[50]

The SBIR program was the first of several other federal efforts to provide a dependable source of capital for young startups. Two other programs—the Advanced Technology Program (ATP) and the Manufacturing Extension Partnership—were eventually created as by-products of the passage of the Omnibus Trade and Competitiveness Act of 1988. To administer these programs, the National Bureau of Standards at the Department of Commerce was transformed into the National Institute of Standards and Technologies (NIST), acquiring a new, invigorated mission based on the assumption that innovation, by itself, does not ensure commercial success. Accordingly NIST, as a world-class center for science and engineering research, positioned itself to help U.S. firms strengthen their competitive performance by speeding innovation and accelerating the adoption by U.S. companies of the most commercially attractive areas of technology. In 1990, it set up the Advanced Technology Program to provide early-stage development funding to accelerate research for promising technologies that might not otherwise be developed quickly enough to be successful in a rapidly changing marketplace. Federal funding of the ATP increased ten-fold between 1991 and the late 1990s, reaching $193 million in fiscal year 1998. Additionally, NIST set up the Manufacturing Extension Partnership, explicitly directed towards small and mid-sized companies to offer access to technology information that might enable them to improve their operations. In fiscal year 1998, that program was funded at $111 million. NIST's Laboratory Research Services are implemented in cooperation with U.S. industry, and it is noteworthy that of 660 Co-operative Research and Development Agreements (CRADAs) implemented since 1988, 50 percent have been with smaller, entrepreneurial companies.[51]

In 1992, Congress continued its support for high-technology startups by establishing the Small Business Technology Transfer Program, overseen by the Small Business Administration. This program permitted cooperative research and development to be conducted jointly by a small business awardee and a research institution that was either a nonprofit or a federally funded research and development center. Funded in 1997 at $70 million and administered by five agencies, the majority of funds ($35 million) still went to the Department of Defense, a reflection of the original national security rationale for federal high-technology support and a way to maintain political consensus between Republicans and Democrats on this issue.[52]

DARPA, moreover, has not been the only agency engaged in making public venture capital investments in young companies. The Energy Department, for example, provided 80 percent of the $3.13 million required by Fuel Cell Energy, a young company engaged in a project to create ultra-efficient power plants. In this case, only 20 percent of funds came from the private sector.[53]

The Federal Government's Role in Organizing and Liberalizing Capital Markets

The financial system in the United States today is based, as never before, on the securities markets rather than on banks, which have traditionally been risk-averse and unlikely to be a significant source of funding for young companies. In "Prosperity and Social Capital," an opinion piece published in 1999 in the *Wall Street Journal*, Michael Milken, now Chairman of the Milken Institute, an economic think tank based in Santa Monica, California, explained the unfavorable context previously faced by young companies:

Back in the 1960s, a small number of money-center banks and large insurance companies pretty much determined who had access to U.S. financial capital. Their customers were large, established corporations—companies with history—and capital was allocated to these 800 or so "investment grade" firms based on a look in the rear-view mirror. Tens of thousands of smaller entrepreneurial companies—companies with prospects—scrambled for crumbs at the tables of the capital club. Wall Street seemed more interested in financing the past than in the future.

Milken compared that situation with the environment of the last third of the twentieth century when:

control of capital in America . . . shifted away from private institutions and towards public markets, making the process of financing growth more forward looking and democratic. Entrepreneurs are no longer limited to the few institutions that used to control the money spigot.[54]

By the late 1990s, the development of private equity markets was so successful that equity financing began to surpass lending by depository institutions for the first time, totaling 20 percent in 1999 compared with a negligible percentage in the 1960s. Lending by depository institutions fell from 60 percent of all financings to 30 percent.[55] Indeed, Federal Reserve Chairman Alan Greenspan in his testimony before the Congressional Joint Economic Committee in June 1999 credited the diversified financial markets in the United States for having the "spare tires" that helped ward off a credit crunch during the Asian financial crisis of 1998.

The federal government, through the Securities and Exchange Commission, played a key role in facilitating the development of competitive, diversified, and liberalized capital markets. By supporting less stringent listing requirements for Nasdaq-listed companies, it allowed young companies to gain access to equity financing. It has worked since then to introduce competitive forces into the stock and options markets and to increase access for the small investor, even when markets are closed, via Electronic Communication Networks or ECNs. Nasdaq, the world's first electronic stock market and a spectacularly successful capital-generating institution for small companies, was created on February 8, 1971. Operated by the National Association of Securities Dealers (NASD) Nasdaq is a self-regulating body governing over-the-counter trading, set up in 1939 under the 1938 Maloney Amendment to the Securities and Exchange Act of 1934. Its explicit purpose was to create an alternative source of equity financing for mid-size and young, technologically innovative, high-growth companies that could provide America with a competitive edge worldwide. Ironically, the federal government was directing that these steps be taken during a period that Japanese and European governments were directing capital through banks (many state owned like the Japan Development Bank) to fund large, often state-owned companies. And in both those economic models, the goal was protection, not increased competition.

The success of the Nasdaq is reflected by its size in comparison to the New York Stock Exchange and by the fact that it not only hosts entrepreneurial behemoths such as Intel and Microsoft but also an ever-expanding number of high-tech and biotech companies whose innovations have boosted productivity, economic growth, and job creation. A study by Cognetics discovered that Nasdaq companies created an estimated one of every six jobs in the U.S. economy between 1990 and 1994. Since 1994, the Nasdaq has exceeded the New York Stock Exchange in volume of shares traded and number of companies listed. Another milestone was passed in 1995 when the market value of Nasdaq companies grew to $1 trillion, expanded to over $3 trillion a year later, and by the end of the decade exceeded $5 trillion.

The acceleration of capital raised on the Nasdaq is illustrated by the fact that while in 1991 there were 172 Initial Public Offerings (IPOs) that raised $4 billion, by 1996 there were 851 IPOs that raised over $50 billion, representing 87 percent of all companies making IPOs that year.[56] More than 400 foreign companies have listings on the Nasdaq, a resounding vote of confidence from foreigners in the ability of American capital markets to allow new entrants, even those from abroad. Having set up institutions to facilitate access to private capital markets for American companies, the federal government has begun working to assist foreign entrepreneurial companies to take further advantage of the availability of U.S. capital. In March 1999, for example, the SEC gave permission to Tradepoint, the small U.K. stock trading system, to become the first foreign market to establish itself in the United States subject to certain restrictions.[57]

In stark contrast, it took until 1996 for Europe to even begin to organize institutions for the generation of private-venture capital firms interested in funding young, emerging companies and to create alternative private equity markets with less stringent requirements geared to younger companies. These efforts included EASDAQ, the pan-European Stock Market, the Alternative Investment Markets (AIM) in London, the Neuer Markt in Germany, and France's Nouveau Marché. Sources estimated that young European technology startups rushed to list on these markets at the rate of two a week. Moreover, according to the European Venture Capital Association, more than $11 billion has been raised there annually, equivalent to the amounts raised in the United States and more than double the levels raised five years ago.[58] However, according to the European Venture Capital Association, in 1997 only 7.4 percent of venture dollars was invested in startup companies, compared with 50.1 percent of those funds going to management buy-outs, with the rest going to mostly safe investments in established companies. In Sweden, for example, 80 percent of venture capital went to more established companies, according to the Swedish Federation of Industries. It has taken American firms like McKinsey to build venture capital networks from scratch. They began a venture capital competition modeled on those begun at MIT and have contributed some 100 million German marks to 40 new companies.[59] Japan did not follow until Nasdaq, in association with the nation's first venture capital firm—Softbank—established Nasdaq Japan in 2000. Only then did the Tokyo Stock Exchange create a subsidiary (called "Mothers") with less stringent listing requirements to raise equity capital for young companies.

Conclusion: America Back on Track

Several studies have confirmed the success of government-led efforts over a twenty-five year period to transform the economy of the United States from one strangled by regulation to the world's most globally competitive and vibrant economy. Once again, after a period of decline, the United States leads the world in intellectual property. This was confirmed in a report by the United Nations World Intellectual Property Organization, which indicated that of 73,023 international patents filed in 1999, 39.8 percent came from U.S. based applicants, with the Germans (at 14.7 percent) and the Japanese (at 10 percent) far behind.[60]

This shockwave of transformation was also reflected in a series of reports compiled by the World Economic Forum. A World Competitiveness Report for 1994 concluded that "The U.S. has regained its place as the most competitive economy in the world for the first time since 1985."[61] The 1996 report added that "the U.S. has reinforced its leadership position in world competitiveness . . . and has even increased its lead over other nations."[62] By 1999 the United States maintained its competitive position against all nations but Singapore and was ranked number two in the Global Competitiveness Rankings compiled by the World Economic Forum.[63] Entrepreneurial capitalism had proved its mettle against all other economic models around the world. It now remained to be seen whether this model could be extended to other nations. Would they be able to successfully adapt American strategies to their very different political and economic systems? Would their cultures endure the shockwave of social change that economic growth inevitably produces? Those questions will be explored in the next chapter.

CHAPTER 6

The Global Impact of Entrepreneurial Capitalism

OVERVIEW

Will the shockwave of entrepreneurial capitalism, having invigorated the American economy over the past twenty years, become a model for other nations? Or is it more likely we have entered an era of "rival capitalisms,"[1] as British economic historian John Gray dourly suggested in *False Dawn: The Delusions of Global Capitalism?*

There are several reasons Gray has been skeptical that the American model will prevail worldwide, even in the industrialized nations, despite efforts to force it upon other countries by the "Washington consensus." He believes that the "managed" capitalist economies of Germany, France, and Italy will be reluctant to embrace what the French have derisively called the "Anglo-Saxon model" of "extreme capitalism," which places efficiency and competition as preeminent goals to the exclusion of social harmony and regardless of social cost. Only post-Thatcher Great Britain, with a past (if buried) history of enterprise (the Industrial Revolution began there), a commitment to free trade (begun when Robert Peel repealed the Corn Laws in 1846), and a global presence dating back to its former colonial days, has seemed receptive to remaking its economy in America's image.

In Asia, Japan has largely been resistant to American pressures for structural change despite a stagnant economy during the 1990s, and change, as it slowly unfolds, will doubtless come as a result of the entry of foreign companies and foreign capital into Japan. Other Asian economies had proudly followed the path of "guided capitalisms" but were forced to introduce economic changes following the Asian financial crisis of 1997–1998. Their success in implementing elements of the American model has varied country by country. South Korea, Taiwan, Hong Kong, and Singapore have been more successful than Indonesia, the Philippines, or Thailand. The forces holding them back are largely cultural and political, and John Gray expressed very grave doubts whether eastern cultures would ever accept individualism and personal calculation in place of kinship and personal relations as the basis for economic life. To do so, he argued, would uproot their economies from their parent cultures and render them uncontrollable. With social cohesion at stake, he suggested that weak states would be destroyed by market forces, while strong ones would find themselves struggling to control them.[2]

Yet, despite an international preference for retaining a "plural global economy," these countries are all facing pressures to adapt or to accommodate some degree of change as the shockwave of entrepreneurial capitalism makes its presence felt worldwide. Despite their former glory days, the "miracle" economies of Germany and Japan were "subsidized, assisted and very closely directed by powerful economic ministries,"[3] but they eventually became overcontrolled and sclerotic by the late 1970s. Slow growth and stubbornly high rates of unemployment have since prevailed, even as the American economy began to be transformed and energized, eventually experiencing growth rates as high as 5 percent and unemployment as low as 3.9 percent. Globalization and technological innovation became forces impossible to ignore, with "entrepreneurial capitalism" fueling American global economic leadership. Economist Edward Luttwak, author of *Turbo-Capitalism*, assessed its impact:

(America's) gain in efficiency undercut prices, or increased quality, or both, forcing the pace of decontrol of that industry in other countries. Thus no country could stop the process by keeping its own controlled capitalism intact within its own boundaries without paying an ever increasing price.[4]

Moreover, increasingly disturbed by the continuing ability of U.S. consumers to absorb the exports of our partners and by a massive trade deficit with the European Union and Japan, U.S. international economic policy by the late 1990s explicitly began to pressure our trading partners to become more like us. The process of economic convergence has already begun. The question now becomes: Will other nations undertake the transition in full? Many countries have focused their efforts on the obvious and necessary conditions for entrepreneurial capitalism: privatization, deregulation, and lowered tariffs. In Europe that process is already well underway. In Asia it is just beginning, faster in some countries than in others. This has become so much the prevailing orthodoxy that even tiny Guyana in South America in 1999 elected a political party, formerly communist, pledged to enact deregulation, privatization, and tariff reduction![5]

The question now becomes whether other nations, with widely different cultural contexts, will be in a position to go "all the way" and implement the policy reforms whose key feature was that they rapidly introduced new entrants into the economy with hypercompetition an inevitable consequence. Will their voters tolerate the social implications of a fiercely competitive and adversarial society? Already political pressures have emerged in Europe reflecting the revulsion of voters against some of the less happy social costs and consequences of entrepreneurial capitalism. Welfare state protections and an ethos of social responsibility have been hard to give up in favor of U.S. style policies slashing welfare protections and emphasizing personal responsibility, replacing them with what global market strategist Edward Kerschner once called "cradle to grave entrepreneurialism." The preference for labor market protections in Europe, along with strong unions, also makes it unlikely that labor market flexibility will be as enthusiastically embraced as a policy goal. Furthermore, business practices in many industrialized nations create a preference for consensus and harmony that translate into cross holdings of German companies, or long-term vendor relationships in Japan, that will be difficult to change. In single-minded pursuit of the goal of making America more globally competitive, successive administrations since the 1980s have decided not to intervene in unfavorable market outcomes. This applied (with a few notable exceptions) equally to workers as well as to corporate America. When workers have lost jobs, the federal government has not intervened to save them. By the same token, when companies have declared bankruptcy or threatened to so do, the government has not helped them either, except temporarily or for short-term political gain exemplified by the extraordinary Chrysler bailout in the 1970s. Governments abroad will find it difficult to allow market forces to prevail and ignore unpleasant consequences, given the intense political pressures they would face. Most important of all, will other countries pursue policies giving strong support to new entrants—or be prepared to pursue antitrust remedies against highly successful, market-dominant companies such as IBM or Microsoft—with the same vigor as we have done? And despite privatizations in France, Germany, and Italy, will the tradition of protecting "national champions" reemerge at some later date? These are all legitimate questions with no clear answers to date.

Reactively, perhaps, European politics actually lurched leftward in the late 1990s, with thirteen of fifteen European Union members electing left leaning governments with mandates to preserve economic models emphasizing social protections. This move to the political left has made the task of the European Union's Competitiveness Commission that much more difficult. Its own mandate has been to impose pro-competitive policies, ensure a level playing field among EU companies, and encourage shareholder activism. While the Commission has been making headway in a few countries, notably the Netherlands and Italy, the largest EU countries, France and Germany, have been resisting those efforts.

The fact of the matter is that the transformation of the American economy—and the ability of both corporate America and the labor force to successfully adapt to the brutal realities of entrepreneurial capitalism—did not occur in a vacuum. A combination of unique historical and cultural factors has provided fertile ground for far-reaching changes in established practices to take root in this country. A comparison of the radically different cultural traditions of our trading partners will help in understanding the limits of American economic influence.

Comparing Cultural Contexts: Assessing the Global Impact of the American Shock Wave

Comparing the two models of capitalism, "entrepreneurial" and "managed," and the cultures in which they are embedded, will serve to help determine the extent to which other industrialized countries can adapt fully to the new global rules of the game set by America.

Chart 6.1
Comparing Cultures

America	Europe and Japan
1. Culture of entrepreneurialism *Breakthroughs *high failure rate/cultural tolerance of failure *acceptance of dislocation	**1. Culture of "champions"** *Continuous innovation to preserve stability and avoid failure
2. Culture of competition *Adversarial labor relations *Emphasis on efficiency/accountability *Flexible labor markets *Few social protections	**2. Culture of social cohesion** *Emphasis on consensus *Social harmony *Inflexible labor markets *Strong welfare state
3. Culture of consumerism *Strong protections for consumers, even as debtors *Emphasis on domestic-led demand/growth of consumer market, by immigration if necessary *Acceptance of diversity	**3. Culture of saving** *Strong protections for producers *Emphasis on export-led growth *Cultural preference for homogeneity

Culture of Entrepreneurialism versus Culture of Champions

Well before the emergence of entrepreneurial capitalism, America's strong entrepreneurial tradition extolled the individual who single-handedly started a company based on a radically new idea. America has had many role models of inventors who made the transition to commercially successful entrepreneurs—from Thomas Edison to Robert Metcalfe, who invented the Ethernet networking protocol and went on to found 3Com, the U.S. networking group. America also enjoys a tradition of entrepreneurial mobility that has no parallel anywhere else in the world. Entrepreneurs leave one company in which they have worked to found another. In the 1960s and 1970, Sperry Rand engineers left to form Control Data, which produced a computer superior to industry leader IBM. Then an employee of Sperry Rand, Seymour Cray left to form Cray Research. The opportunities presented by the Internet era accelerated the trend of individuals who have left as employees of one company to start their own. Marimba, an Internet applications and management startup, was founded by four ex-employees of Sun Microsystems, who had worked there to develop the Java browser. Mindspring was founded by ex-employees of Palm Computing. And the list goes on and on.

America has also produced more "serial entrepreneurs" than any other country, a trend accelerating with new sources of venture capital and new avenues for taking companies public. For example, Jim Clark (whose extraordinary career was chronicled in Michael Lewis' *The New, New Thing* [2000]), after founding Silicon Graphics in 1982, co-founded Netscape in 1994, then invested $50 million of his own money to found online medical data provider Healtheon in 1995, a company he took public in 1999, following that up with another startup, MyCFO Inc., a year later.[6] Steve Jobs, co-founder of Apple Computer, left under acrimonious circumstances to found his own computer company, NeXT, followed by Pixar, a movie animation company. He returned triumphantly, and by invitation, to serve as interim, then permanent, CEO of Apple, reinventing the company and its products. The flip side of this embedded culture of entrepreneurship is the high tolerance in America for failure and the willingness of failed entrepreneurs to start over. Steve Perlman, who founded WebTV, then sold it to Microsoft, had failed at several startups before he succeeded—and it was not long after he joined the Microsoft team that he left to start another new venture. Ian Hendry in *Innovating for Failure: Government Policy and the Early British Computer Industry* blamed Britain's lack of a similar "entrepreneurial spirit" for hindering the British government's attempts to jump-start their computer industry, while one German CEO commented that fear of failure was very great in his country, unlike the United States, where "filing for Chapter 11 is seen as a valuable lesson in building a career."[7]

This phenomenon, together with the gargantuan financial rewards accruing to the successful, may be one reason why America, more than any other country, has produced what Paul Johnson and Geoffrey Moore have called "discontinuous innovation," which they defined in their book about high-technology investing, *The Gorilla Game*. "Discontinuous innovation," according to Johnson and Moore, destroys the technology that preceded it and, in turn, creates new markets that the predecessor technology never reached. In the process, old technologies, old companies, old ways of doing business are destroyed in a whirlwind of Schumpeterian "creative destruction." It has been described in this way:

each discontinuous innovation produces a whirlwind of growth as business and then consumers, undertake a wholesale migration to the new technology. These "growth tornadoes" . . . occur when a company emerges to set the standard for a new technology and that technology is widely adopted. The standard-setting company's revenue grows at triple digit rates even as the price of its technology falls. Virtually overnight, whole new markets and industries spring up around that standard.[8]

Americans have been better able to adapt to the dislocations this process has produced without necessarily seeking political remedies.

In contrast, England, while it has long had a tradition of "discontinuous innovation," has been unable to convert that tradition into similar "growth tornadoes." Ian Hendry's *Innovating for Failure: Government Policy and the Early British Computer Industry* offered a case study of what has been called the "British problem," the chronic inability of British industry to convert high levels of technological expertise into commercial success in the marketplace, a problem recognized in political debate for fifty years. This failure to market technological innovation has been attributed to Britain's anti-entrepreneurial business culture. Not only have British entrepreneurs lacked the management, marketing, and capital to build global presences, but established British companies have been reluctant to partner with entrepreneurial startups in the same way that American companies, such as Cisco Systems, have done, embracing the innovation of competitive upstarts.

Adding to the cultural antipathy towards entrepreneurialism was the unfortunate detour in British public policy during the 1950s, 1960s, and early 1970s, when successive governments, both Conservative and Labor, tried to copy the "managed" economies of France and Germany by creating national plans through the National Economic Development Council while directing public funds to established champions and discouraging technologically innovative young companies. The first significant public policy measure put in place in the 1950s focused on the computer industry. The National Research Development Group (NRDC) was charged with ensuring that commercial opportunities to develop the computer industry succeeded. To address the problem of a shortage of venture capital for new technology projects, especially those at the prototype stage, the NRDC selected three computer firms to receive direct financial assistance, deliberately discouraging smaller rivals.

Ultimately, this focus on a few champions proved unsuccessful and was followed by a succession of attempts to support a variety of programs in fields like electronics, machine tools, and information technology. The Thatcher government by the early 1980s was the first to recognize the failure of this exclusive focus on established champions; hence, England traveled furthest in the direction of "entrepreneurial capitalism" under reforms initiated under Thatcher's leadership. These reforms were consolidated by her successor, John Major, and continued under Labor Prime Minister Tony Blair, who proved a most ardent advocate for adopting the American model, even taking his case for reform to his European socialist counterparts.

Like America, Britain also used the defense procurement budget to fund commercially viable technological innovation. The Ministry of Technology, while initially following a policy of supporting "champions," had by the 1990s moved, along with the Department of Trade and Industry, to provide substantial programs of user support and training intended to help British innovators achieve commercial viability. In 1993, as a result of government panel recommendations, the British government introduced the Technology Foresight Programme [sic], which aimed to set long-term guidelines for public and private sector research and development. The program noted that science and technology played a vital role in wealth creation and long-term international competitiveness.[9] Nevertheless, without a sustaining culture of entrepreneurship the British government has not yet succeeded in achieving its primary goal of establishing internationally competitive national industries.

In comparison with America, or even Great Britain, the European and Japanese historical preference has been openly anti-entrepreneurial. The Japanese, in particular, have long expressed open distaste for the American model of entrepreneurial innovation, which they considered too focused on "breakthroughs" and hence far too risky. They were not surprised at the high failure rate of American firms (85 percent by some estimates) particularly in the fields of high technology and biotechnology and would not tolerate such failure in Japan. Instead the Japanese have preferred to emphasize the *kaizen* approach based on step-by-step continuous improvement with several people involved at each stage, rather than American-style "discontinuous innovation."[10]

The Japanese antipathy for American-style entrepreneurialism has deep roots. Before the Second World War this cultural preference was embodied in government policies supporting and, in some cases mandating, cartels—groups of independent producers who would jointly set prices and be protected from foreign competition. The infamous 1931 Major Industries Control Law, under which the state-owned Yawata Iron Works and five private firms were combined to create the giant Nippon Steel, exemplified this. It was also during the prewar period that the government presided over the creation of several other industrial behemoths such as Sanwa Bank and Mitsubishi Heavy Industries,[11] which were ultimately to play a large role in sustaining the Japanese war effort.

After the Second World War, and despite considerable American pressure, Japan continued to display a strong commitment for industrial policies supporting "champions" whose activities would be directed, even funded, by government bureaucrats. Behind this preference for a "managed capitalist model" was the belief that unbridled competition would be ruinous for producers and that a more rationalized approach to innovation, one that protected jobs, was better for countries coming late to capitalism. Thus, postwar Japan, despite the proddings of the American Occupation, saw the reemergence of large industrial *zaibatsu*, now resurrected as *keiretsu*, or holding companies with cross-holdings in other companies, tied to captive suppliers.

Moreover, compared with America, where suspicion of the government is endemic, the Japanese respect government bureaucrats as partners and have long relied on government planning and state guidance of the private sector. The Japanese government, through the Ministry of International Trade and Industry (MITI) and the Bureau of Economic Planning, openly favored its "national champions" and rewarded them with government-directed funding through the Japan Development Bank. Kenneth Flamm, in two exhaustive studies of the American computer industry in the 1980s, made these observations about Japan: "National champions received a steady diet of financial subsidies and preferential procurement policies."[12] Yet, unlike the policy response in America, "no support was given to new entrants in a position to go after new markets in a manner that was to prove successful in the United States."[13]

The Japanese have been slow to embrace structural reforms such as privatization. When Japanese Prime Minister Yoshiro Mori suggested during an election campaign in June 2000 that NTT, the Japanese telecom giant in which the Japanese government owns a 59 percent stake, be fully privatized it was the first time such a radical move had been proposed.[14]

While Europe, too, has a history of government planning and support for national champions, their governments have been more prepared to embrace structural reform. The 1990s witnessed a wave of privatizations in Germany, France, and Italy, especially in sectors such as banking and telecommunications. This new direction stands in stark contrast with the policy directions those governments followed immediately after the Second World War and for thirty years thereafter. Successive governments in France, Germany, and Italy had all overseen the creation of large, consolidated champions, especially in sectors such as computers where their governments perceived they were losing to American technological innovation.

The West German government, for example, had selected Siemens as its "national champion" in the electronics sector and directed state funding to it, but was forced to reconsider this policy after Siemens was bested by a small entrepreneurial pioneer, Nixdorf, which, with no state help, came to dominate the PC market. By the 1990s, former Chancellor Helmut Kohl openly expressed his admiration for American technological entrepreneurship, and suggested that Germany should take steps to foster an entrepreneurial sector as one way to create new jobs. His successor, SDP leader Gerhard Shroeder, went so far as to issue a call to any entrepreneurial company to relocate to Germany, and he offered state subsidies to those who came! Nevertheless, by the late 1990s, Germany had come a long way. One study found that 56 of Europe's 150 Internet-related companies were German and that Germany's Neuer Markt had grown to 330 young companies listed.[15]

The French government, also concerned about technological underperformance, similarly took the path of government direction, introducing its Plan Calcul in 1967 through which the CII (Compagnie International pour l' Informatique) was created. In 1975 CII and Honeywell Bull merged to form CII-Bull, a state enterprise.[16] Yet even after two decades of protective nurture for its single national champion, France still found itself unable to prevail over its rivals in the open market.

In the 1980s and 1990s, European partner governments tried to encourage technological innovation through the jointly funded Eureka project but few technological breakthroughs resulted. Consequently, France and Germany have come shopping for entrepreneurial alliances, mergers, and partners in the United States.

Culture of Competition versus Culture of Social Cohesion

Entrepreneurial capitalism, under which competitive pressures are maximized, requires flexibility on the part of both business and labor. American labor market policies, in a culture which is adversarial rather than cooperative, have always been flexible and, with the decline of unions, have become more so. In fact, the culturally embedded preference for entrepreneurialism is being gradually extended to the working population who face a future of "cradle to grave entrepreneurialism," a term used by Edward Kerschner, Chief Global Strategist at a major brokerage house. He has suggested that bureaucracies that used to take care of workers have been dismantled, with union membership at an all-time low. He noted that workers who spent twenty-five to thirty years working at one company will, in the future, likely spend their working careers at several different companies. This is reflected in the fact that one-quarter of Baby Boomers and one-sixth of the pre-retirement age group have worked less than two years at the same job. Moreover, the last five years have witnessed an accelerating dismantling of the social safety net, while government spending as a percentage of GDP continues to shrink, giving the United States the lowest level of public spending among all OECD (Organization for European Co-operation and Development) countries.[17] The American policy debate for the twenty-first century turns on whether "cradle to grave entrepreneurialism" can be extended even further in the United States to previously subsidized populations such as farmers and welfare recipients!

Leading European countries, notably France, Germany, and Italy, have all faced pressures to adopt "flexible labor markets," cut back on social welfare spending, and make the kinds of structural reforms that in the United States facilitated the emergence of "entrepreneurial capitalism." Yet European voters have continued to display a strong preference for labor market policies promoting social cohesion and a disinclination to shred their social safety nets, and there are few signs that this will change in the foreseeable future.

Nevertheless, there is a growing recognition among some observers in Europe that flexible labor markets have a positive impact on job creation, and Britain has come the farthest in making labor market changes. However, with England's long history of trade union militancy, Conservative reformer Margaret Thatcher had to fight hard to break the power of unions in the early 1980s. Still, the positive impact on the flexibility of labor markets was so evident that these policies were eventually endorsed by New Labor when they came to power in 1997. Indeed, it was British Labor Party Prime Minister Tony Blair, who took the reformist message to the Congress of the Party of European Socialists in 1999. Blair's exhortations for change were endorsed by Italian Prime Minister Massimo D'Alema, who said: "The extraordinary capacity of the U.S. to create wealth and work should encourage Europe to create a younger, more dynamic society."[18] Though proposals for structural reforms were ignored by participants, a plan adopted by the Congress and prepared by Portuguese Prime Minister Antonio Guterres warned that the "European social model must be modernized in order to survive."[19]

This chorus of voices urging structural reform to weaken union militancy and to lessen social protections was joined independently by the head of the European Central Bank, Wim Duisenberg, who admonished the German government in particular: "The main cause of unemployment is not lack of domestic demand, it is structural . . . Labor and goods markets must become more flexible, like in the U.S."[20] In fact, the lack of labor market flexibility has had far-reaching repercussions. It helps to explain why Europe has been unable to benefit, in terms of increased growth, from a similar technology-driven productivity surge to the same extent as the United States. That is because productivity enhancements have direct implications for labor. Less labor may be needed, jobs may need to be cut, or workers may need to be transferred to other types of work.[21] Labor market inflexibility also helps to explain why initiatives to bolster technology transfer, such as the *Eureka* project—a Europe-wide network for industrial research and development—have failed. Despite intensive efforts to make it more market-oriented and to reduce bureaucratic input, Eureka's 1997 Annual Report despondently acknowledged that converting technological success to commercial results had been a failure and that *"Eureka's principal effect (has been) to safeguard jobs rather than create significant new ones"* (emphasis added).[22]

There are important cultural forces preventing social welfare and labor market reforms from being seriously considered, let alone implemented, in many European countries. France and Germany, in particular, have a long tradition of commitment to a "social model," rather than a competitive market model, rooted in their particular cultures and histories. Bismarck in the late nineteenth century merely formalized a long German tradition of working cooperatively with workers, while the French have had a radical past which, after the Second World War, almost tipped them into electing a communist government. In comparison with the American model of capitalism, where the state is officially neutral but accessible to adversarial labor and business lobbying, the "social model" views employers and trade unions as "social partners" working alongside the government to make wage policy. Chancellor Gerhard Schroeder's working group, "alliance for jobs," which brought together "employers, the states and trade unions" in order to improve social solidarity, typified this effort.[23] It has been triumphantly characterized as the "Rheinish model," in contrast to the despised "Anglo Saxon model" of adversarial relations between business and labor, with government playing only a neutral role.

The social market model is one Europeans are reluctant to abandon and one which, in the late twentieth century, was, in fact, being extended and strengthened as French, German, and Italian voters elected Socialist governments that were even less likely to initiate changes that would deregulate the labor market or shrink the welfare state. Indeed, these governments actually reversed course and enacted even more social welfare legislation and enhanced worker protections.

Germany is a particularly striking example of this trend. The German social justice agenda and an emphasis on social consensus were invigorated by the election of the Social Democrats. Despite Schroeder's sum-

mer 1999 commitment to join with Tony Blair to sign a "strategic blue-
print" advocating an overtly pro-enterprise Neuer Mitte or New Center,[24] by the fall an embattled Chancellor Gerhard Schroeder played to
his party's left wing at its 1999 three-day SDP Conference when he made
frequent references to the core socialist value of social justice. In fact,
expanded social protections had been enacted by the Social Democrats
within weeks of taking power. To promote a "socially just" tax structure,
for instance, the new government enacted electoral pledges raising child
and personal allowances, cutting personal tax rates while threatening to
raise them for business—a move so unpopular that outspoken Finance
Minister Oskar LaFontaine, who had defended them, was forced to
resign.

So, too, does labor market flexibility appear to be receding in Germany. The election of Social Democrats strengthened union militancy in
a country where 50 percent of workers in the country's western half were
unionized. In 1999, the nation's largest trade union, IG Metall, secured
an annual wage increase of 4 percent that employers complained would
only price companies out of markets and workers out of jobs.[25] Germany's labor market inflexibility and union protections have already
made it less attractive to investors. In 1999, Germany attracted only $343
million dollars in investment dollars compared with the United States,
which attracted $93 billion.[26]

Under pressure to reduce unemployment, the Social Democrats suc-
cumbed to pressures not only from labor, but also from business, to
intervene in impending unfavorable market outcomes in ways that suggested that Germany was far from able or even willing to adopt the
entrepreneurial capitalist model. In late 1999, two situations arose that
tested the government's resolve to implement structural changes being
urged by the European Central bank and by the European Commission.
When Phillipe Holzman, Germany's second largest construction company, faced collapse, the government rushed in with promises of over
$130 million in state funds to save Holzman, its suppliers, subcontrac-
tors, and, of course, jobs. Defending his decision to intervene in the Holzman matter, Chancellor Schroeder commented: "Politics must intervene
when a company is (fundamentally) unable to maintain itself in the market."[27] Nevertheless, the participation of public sector banks in politically
motivated bailouts became the subject of European Union scrutiny and
led Wim Duisenberg, president of the EU Central bank, to caustically
comment that the bailout did "not enhance the image of the euro-zone
as 'market driven.'"

Having rushed to save jobs in the Holzman case, the government now
intervened to save German corporations from external forces. When telecommunications company Mannesmann received a hostile buyout offer
from the British company Vodaphone/Airtouch, the affair escalated into

comparisons of different cultural approaches to business. Believing such a takeover would expose German companies to outside forces that would undermine their culture of social consensus, Shroeder again intervened, ultimately unsuccessfully, to defend the "Rheinish" model of deal making by consensus between managers, government, publicly owned banks, and even unions, versus the "Anglo-Saxon" model which valued only efficiency. Wolfgang Clement, the Social Democratic Prime Minister of North Rhine, Westphalia, where Mannesmann was headquartered, backed the company's fight for independence by saying: "We should hold on to our culture—and that applies to our business culture as well."[28] Not to be outdone, Gerhard Schroeder even called for new European Union rules to ban hostile takeovers, a call initially ignored in Brussels and certainly by Mannesman itself.

France, under Socialist Prime Minister Lionel Jospin, chose to expand its welfare state by unveiling plans, in 1999, to extend full public health insurance to low-income groups, even though the French Government already spent 9.6 percent for health compared to an European Union average of 7.9 percent.[29] And far from promoting labor market flexibility, the Jospin government enacted a plan to boost jobs by reducing the work week to thirty-five hours, a form of job sharing. The French, moreover, have been particularly critical of the "Anglo Saxon model," which views the individual as rational, calulating, and competitive. While Americans may be predisposed to reward merit, even to the point that it produces gross inequalities of income, French culture has historically prized social harmony over incentives to stimulate efficiency and initiative. Jospin, however, recognized the need for reform and made efforts to downsize the French state by permitting privatizations.

Japan is similar to Europe in its cultural preference for social cohesion and in its distaste for the mass firings that characterize American markets. For example, in 1999, Japan's largest banks were forced to promise to cut 21,000 jobs as part of a broader restructuring in order to qualify for recapitalisation loans of $60 billion from the Japanese government. Yet, as one informed observer stated, the job cuts were unlikely to be achieved through direct elimination of jobs and more likely through "early retirements, sharp cuts in graduate recruitment, reductions in non-Japanese employees and transfers to subsidiaries rather than through compulsory redundancies."[30]

Yet Japanese companies have not been able to escape the pressures of global competition. Despite John Gray's insistence that "Japanese capitalism differs profoundly from Anglo Saxon market individualism," when NEC was faced with a $1.25 billion loss, its largest ever, it reluctantly announced it would shed 15,000 jobs. News reports commented: "The job losses will come as a shock to many Japanese for whom lifetime employment has been a hallmark of corporate culture."[31] Moreover the entry of foreign companies and foreign capital to rescue bloated and debt-ridden Japanese companies will forcibly expose the Japanese market to the global forces of efficiency, competition and accountability as never before. It will force labor market changes as well as changes in established business practices, even if the Japanese government is unwilling or unable to initiate structural reforms urged upon it by America and the International Monetary Fund.

The fate of Nissan is a case in point. After being rescued by an investment from the French company Renault, job cuts affecting Japanese workers were made. Carlos Ghosn, a Brazilian-born Renault executive, drafted a plan to help revive Nissan, warning that in order to become globally competitive, the company would have to endure plant closings, as well as changes in supplier relationships, dealerships, purchasing, and product development—a revolution in business culture. In particular, much prized long-term vendor relationships, which may be stable and harmonious but leave Japanese companies unable to seek the lowest cost vendor, would have to be abandoned. Under these circumstances, the relationship with Renault might eventually be used as an excuse to break up the Nissan *keiretsu*. This would mean that Nissan might become free to weed out weaker suppliers from its *keiretsu* at the same time that strong suppliers could also seek out partners and relationships with other car companies. As one consultant said: "Why honor traditional ties when your parent can't stop talking about the cold reality of global competition and threatening to dissolve *keiretsu*."[32]

Other cultural traditions are being tested in Japan. John Gray had written that, "In their dealings with their employees and the rest of society, Japanese institutions rely on networks of trust rather than upon a culture of contract."[33] That, too, may be changing. As Nissan CEO Yoshikazu Hanawa said in response to the Renault report on changes to be made at his company: "There is no alternative for us. It is not going to be an easy process."[34]

And even though John Gray maintained that "economic and industrial development (has) been animated and concerted by the institutions of the state at every point in Japanese history,"[35] this time may be different. Although the Japanese government, faced with a decade-long stagnation, has relied only on fiscal stimulus and government spending on public works, outside forces seem likely to become the agents of change as massive debt and declining profits continue to force Japanese companies to seek partnerships with foreign companies. Mazda allowed Ford a 33.4 percent stake in the company, while Izuzu and Suzuki have permitted investment by GM, which now controls 49 percent of Isuzu and 10 percent of Suzuki.[36]

Whether or not Japan can preserve its culture of social harmony and full employment while moving towards labor market flexibility and eliminating the traditional promise of lifetime employment, is open to question. But the Japanese have a history of successfully adapting to changes forced upon them since Commander Perry's visit in 1868, and exigency may force them to adapt now. Doubtless, the availability of capital to the Japanese entrepreneurial sector through the opening of Nasdaq Japan and a subsidiary of the Tokyo Stock Exchange will bring to bear still more drastic changes in Japanese culture and business practices in the coming years.

What of other Asian countries? South Korea, since the election of its first democratically elected President, is proceeding to dismantle the chaebols or conglomerates with their oligopolistic domination of the domestic market and to invite foreign ownership for the first time ever. It was reported[36] that the South Korean government banned financial transactions between twenty-five units of troubled Daewoo Group to prevent the practice of stronger businesses propping up weaker ones. Daewoo itself was dismantled and forced to restructure as it faced debts of over $50 billion,[37] and tried to seek foreign buyers for its auto division.

Culture of Consumers versus Culture of Savers

Entrepreneurial capitalism, with its emphasis on the commercialization of technological innovation, requires a ready and expanding market of consumers for new products and services. The United States has shown a clear preference for developing its domestic market and has urged the private sector to expand and extend credit, even to the "subprime" market, in order to boost consumption.[38] Thus, when Robert Rubin, former U.S. Secretary of the Treasury during the Clinton Administration, traveled the globe urging governments in Europe and Japan to stimulate "demand-led growth," he did not take into account their cultural preference for saving over consuming, which has led many of our trading partners to favor export-led growth.

The cultural preference in favor of consuming over saving has been translated into extensive political protections for consumers in the United States, and economic deregulation, far from altering that focus, has intensified it. In all antitrust actions, harm to the consumer has been the key factor forcing a governmental decision to take action. AT&T, IBM, and then Microsoft faced antitrust lawsuits on behalf of consumers. When Microsoft was deemed a "predatory monopolist" by Judge Penfield Jackson, the company was assumed to have harmed consumers by stifling innovation and keeping prices for operating systems higher than they might otherwise have been in the presence of innovative competitors. Moreover, the United States has a long history of protecting debtors over creditors, even if reforms proposed in 2001 appear to be tilted in favor of the latter. As one example, for not properly filing "reaffirmations" made by bankrupt customers to avoid repossessions, in 1998 Sears was forced by the courts to pay over $400 million in restitution and punitive damages.

Europe, especially Germany, has a much more conservative population, which has preferred saving over consumption. Historically the government has protected producers from price competition, and not consumers who have been forced to pay higher prices as a result. Japan, especially during its 1990s recession, has been unable to ignite consumer demand despite tax cuts and spending vouchers, forcing the Japanese government to embark on a program of public spending that by 1999 led to a Japanese budget deficit of 10 percent of gross domestic product.

The United States, unlike its trading partners, has also been prepared to take all necessary steps to assure domestic demand-led growth. Facing a future of stagnant population growth and an aging population, fates all the industrialized countries share, America has chosen to expand the growth of its population and its domestic markets through a policy of steady immigration. Of course, Lyndon Johnson's 1965 immigration reform law was rationalized in far more noble terms at the time, but the effects have been to keep consumer demand ignited, with 30 percent of population growth in the United States since the 1970s coming as a result of immigration. In the process, America has been willing to accommodate, and to prepare for, the social strains of diversity and to accept both the cultural consequences of immigration as well as the demographic changes it will bring to our national identity. This includes predictions that by 2050 the white population will have shrunk to 51 percent. When the year 2000 census indicated the largest ever census-to-census increase in America's history, the *Wall Street Journal* ran a triumphant editorial, "The More, The Merrier."

In contrast, Europe and Japan, both more committed to cultural and racial homogeneity, appear unlikely to boost consumer demand by adopting policies encouraging expanded immigration, despite United Nations' projections of worker shortages and other imbalances caused by an aging, shrinking population. Germany, however, according to a United Nations' Population Division report, has boosted net immigration to 2.9 per 1,000, levels similar to that of the United States. By comparison, France and Britain's net immigration rates were 0.7 per 1,000. Japan's, according to the same report, was zero![39]

Conclusion: Will the American Shockwave have a Global Impact?

Under these circumstances, can American economic leadership transform the economies of the major industrialized countries? Without a cultural context sympathetic to rapid change, it seems unlikely that structural reforms in Europe and Japan, identical to those undertaken in

America in the 1980s and 1990s, would result in a complete transformation to "entrepreneurial capitalism," even though the forces of global change and competition are shaking those countries to the core.

England exemplifies the limits of adaptation to the new rules of the game set by America. It has taken the greatest leap forward in abandoning the European model under Thatcher, has consolidated the new rules under John Major, and extended them under Tony Blair. Structural reforms have weakened trade unions, lowered taxes so that they are 40 percent lower than in Germany and 80 percent lower than in France, abandoned national planning and dismantled its National Economic Development Council, and embraced a "welfare to work" ethos similar to that of the United States. Its unitary and parliamentary system of government allowed for rapid change and, indeed, Great Britain has made huge strides. By the late 1990s it enjoyed lower unemployment and faster growth than France or Germany. Labor Prime Minister Tony Blair frequently urged his fellow Socialists in Europe to follow his lead in embracing a "culture of enterprise." Under his leadership, Britain invested heavily in worker retraining as it embraced labor market flexibility. But one piece has been missing—namely, a culture fully supportive of entrepreneurial innovation. Although that is slowly changing, Britain has yet to produce the accelerated rates of entrepreneurial innovation America has achieved.

In the twenty-first century, Japan, France, and Germany can no longer rest on the laurels of their postwar economic miracles. In France, in particular, high levels of unemployment combined with slow growth have forced French companies like Vivendi to turn to the United States in search of merger partners in order to achieve enhanced profit growth. Germany, too, has remained unable to reverse high unemployment, slow job creation, and slow economic growth and has been only slightly better off than Japan, which experienced recession, slow growth, and a stagnant economy throughout the 1990s.

The obvious structural solutions urged by the United States, the European Union's Competitiveness Commission, and Tony Blair—namely, reforms of the labor market and cutbacks in social welfare spending—will probably continue to be held back by historical tradition. Cultural preferences, which hold social cohesion and cooperation between the forces of business and labor in high regard and which prefer the state to play a large role in guiding private sector decisions, still dominate. Clearly, this "managed capitalist" model has been breaking down amid the forces of global competition and the impact of American-led technological innovation, but these countries still have far to go in adapting to our ultracapitalist model of extreme competition, adversarial relations between business and labor, plus a strong government commitment to enforced competition and new entrants. So far they have been willing to spur economic growth by embracing some reforms such as privatization. Some signs of progress have emerged. The SDP in July 2000 began the process of modernizing Germany's financial markets, taking steps to introduce tax incentives for business that opened the way for the restructuring of German financial markets. In particular, the SDP eliminated the 50 percent corporate capital gains tax on companies that sell their cross-holdings in other companies. This system of cross-holdings, begun in the postwar period when banks took equity positions in German companies in exchange for loans, had been a major barrier to corporate mergers, preventing the streamlining of German business.[40] In Japan the ruling LDP, for the very first time in July 2000, abandoned a plan for a state-sponsored bailout of a bankrupt company, the retailer Sogo, ignoring business pressures to prop it up. Nevertheless, it seems unlikely that "entrepreneurial capitalism" in its uniquely American form will rapidly appear in Europe and Japan, no matter what the economic merits may be.

If change does occur, governments will not conceivably be the primary catalysts since they will be held back by political pressures and cultural preferences. It appears much more likely that European, as well as Japanese, corporations will seize the initiative to induce economic change. In their quest to maintain global competitiveness, they are buying into the more liberalized American markets. For example, one year after Daimler's merger with Chrysler in 1998, French telecommunications equipment maker Alcatel purchased data-switching specialist Xylan, while Vivendi purchased first U.S. Filter, America's largest water treatment company, then Seagram, now an entertainment conglomerate. Corporations appear to be escaping constraints inside their own countries. In France, for example, the employers' organization, Medef, has become increasingly defiant of laws that limit the ability of French companies to compete globally.[41] In Germany, the SDP's renewed emphasis on social consensus and social justice has aroused the ire of Hans-Olaf Henkel, President of Germany's largest industrial federation, the BDI, who strongly criticized the "wrong" positioning of Germany in the world economy. Comparing America's emphasis on personal responsibility over social protection he stated: "We have to get away from a society overly occupied with social justice and consensus and move toward policies promoting self-responsibility. We have to discover freedom— and not just equality."[42] Henkel affirmed his support for social consensus but added, "as long as we don't all agree to walk at the speed of the slowest."[43]

In Japan, foreign companies for the first time have been permitted to purchase stakes in Japanese companies. This particular development could have important implications for Japan's preference for "managed capitalism" and for the *keiretsu* form of business structure. Given that long tradition (and the prewar *zaibatsu*) change in Japan is most likely to come from outside pressures or *gaiatsu*, which increased in the wake of Japan's decade-long slow growth recession. By the late 1990s, for the first time, foreign acquisitions and mergers took place: AT&T/BT bought into Japan Telecom, Cable and Wireless bought International Digital Communications, Merrill Lynch and GE Capital entered the financial services sector, and Renault bought part of Nissan.

Thus, it is conceivable that entrepreneurial capitalism may eventually alter, if not replace, managed capitalism in Europe and even Japan. If it does, it will not come about through structural changes made by their governments, but through the back door—via business galvanized by the cold realities of global competition and technological innovation that threaten their survival. A new factor entered the equation with the introduction of the "euro" in 1998. Within two years the "euro" economy was transforming European capital markets faster than anyone could have anticipated, making them more liquid and accessible to new entrants than ever before. Perhaps this development will "Americanize" Europe's economy, even if the harsher social aspects of entrepreneurial capitalism are mitigated by welfare state protections that France and Germany, among others, appear reluctant to abandon.

It seems equally likely, however, that political and historical realities in those countries may short-circuit structural reform, as reflected by this observation:

Clearly Europeans and Asians long for some non-American route to prosperity, with more consensus, more government than in the U.S. (with) less harshness and less risk of failure. . . . Europe's bloody twentieth century history proves that maintaining "social cohesion" or "solidarity"—even at the expense of faster economic growth—is imperative, some Europeans argue. Disaffected Europeans are more easily drawn to dangerous extremes than their American counterparts.[44]

Under the circumstances, it seems more likely that a hybrid version of entrepreneurial capitalism, shorn of its harsher social aspects,[45] may yet take shape.

CHAPTER 7

Backlash: The Limits of Entrepreneurial Capitalism

Some Cassandras have drawn an ominous parallel between Great Britain one hundred years ago and America today. At the dawn of the twentieth century Great Britain was globally ascendant and economically prosperous. Few could see, or even imagine, a single cloud on the horizon to threaten her future prospects—yet war, depression, and misguided public policies removed Britain from the front rank of global leaders, a position she is still struggling to regain. Entering the twenty-first century, America's economic leadership is unquestioned, but are there dark clouds looming, perhaps more visible to us than they had been to the British several generations earlier.

Even if the dimensions and genesis of entrepreneurial capitalism are not yet fully understood, there is growing recognition that the New Economy has been sustained and energized by the twin competitive pressures of globalization after World War II and by the entry, after the 1980s, of technologically innovative entrepreneurial companies into a domestic marketplace in which regulatory protections for more established companies were being dismantled. Both international and domestic competitive pressures were imposed upon corporate America as a direct consequence of incremental policy choices made at the federal level. The private sector would never have chosen to operate of its own volition in such a hypercompetitive environment! To the extent that these forces are attacked and wane, entrepreneurial capitalism will cease to thrive.

Two disquieting trends have emerged. The first, which only became clearly apparent at the end of 1999, was the antiglobalization movement.

In order to protect American jobs from going overseas and cheap goods from flooding the market, unions and other groups cynically manipulated public opinion, using legitimate concerns about child labor and environmental degradation in the Third World, to justify what amounted to trade protectionism. The adoption of policies denying developing countries entry into global markets, or worse still, pulling back from free trade altogether would be the first step in destroying the competitive forces of free trade and the free flow of capital that have been vital underpinnings for entrepreneurial capitalism. One observer offered a timely reminder that postwar global prosperity and an expansion of the global economy were a consequence of a sixteenfold expansion of trade brought about by liberalized markets.[1]

Second, the future of entrepreneurial capitalism rests on the continuance of competitive pressures from technologically innovative new entrants. Whether or not the private sector is in a position to produce this condition on its own depends on the continued willingness of investors to take risks. By the end of the 1990s, several factors emerged to threaten and undermine investor confidence in underwriting technological innovation, especially among those unlucky enough to have joined the 99 percent club (a reference to Internet companies that had lost 99 percent of their market value). A prolonged bear market in the technology or biotechnology sectors, the use of sustained high interest rates imposed by a Federal Reserve determined to quash "irrational exuberance," or any other combination of factors could severely undermine investor support for equities in general and new entrants in particular. Even more ominous, perhaps, persistent and overbearing regulatory intrusion into the activities of market-dominant companies (like Microsoft) seeking to retain market share in a hypercompetitive environment could undermine investor confidence. Each of these trends will be examined in greater detail.

WILL COMPETITIVE FORCES DIMINISH?

The Attack on Globalization

Is a political backlash gaining momentum as more Americans battle the impact of globalization and technological innovation?

The social costs of globalization and its impact on blue-collar Americans has been well documented. In two books, *America: Who Stole the Dream?*, published in 1996, and the earlier *America: What Went Wrong?*, Pulitzer prize-winning journalists Donald L. Barlett and James B. Steele chronicled the litany of social costs attributable to global competition. These included rising income inequality between what they called the "Have-Mores" and the "Have-Lesses"; the movement of manufacturing jobs abroad; and the influx of millions of immigrants who compete for lower skill jobs, depressing wages for American workers. They characterized attempts to rectify these matters as "retraining for nonexistent jobs." To be sure, as corporations have adjusted to the realities of global competition, especially in stagnant industries where top-line revenue growth is impossible, job cuts have become a permanent feature of American economic life. In a now familiar vein, Exxon–Mobil, following their merger in 1999, issued a pre-Christmas announcement that they would eliminate 14,000 jobs at a savings of over $3.8 billion dollars, far more than they had anticipated.[2]

Unions, moreover, have largely been unable to protect workers from either job losses or from shrinking wages. In fact, unions have been in decline for some time, so far unable to mobilize more workers to join their ranks. This is exemplified by a steady decline in union membership from 35 percent in the 1960s, to 20.1 percent in 1983 to 13.9 percent in 1998. Thus, the domestic labor market has been quiescent, despite job losses and lowered wages resulting from the competitive pressures of globalization. Strikes by workers are at an all-time low. According the the Bureau of Labor Statistics, between 1990–1998 there were on average only 36 big strikes compared with 337 annually between 1947 and 1957.[3]

However, even as the blue collar manufacturing segment of the labor market shrunk to 15 percent by 1999 (from 26 percent in 1973) and professional and technical employment grown (to 60 percent),[4] as America makes the transition from a manufacturing to an information economy, middle class workers, who may benefit from globalization, are being threatened by technological innovation that has brought with it job obsolescence, hence job insecurity. "Cradle to grave entrepreneurialism" now threatens to become the lot of all working Americans, who face futures of constant career changes and upgrades of their work skills.

Thus, despite a more educated, professional labor market, the middle class is not immune to the dislocations and chronic job insecurity that have long plagued blue-collar workers. In addition to normal competitive pressures, the transition to the information age continues to make entire categories of jobs obsolete, many of them white-collar and professional. The Internet, in particular, is remaking relationships between suppliers, vendors, and clients, eliminating middlemen and brokers. For instance, two thousand travel agents closed their doors in 1999 as travel web sites multiplied. When medical supplies company Bergen Brunswig announced its e-commerce venture to sell its products directly to hospitals and doctors directly via the web, medical supply salesman abruptly found their jobs eliminated or redefined. Will publicly traded Internet ventures such as eCollege redefine higher education? In 1999 the American Association of University Professors informed its members in an article in its journal *Academe* that more and more colleges and universities were relying on contingent teachers rather than on tenured college professors, and that innovations such as distance learning and web-delivered courses were exacerbating this trend. Wall Street, too, has begun to come under pressure. In December 1999, the first Internet-based bond auction was held by a Pittsburgh-based company, Muni Auctions, and, though their computers crashed due to excessive demand, it was a clear signal that even bond investors were willing to embrace the Internet. Bond auctions threaten the livelihoods of Wall Street broker dealers, who have made careers charging commissions as middlemen for bond transactions.[5] The spread of ECNs (Electronic Commerce Networks) threatens the careers of specialists and market makers on the New York Stock Exchange, which has come under pressure to list its stocks with outside exchanges.

If the era of the middleman and broker are over, so may be the era of the "gatekeeper." In fields such as music, publishing, and filmmaking, the Internet offers a future where artists and writers offer their work directly to the consumer and "scarcity" is no longer a concern. For example, Seagram (now a unit of Vivendi) established a music site where new recording artists can reach new audiences; iuniverse.com and fatbrain.com are web sites that will digitize, store, print, and distribute self-published books; while ifilm.com will store new work by independent filmmakers in digital form. Low cost, bandwidth, and access to the consumer may make the "gatekeeper"—the editor—redundant, especially for already established authors like Stephen King, who have little need for the marketing and publicity services of publishing houses. The potential for job loss is endless. Technological change is disruptive and will continue to intensify in the twenty-first century.

These dislocations may, of course, eventually be overcome as newer workers transform and upgrade their skills. Indeed, for those willing to adjust and adapt, new and more lucrative careers have appeared. Even for the less adaptable, the Internet has created self-employment opportunities. Some 20,000 Americans by the end of the 1990s made a living selling goods on eBay, the Internet auction site! And Internet-based home delivery services—for groceries, for example—may continue to create blue-collar jobs for delivery van drivers, as the upgrading of broadband cable and DSL lines has created jobs for construction workers.

Nevertheless, the adjustment to globalization and technological innovation will take time. In the interim, the trauma and pain of economic dislocation have produced a political backlash that has been fanned by the presidential campaigns of Patrick Buchanan and earlier by Ross Perot, whose Reform Party became Buchanan's adopted destination in the 2000 presidential campaign when he found himself unable to get his Republican colleagues to support the once-traditional Republican agenda of isolationism, protectionism, and nativism.

Buchanan has been staunchly unwilling to acknowledge any economic benefits of the changed economy. Indeed, in *The Great Betrayal*, published in 1998, he chronicled the decline of the manufacturing sector in mind-numbing detail. From his perspective, America's current economic status is far from ascendant. On the contrary, the nation remains in a grinding decline, and, worse still, it has been a decline orchestrated by its own government: ". . . the era of economic hegemony had come to a crashing close. Having organized its own decline the United States had masterfully executed its plan."[6]

Buchanan's book, though written at a time when the unemployment rate was falling, ignored the jobs created by the information economy. It chose to focus instead on the job losses sustained by industrial America, a sector he viewed as critical to the national security of the nation. The fact that manufacturing jobs went abroad was, he agonized, a symptom of "a nation in an advanced stage of industrial disarmament."[7] Elsewhere in the book he reiterated this point: "If trade is war, then free trade amounts to unilateral disarmament."[8]

His political ambitions turned him into a populist, forcing him to assess the implications of these job losses for social justice: "Social stability depends on a rising standard of living for all our people, those who work with lathes as well as those who work with laptops. And as we go surfing in Third Wave America, we best not forget those left behind on shore."[9]

In sum, Buchanan offered the view that nothing less than American sovereignty was at stake if America's postwar commitment to the global economy did not end: "free trade is shredding the society we grew up in and selling out America's sovereignty . . . free trade is truly a betrayal of Middle America and treason to the vision of the Founding Fathers."[10]

On the political Left, the year 2000 presidential campaign of Green Party candidate Ralph Nader promised to bring environmental and labor concerns to national attention, threatening a backlash against globalization from the opposite end of the political spectrum. Nader used the issue to reiterate the concerns of the Old Left, which remained critical of the shrinking of social protections and the shredding of the safety net, even as the New Democrats had embraced welfare reform and a shrinking of the public sector. If the "Naderites" eventually force the Democrats to take steps to ameliorate the harsher effects of globalization, will the party apply the salve of re-expanded welfare protections to ease the pain? Or will it accede to an invigorated labor movement demanding more labor market protections for workers, jeopardizing labor market flexibility? Or will the party take a stand against globalization and free trade?

While the political future of the antiglobalization movement is uncertain at this point, no politician could ignore the fact that these simmering forces had already erupted suddenly and unexpectedly during the "debacle in Seattle" in November 1999, when thousands of angry demonstrators disrupted a World Trade Organization meeting. The loosely organized forces of the "mobilization against globalization" had quickly brought to public attention the intensity of feeling against global trade, not just in America, but among workers in industrial nations worldwide. Union activists in America saw trade issues and the Seattle protests as a rallying point for a reinvigorated labor movement. A Teamster official had described the protests as a "defining moment for labor in redefining ourselves as a force to be reckoned with."[sic][11] and the pressure of international protest continued.

Not long before, political economist Ethan Kapstein had presciently predicted that a backlash of global proportions was gathering and would emerge, sooner rather than later, and events bore him out. But whereas Buchanan lamented only the loss of American jobs, Kapstein's book *Sharing the Wealth: Workers and the World Economy*, published in 1999, took a much broader view of the negative effects of globalization: "Today, workers everywhere are being overwhelmed by the raw power of unleashed market forces. . . . This book addresses the issue of how working people and especially the unskilled, are faring in the world economy. My argument is that they are not doing very well."[12] He went on to elaborate that his book "takes up the challenge of addressing the policy steps that are necessary to help labor, and especially unskilled workers, cope with the forces that have been unleashed."[13]

Kapstein continued:

If the process of globalization is to be sustained, easing pressure on the "losers" of the new open economy must now be the focus of international economic policy. Otherwise, demagogues will promote xenophobia and protectionism. These politicians are playing to those who see inequality and unemployment as the flip side of globalization.[14]

These doubts about the postwar order have, in his view, "potentially grim consequences for globalization." He reminded readers that the greatest catastrophes of the twentieth century were social disruptions caused by rapid economic change. If history is to be our guide there are lessons we would do well not to ignore in our quest for a global economy:

To readers who are prepared to dismiss the possibility of a backlash against globalization and the neo-liberal economic agenda, I would point to the period surrounding World War I and its aftermath. The Great War destroyed a global economy that in many respects was as highly evolved as our own, with trade and investment crossing borders at rates that would not recover until the 1970s

... But accompanying these changes was massive social dislocation, including the widespread movement of agricultural workers to cities, or the break-up of community based support systems. With the failure of national governments to fill this vacuum, workers naturally turned towards radical political solutions in addressing their grim economic fate—communism and revolution and later fascism and war.[15]

Kapstein raised several questions. Do governments, he asked, have any responsibility to help workers adapt to changing economic circumstances? If so, how? Should the losers from economic change be compensated? What role should international institutions and bilateral assistance programs play in helping the losers cope with the future? How should governments help workers cope?

The focus of American government's response to global competition from the late 1970s until the mid-1990s did not focus primarily on workers, the "losers" in the global economy. Policy makers had focused, instead, on policies to spur commercially viable technological innovation and measures to increase productivity by the private sector in order to revive its competitiveness in the global economy. Washington had sought to accomplish this goal by encouraging new entrants into the American economy in a variety of ways and then relying on them to create the new jobs for the next century. Indeed, it was estimated that one out of six new jobs during the 1990s was created by these new entrants.

While corporate America struggled to make itself fit for competition in order to ensure its survival on the global battlefield, the federal government cheered it on. If restructuring and mergers meant job losses, Washington did not succumb to intense political pressures to intervene. If industries went under, the government allowed them to fail and intervened only on a case-by-case basis and not as a general matter of public policy.

By the late 1990s, as an economic boom gathered force, the Clinton Administration paid more attention to the plight of workers who lost their jobs due to economic dislocation, passing job retraining acts and education tax credits. However, labor market flexibility had been a cornerstone of corporate America's ability to restructure, and not even the unions have been able to successfully intervene to stop it. Nor is it likely that the federal government will create jobs for displaced workers and the low-skilled unemployed as Roosevelt had done during the Great Depression and as William Julius Wilson had called on the government to do in his 1996 book *When Work Disappears*. More likely, subsequent presidents will seek nongovernmental solutions. In 1999 Clinton unveiled his New Markets Initiative to spur corporations to target and invest in areas of deep poverty in the same way they set up factories in developing countries. George W. Bush, the Republican candidate in the year 2000 presidential campaign, suggested instead that greater reliance be placed on private philanthropy. Upon taking office in January 2001, he immediately established a White House Office of Faith-Based and Community Initiatives.

A less charitable twist on how policy makers had handled the social costs of globalization came from Edward Luttwak, who pointed to America's willingness to put the low-skilled, displaced by the elimination of industrial jobs, into prison if they turned to crime. Indeed, America by the 1990s had the highest rates of incarceration in the industrialized world, with an estimated five million in the criminal justice system, including over 1.9 million in prison.

The potential unraveling of globalization due to a political backlash in the United States would be damaging to American prosperity and catastrophic for many developing countries. Forcefully arguing on their behalf, Kofi Annan, Secretary General of the United Nations, declared that: "The movement of jobs to Third World countries has been a boon to these economies and their governments look with deepening alarm upon attempts by First World unions to introduce issues such as labor or environmental standards into discussions of trade at the World Trade Organization."[16]

In sum, a movement against globalization, a crucial underpinning of entrepreneurial capitalism and the New Economy, is gaining momentum in the United States, although the outcome is uncertain at this time. Thus far the antiglobalization forces remain on the fringes of American politics, with both Republicans and Democrats continuing to express support for free trade. Should that change, however, under pressure from the "losers" galvanized by the social upheaval many scholars believe imminent, or by demagogic politicians seeking political advantage, then one of the underpinnings of entrepreneurial capitalism will most surely be removed.

The Attack on Investor Confidence

The second factor that could undermine entrepreneurial capitalism would be permanent damage to investor confidence caused, for instance, by any lengthy decline in the stock market. Investors, once willing to provide capital to young companies, could become gunshy. The impact of closing capital markets will be fewer innovative new entrants into the marketplace and hence a lessening of competitive pressures. Throughout the 1990s, investor confidence had been nurtured under the protective umbrella of a prolonged bull market, which had, perhaps overexuberantly, allowed valuations of innovative young companies—particularly in the Internet, technology, and biotechnology sectors—to become severely overstretched. What can be expected to happen to investor psychology under conditions of a sustained bear market? While we have yet to find out, the savage 2000–2001 stock market decline offered some important clues as venture capital shrank and only 21 companies went public in the first quarter of 2001, compared with 123 in the same period a year earlier.[17]

It is important to remember that private sector entrepreneurial innovation was fueled by the willingness of investors to take risks by providing early-stage seed capital to innovative startups in high-risk sectors, a task formerly undertaken almost exclusively by public sector (government) funding. Investments in future technologies are inherently risky. Young companies, particularly in the nascent Internet sector, all too often had tiny and unpredictable revenue streams and nonexistent profits. As the venture market gathered steam, venture capitalists were knowledgeable enough to bear such risks, but the prices they had paid for their investments in young companies had been minuscule (and profits huge) relative to the market prices paid by unsophisticated investors, many of whom bought at the initial public offering price, only to be "slaughtered" in the carnage of the "dot.com crash" that began in spring 2000. For example, one venture capital company and business incubator, Idealabs, paid half a cent for each of its shares in a company called "eToys"—for a total of $100,000. It subsequently sold 3.8 million of its shares in December 1999 for prices between $47.5 and $69.58, making a profit of $193 million. By May 2000, eToys was down 72 percent from its offering price! Within a year the company closed down.[18] Indeed by spring 2000, half of all 1999 initial public offerings were stuck below their offering prices.[19] By the following spring many, like garden.com, had ceased to exist. The depth of the decline was exemplified by globe.com's stock price. Briefly at $97, from an offering price of $9, it plummeted to a pre-split adjusted price of $3.625 by May 2000.[20] By 2001, that kind of decline had become routine in the entire technology sector even for well-established and profitable companies like Cisco Systems and Sun Microsystems, whose own viability and profitability came under scrutiny.

If investors feel permanently foolish for having made investments in new entrants and decide to stick to companies with predictable revenues and earnings, then equity capital, once so abundant to fuel the boom in new products and new markets, will eventually shrivel and the IPO market close to all but a few, as it began to do by mid-2000. Competitive forces emanating from private-sector initiative and innovation will lessen. Part of the blame for the Internet debacle, which spread to the entire technology sector, should go the investment bankers for devaluing underwriting standards in order to take companies public that under other circumstances would not have been deemed ready, as well as to the brokers and research analysts who touted them. A mixture of greed, cynicism, and suspension of belief fueled the "Great Internet Bubble," so that the business fundamentals and future prospects of new entrants were ignored. If investors remain bruised by their experiences, they will not be eager to buy stock in new companies. And without an "exit strategy"—access to the equity markets for their investments—private-venture capital may also shrink, endangering the technological innovation that has been such a key feature of entrepreneurial capitalism and has undergirded America's return to economic growth and prosperity. In *The Coming Internet Depression*, written well before the full dimensions of the debacle had unfolded,[21] Michael Mandel, economics editor for *Business Week*, seemed to argue that too much technology-driven growth could become a problem and predicted technology overcapacity would follow a brief period of "hypergrowth." A far bigger concern, he suggested, was that technology-driven productivity gains might shrivel as private venture capital grows scarce. Should that occur, Mandel predicted "that government might have to take a hand in the high-tech sector to stabilize the New Economy," a role I believe it has already undertaken over the past twenty years!

Political misunderstandings from federal regulators about the source of what in hindsight appears to have been "hypergrowth" is a cause for concern as well. The fragmentation of American government meant that it took over two decades to forge and maintain a bipartisan consensus of the legislative *and* executive branches to reverse the decline of U.S. productivity and to spur competitiveness. Incrementally enacted public policies simultaneously removed regulatory protections for established companies and introduced public policies supportive of entrepreneurial innovation. Those policy steps unleashed a highly competitive technology-driven economy with both higher productivity and higher growth rates. Corporate America experienced a concomitant spurt in growth rates and profits during the 1990s, with even established companies such as General Electric benefiting from growth rates of 20 percent annually, up from a more "normal" 8–10 percent in the 1980s. This has been reflected in an expansion of market "price to earnings" ratios (to 20–25 times earnings), resulting in higher valuations for stocks in general. Jeremy Siegel, a finance professor at the University of Pennsylvania's Wharton School, was once a vocal apologist for higher market valuations given the more beneficent economic conditions and doubted, at least before the 2001 bear debacle, whether the stock market would ever return to historic valuations of 10–15 times earnings.[22]

These forces shaping the economy and markets were real, yet Federal Reserve Chairman Alan Greenspan, as part of repeated attempts to "talk down" the stock markets, enunciated new parameters for setting the future course of monetary policy, with ominous implications. By early 2000, he was suggesting that productivity gains and wealth creation—

"the wealth effect"—were a cause of imbalances that led to inflation as investors spent their new-found wealth. Henceforth, stock market gains in excess of household income would be viewed as inflationary by the Federal Reserve, with a concomitant bias towards higher interest rates.[23] When those higher interest rates were put in place, they rapidly slowed down growth, undermined business confidence and restrained capital spending. Taken together, these forces ironically created conditions of technology overcapacity—which caused profits and stock prices of high-tech companies to fall quickly and dramatically. Under a worst case scenario, if a similar stance is adopted by future Federal Reserve chairmen, this could keep equity markets almost permanently constrained, creating a much less hospitable environment for the launch of new companies with innovative products and services. This clearly would undermine one of the defining characteristics of entrepreneurial capitalism and restrain competitive pressures.

Still other threats to technological innovation and the viability of entrepreneurial capitalism emerged by the end of the 1990s. Antitrust regulators, it became clear, showed little understanding of how the New Economy has altered the marketplace. Entrepreneurial capitalism has been characterized by ferocious competition galvanized by disruptive technologies. The balance of power has shifted to consumers as never before. The bottom line for corporations has been that they face unprecedented market risk since market conditions can change rapidly and unexpectedly. Market leaders, even a market darling such as Cisco Systems, could be challenged overnight by new entrants such as Sycamore or Juniper Networks—something apparently lost on federal regulators and the courts as they launched an antitrust investigation of Microsoft in 1998, naming it a "predatory monopolist" at the very moment the company's temporary monopoly of PC operating systems was being challenged by the non-PC-centered world of web-based information appliances with alternative operating systems. In this new world Microsoft was being challenged by Sun's Java, Palm Computer's OS, and others, even while its server software, Windows 2000, faced challenges from a free (open-source) rival, Linux. As economist Lawrence Kudlow pointed out, the Microsoft case created uncertainties in the marketplace about whether there would be similar regulatory intrusions into the operations of other market-dominating companies, causing downdrafts in their stock prices and ultimately threatening their ability to find, acquire, and expand the technologies of young companies. Beyond this concern was a new one: that antitrust policy during the Clinton Administration[24] had shifted from protecting consumers to protecting competitors.

At issue in the Microsoft case was the company's inclusion of a free version of Internet Explorer in its Windows 98 operating system. Charging that Microsoft's monopoly of operating systems posed a serious threat to rival Netscape, the Justice Department sought to force Microsoft to remove Internet Explorer from Windows 98. While there were several issues in the trial—such as Microsoft's freedom to innovate in order to serve consumers better and Microsoft's contention that its rivals had failed to take advantage of market opportunities—as the year progressed the competitive landscape changed so dramatically that it became clear that all Microsoft's PC operating system monopolies were under attack. A Microsoft spokesman, albeit not a disinterested observer, assessed the situation: "Microsoft faces so many threats from so many different directions that it's impossible for anybody to dictate prices or exclude competitors from the marketplace."[25]

The course of events that year proved him correct. First, during the course of the trial, Netscape merged with AOL and agreed to work on a rival application, Java, a programming platform from competitor Sun Microsystems that Microsoft in its trial claimed was being explicitly developed to make Windows obsolete.[26] Microsoft founder and Chairman Bill Gates himself complained that "The deal (between AOL and Netscape) demonstrates how intense competition is in this business."[27] Early the following year, AOL set about transforming itself into an even more formidable competitor when it announced its merger with Time Warner.

Next, Linux, an "open-source" server operating system developed by a young software engineer from Finland, Linus Torvalds, directly competed with Microsoft's server software, Windows NT, as well as its successor, Windows 2000. By 1998, Linux had gained an almost 17 percent share of the server software market, and a *New York Times* magazine article informed a national audience that:

A formidable array of Microsoft's competitors, including IBM, Intel and Oracle are lining up to back the orphan program. New companies like Red Hat Software in Durham, N.C. are aiming to make money by providing technical support for the software they can never own. In a bow to Linux's growing stature, Netscape and Intel invested last Fall in Red Hat . . . In an internal memo that somehow found its way onto the Internet, a Microsoft engineer outlined the circumstances in which "Linux can win" and proposed strategies for defeating the advantages of its new competitor. Microsoft has also cited its fear of Linux in its antitrust battle with the Justice Department.[28]

Some months later in 1999, other leading companies such as Compaq, Novell, and Oracle took equity positions in Red Hat Software, while Hewlett-Packard (and later IBM) adapted it to work on their own computers.[29] Following their lead, Germany's Siemens and SAP agreed to support Linux. Karl Heinz Hess, executive vice-president of systems technology development at SAP commented: "In view of the market interest in Linux, its stable technological foundation and our commitment to platform independence, it was incumbent to SAP to step up delivering (its newest model) SAP R/3 on Linux."[30]

Compounding Microsoft's problems, "Solaris" from Sun Microsystems was introduced in January 2000, joining Linux as an open-source operating code, even beating Microsoft's own new server software Windows 2000 by one month. By 2001, yet another different, free, open-source operating system—Free BSD—joined Linux, similarly developed by volunteer software engineers. In the interim Linux itself gained greater acceptance from companies as diverse as Home Depot and Amerada Hess. In fact, the Linux operating system, with over 16 percent of server market share in 1998 had grown to a 27 percent market share by 2000.[31]

Microsoft found itself embattled on other fronts as the year ground on. Non-PC applications were threatening Microsoft's purported dominance of the personal computer, challenging Windows 98's threat as an entry point to the Internet. Many personal computer makers and other vendors in the cell phone, pager, and other industries were at work on a new generation of "information appliances." While Microsoft had also developed an operating system for "information appliances"—namely, Windows CE—it faced fierce competition from other appliance-operating systems such as the Palm OS and even from cellular phone makers. AOL announced plans to expand delivery of its online service service through a new generation of Internet devices that would use Sun Microsystem's Java programming, even as it invested 5 percent in the Palm spinoff. As a consequence of these competitive pressures, Microsoft began the new century with a strategy to "webify" its products, now ensuring that its net initiative supported a variety of programming languages, thereby reversing the company's prior emphasis on proprietary and incompatible software products.

Dismissing all these drastic marketplace changes, a senior Justice Department official commented: "Ambitious plans (by Microsoft rivals) do not change the fact of Microsoft's monopoly and how it used it." And even though Judge Thomas Penfield Jackson had begun to cite "very significant changes in the playing field as far as this industry is concerned," he nevertheless rocked financial markets when he issued his "finding of facts" on Friday, November 5, 1999, agreeing with the Justice Department by naming Microsoft a predatory monopolist whose business practices had stifled innovation.[32]

After several arbitration attempts failed, the judge issued his final ruling in 2000, calling for a breakup of Microsoft, which the company immediately appealed. In June 2001, the appeals court reversed the breakup order but upheld the finding that Microsoft had broken the law. The case serves as an example of the time lag between government reform—so incremental that it took more than a decade before its impact on the competitive landscape became clearly apparent—and the recognition of this new paradigm by government officials.

Conclusion

What factors could unravel America's economic dominance and technological ascendancy? The threats have not, as yet, become so worrisome that Americans should visualize a future in which the nation, like Britain before her, becomes a "declining hegemon"—even though by the late 1980s so many academic observers, including Paul Kennedy, foresaw just such a dismal future.

At this point we can only guess. Perhaps the underpinnings of entrepreneurial capitalism, such as global free trade, will crumble under the pressure of labor and environmentalist concerns; or perhaps, as John Gray suggested, a global free market functions only so long as its institutions are underwritten by an effective global power. His best guess had been that the United States today "lacks the will, perhaps the capacity, to assume the burdens of an imperial power, because, despite its 'unchallengable military superiority,' (America) can sustain no military engagement that seems likely to be protracted or which comes at a significant risk of high casualties."[33]

Perhaps the newly emerging powers will challenge the rules of the game if their needs are not met (for example, they will infringe on copyright laws), and without America's willingness to enforce them, the rules will collapse. Or perhaps America will be a victim of its own success. As the Nasdaq organizes global capital markets in Japan and Europe, and assuming its 70 percent collapse in the United States during the 2001 bear market does not undermine confidence in emerging companies, other nations will gain access to American capital. Then, as entrepreneurial enterprises grow and prosper, they may change their host cultures, albeit slowly. In the interim, other nations may rise to challenge our economic dominance. China is currently a sleeping giant, but one with an entrepreneurial heritage. In December 1999 the Hong Kong Stock exchange took the first steps towards creating the access to capital young companies need by organizing the Growth Enterprise Market[34] and China itself may awaken from its long economic slumber.

On the other hand, other scenarios may play out. Many Americans who remain uncertain of the role played by public policy in underwriting growth and prosperity may pressure policy makers to alter direction in ways that undermine American competitiveness, technological innovation, and entrepreneurial energy. A lessening of public support for privatization and globalization as a result of the terrorist attacks of September 11, 2001 is one possibility. Only time will tell.[35]

Notes

CHAPTER 1: AN OVERVIEW

1. By February 2000, the National Bureau of Economic Research measured the economic expansion at 107 months, exceeding by one month the longest previously recorded economic expansion, which lasted from February 1961 to December 1969. During that expansion unprecedented household wealth was created. For example, as of 1994 only 90,000 U.S. households had net worths in excess of $5 million, yet by 2000, 531,000 U.S. households had net worths exceeding that figure. Source: The Spectrem Group, cited in *Investor's Business Daily* (March 19, 2001): A6.

2. By the late 1990s the American economy recorded unheard-of levels of growth, as well as low unemployment and low inflation, a combination not thought possible. By 1999, third quarter GDP growth roared along at 5.7 percent surpassed by fourth quarter rates of 7.3 percent, considered unsustainable, with an average annual growth rate of 4 percent recorded for the last few years of the 1990s. Unemployment rates dipped as low as 4.1 percent and inflation remained a tepid 2.6 percent. Department of Labor and National Bureau of Economic Research statistics reported in the *Wall Street Journal* (January 25, 2000): B1. Not only did the economy grow, but corporate profit growth exceeded previous levels. Between 1992 and 2000, for example, profit growth for the S&P 500 averaged 11.5 percent a year, compared with 7.1 percent for previous decades, with only one down year (1997) recorded between 1994 and 2000. Source: *Wall Street Journal* (April 9, 2001): A12.

3. There is ample statistical evidence to support the claim that after 1980 there were dramatic increases in R&D investments, as well as in the rate of technological innovation, compared with the preceding pre-1980 period:

(a) Whereas total R&D expenditures increased 34 percent between 1970–1975, they increased by over 80 percent from 1980–1985. Using more extended time periods, total R&D expanded 249 percent from 1980–1998 compared with a 175 percent increase from 1965–1979.

(b) The number of natural scientists and engineers employed in R&D grew by 83 percent from 1980–1997 versus an increase of only 21 percent in the period 1960–1980.

(c) Federal outlays for general science, space, and other technology increased 58 percent from 1980–1990.

(d) Patents issued to U.S. residents increased by 75 percent from 1980–1997, whereas the rate of increase had been virtually flat from 1960–1980.

(e) Patents issued to U.S. universities increased 500 percent to 1,500 annually after 1980 compared with fewer than 250 annually prior to 1980. This effect has been directly attributed to the Bayh–Dole Act of 1980 by many observers, including the Association of University Technology Managers. Moreover, this act is credited with creating the U.S. biotechnology industry, since it is generally recognized that university R&D is responsible for developing 44 percent of all new U.S. drugs and 37 percent of all new pharmacological processes. Source: www.nttc.edu.

Source for footnotes 3(a)–3(d): For the period 1960–1970: *Historical Statistics of the United States: Colonial Times to 1970, Part 2* (U.S Department of Commerce: Bureau of the Census, 1975). For data from 1980–1997, *The Statistical Abstract of the United States: National Data Book*, 119th ed. (U.S. Department of Commerce: Bureau of the Census, 1999). Data after 1997 obtained from U.S. Census Bureau, *Statistical Abstract of the United States 2000* (PDF file at www.census.gov).

Historians will doubtless be tempted to draw parallels with a similar period of entrepreneurial innovation during the turn of the last century. They should bear in mind, however, that industrial era "laissez-faire" capitalism, which was led by the private sector, emerged behind a wall of protectionist tariffs, grew unimpeded by antitrust, which was in its infancy, and produced monopolies whose dismantling required drastic political solutions. This point is elaborated upon in Chapter 2.

4. The German and Japanese economic miracles had long since faded into memory. European economies in the 1990s recorded stagnant growth rates. The Euro-zone economy expanded at just 2% in 1999, with Germany (1.4% growth); France (1.1% growth), and Italy (0.9%) holding back the average growth rate. While inflation remained low (1.6% by November 1999), unemployment rates remained high, with average rates around 12 percent *The Financial Times* (December 21, 1999): 12. Unemployment rate quoted in the *Wall Street Journal* (February 20, 1998).

Japan remained in dire straits throughout the 1990s. The Japanese Economic Planning Agency announced a growth target of 0.6 percent for the fiscal year ending March 31, 2000 and had expected growth of 1 percent starting in April, 2000. Source: *Investor's Business Daily* (December 18, 1999): A8. By early 2001, however, the Japanese government conceded for the first time that its economy was in a state of mild deflation and that its fragile recovery was faltering even as most observers believed it had slipped into recession. *Investor's Business Daily* (March 19, 2001): A2.

5. Even proponents of the New Economy had their faith sorely tested when early in the twenty-first century an economic downturn and plunging stock markets cast doubt on its longevity, even its existence. By the first quarter of 2001, growth in the American economy slowed to almost zero, plunging from a previously robust rate of 6 percent one year before. The unemployment rate, however, remained at a level that in prior years would have been considered full employment (under 5 percent) and inflation remained subdued. The technology sector was hit particularly hard as business investment in equipment and software which, since 1992 had been growing at a rate of 13 percent annually, was projected to fall by 2–3 percent in 2001. *Wall Street Journal* (April 9, 2001): A 12. Surprisingly, however, an initial growth rate of 2 percent was estimated for the first quarter of 2001.

6. Although the chairman of the Federal Reserve Board, Alan Greenspan, refrained from speculating about the genesis of the New Economy, he has been a firm proponent of its existence. In 1999 he recognized that "something special has happened to the American economy." See the *Wall Street Journal* (June 15, 1999): A2. A year earlier, in his June 1998 testimony before the Joint Economic Committee of Congress, he acknowledged that "the current economic performance . . . is as impressive as any I have witnessed in my half century of daily observation of the American economy." *Wall Street Journal* (June 11, 1998): A2.

7. Productivity growth had been mentioned by Mr. Greenspan as a factor spurring economic growth, and although the rate had slowed in the 1970s to 1.5 percent, in the last years of the 1990s it had expanded to 3 percent annually. See "The Magic Elixir of Productivity," in the *Wall Street Journal* (February 15, 2001): A1. Despite the stock market crash of 2000–2001 and lackluster productivity numbers, Mr. Greenspan was quoted as saying that high-tech investments in recent years had permanently improved the productivity outlook. Gains, he suggested, had merely been moderated because of the slowing economy, but he had faith that the lull would only be temporary. Source: *Investor's Business Daily* (April 30, 2001): A1.

8. If Reagan-era tax cuts indeed spurred economic growth, the question begs to be asked: Why then did Bush- and Clinton-era tax increases not end it?

9. Historians will surely underscore this point of comparison with the era of laissez-faire capitalism. With budgets averaging $617 million from 1900–1915, the federal government in the early twentieth century had neither the resources nor the political will to underwrite the intense entrepreneurial innovation of that period. See *Historical Abstract of the United States* 2000, p. 887.

10. Josh Lerner, "The Government as Venture Capitalist: The Long Run Effects of the SBIR Program," *Journal of Business*, 72 (July 1999) 285–318. See also "The Problematic Venture Capitalist," *Science* 287 (February 11, 2000): 977–979.

11. During the 2000 presidential campaign, Democratic candidate Al Gore's claim to have "invented the Internet" was met with derision. However exaggerated the claim, and in the absence of any cogent defense by Mr. Gore himself despite his interest in government support for the "information superhighway," I would like to offer a partial defense of his claim to have played a critical role in the development of the Internet. His sponsorship of the High Performance Computing and National Research and Education Act, mandating a leadership role for the United States in supercomputing, led to National Science Foundation

funding for the National Center for Supercomputing Applications at the University of Illinois, which developed an early Internet browser, Mosaic. Marc Andreessen, a student employed at the Center, subsequently joined with entrepreneurs Jim Clark and Jim Barksdale to engineer an improved graphical interface, the Netscape internet browser, which the trio successfully commercialized, making them billionaires.

By the end of the 1990s, even obscure Third World nations were looking to emulate the American economic model. In Guyana, the 1999 election of the People's Progressive Party (PPP), a formerly Marxist party, affirmed its commitment to a market economy and pledged to implement reforms to reregulate, privatize, and lower tariffs. *Financial Times* (November 23, 1999): p. 7.

12. Peter Eisinger, *The Rise of the Entrepreneurial State: State and Local Economic Development Policy* (Madison: University of Wisconsin Press, 1988), 334.

13. Ibid., p. 2.

14. Ibid., p. 2.

15. By the mid-1980s, the subject of declining U.S. competitiveness so dominated informed discussion that a senior bibliographer in science policy at the Library Service Division of the Congressional Research Service compiled a list of academic sources on the subject exclusively for members of Congress. See B. F. Mangan, *Science, Technology and the International Competitiveness of American Industry: Selected References, 1985–1988* (Washington D.C: Library of Congress, Congressional Research Service, August 1988).

16. Paul Kennedy, *The Rise and Fall of the Great Powers* (New York: Random House, 1987). See also Henry Nau, *The Myth of America's Decline: Leading the World Economy in the 1990s* (New York: Oxford University Press, 1990). Also Paul Krugman, *The Age of Diminished Expectations: U.S. Economic Policy in the 1990s*, revised 3rd. ed. (Cambridge, MA: MIT Press, 1997).

Illustrative of the lag effect on public opinion, as late as September 1991, the Council of Competitiveness reported that 73 percent of respondents had answered that they believed that difficult times with respect to foreign competition were "still ahead of us." The question had asked:

Thinking about the challenge to America posed by foreign economic competitors would you say that the most difficult period is still ahead for America or that the most difficult period is still ahead for us. Source: *Wall Street Journal* (October 1992).

17. A series of Congressional Research Reports addressed the problem of declining U.S. competitiveness, among them: Wendy Schacht, *Commercialization of Technology and Issues in the Competitiveness of Selected U.S. Industries: Semiconductors, Biotechnology and Superconductors* (Library of Congress: Congressional Research Service 88–879, 1988); Gary L. Guenther, *Semi-Conductor Devices: The Changing Competitiveness of U.S. Merchant Producers 1977–1987*, (Library of Congress: Congressional Research Service, rev. June 1998).

18. Kenneth Flamm, *Targeting the Computer: Government Support and International Competition* (Washington, DC: Brookings Institution Press, 1987), 189.

19. *Statistical Abstract of the United States 2000, Federal Funding of R&D by Agency 1980–2000* (U.S. Department of Commerce: Bureau of the Census), 603. The 1970 figures are from *Statistical Abstract of the United States Bureau of the Census*, 119th ed.

20. Malcolm Gladwell, *The Tipping Point: How Little Things Can Make a Big Difference* (Boston: Little, Brown, 2000).

21. Source: https://radius.rand.org/radius/radius_info.html. Prior to Ra-DiUS, developed by the RAND Corporation on behalf of the federal government, data on how much the federal government was spending and through which agencies was incomplete, fragmented, and out of date.

22. Josh Lerner, "The Government as Venture Capitalist," 1999. Academic opinion remains divided on this subject. See Linda R. Cohen and Roger C. Noll, *The Technology Pork Barrel* (Washington DC: Brookings Institution Press, 1991). In March 2001, Ralph Nader in an Op/Ed piece in the *Wall Street Journal* derided as "wasteful duplication" the fact that seven federal agencies, twenty federal laboratories, and the Big Three automakers were involved in the PNGV (Partnership for a New Generation of Vehicles). See "Ending Corporate Welfare As We Know It," *Wall Street Journal* (March 7, 2001): A22.

23. Peter Eisinger, *The Rise of the Entrepreneurial State*, 342.

24. John Kingdon, *Agendas, Alternatives and Public Policies* (New York: Harper Collins, 1984). For a detailed discussion about how agendas rise to prominence or fall from attention, see Chapter 1.

25. *Small Business Innovation Research*, a descriptive booklet published by the Department of Defense, 4.

26. Kenneth Flamm, *Targeting the Computer*, 175.

27. Ian Hendry, *Innovating for Failure: Government Policy and the Early British Computer Industry* (Cambridge, MA: MIT Press, 1990), 162.

28. Sten Thore, *The Diversity, Complexity and Evolution of High-Tech Capitalism* (Boston: Kluwer Publishing Company, 1995), 1.

29. Ibid.

30. Alvin Toffler and Heidi Toffler, *Creating a New Civilization: The Politics of the Third Wave* (Atlanta: Turner Publishing, 1995).

31. Robert Kuttner, *Everything for Sale* (New York: Alfred P. Knopf, 1997), 1.

32. Lester Thurow, *The Future of Capitalism* (New York: Penguin, 1996).

33. Donald L. Barlett and James B. Steel, *America: Who Stole the Dream?* (Kansas City, MO: Andrews and McMeel, 1996).

34. John Gray, *False Dawn: The Delusions of Global Capitalism* (New York: New Press, distributed by W. W. Norton, 1998).

35. Edward Luttwak, *Turbo-Capitalism: Winners and Losers in the Global Economy* (New York: Harper Collins, 1999), 12.

36. Paul Krugman, "America The Boastful," *Foreign Affairs*, volume 77, no. 3 (May/June 1998), 32–45. Although Krugman acknowledged that the U.S. economy seemed to be experiencing a period of robust growth, he wrote: "Its long-run growth rate has not accelerated, productivity has not risen, and the structural unemployment rate has fallen by one percentage point at most." Krugman himself may have changed his mind about the temporary nature of the New Economy. In an article by Gerard Baker in the *Financial Times* on December 14, 1999, page 11, he appeared prepared to acknowledge that positive changes in productivity, growth, and unemployment rates had occurred, and may be permanent.

37. Alvin Teffler and Heidi Toffler, *Creating A New Civilization*, 1.

38. David Hale quoted in the *International Herald Tribune* (January 12, 1999): 11.

39. Ibid.

40. *The Statistical Abstract of the United States*, 119th ed. (U.S. Department of Commerce: Bureau of the Census, 1999). There is a strong case to be made that increases in private sector R&D were heavily dependent on the temporary R&D tax credit that went into effect in 1981. Although by spring 2001, a permanent extension of the investment tax credit was still in doubt, on the campaign trail a year earlier, Presidential candidate George W. Bush had acknowledged that extending it permanently would "create an environment that rewards investment in innovative technologies and spurs the long-term investment in R&D that America needs to develop the next generation of critical technologies both civilian and military." However, estimates of what that would cost through 2011, according to the chief of staff of Congress' Joint Committee on Taxation, rose from $24 billion in 2000 to $47 billion in 2001. See the *Wall Street Journal* (February 28, 2001): A1.

41. *The Statistical Abstract of the United States*, 119th ed. (U.S. Department of Commerce: Bureau of the Census, 1999), 562.

Venture capital has been credited with financing the nation's broadband capacity (perhaps overcapacity by 2001), yet the policy priorities undergirding this effort were set a decade earlier when Senator Al Gore and Representative Boucher introduced S 2937 and HR 5759, respectively—two bills that led to the Information Infrastructure and Technology Act of 1992, which did not become law but nevertheless raised as a policy priority the development of a coordinated federal program "to accelerate development of an advanced information superstructure." A year earlier, in 1991, Title One of the Communications Competitiveness and Infrastructure Act, introduced by Representative Boucher as bill HR 2546, had amended the Communications Act of 1934 to "establish a new national goal that by 2015 the U.S. will have established an advanced, interactive, interoperable broadband system nationwide." Source: www.loc.gov.

42. The Small Business Innovation Research Program booklet. Since the inception of the program in 1982, DARPA reported that over 40,000 SBIR awards totaling over $6.5 billion have been made.

43. With respect to space-related research and development, the Department of Commerce, in keeping with the federal government's new policy goal of commercializing defense-related expenditures, produced a 136-page report titled: *Space Commerce: An Industry Assessment* (Washington, DC: U.S. Department of Commerce, 1988). Ebola virus information: *Wall Street Journal*, (January 24, 2001): A4.

44. Ironically, only Israel seems to have followed this aspect of the American model. Its "Silicon Wadi" has produced over 4,000 high-technology companies with strong ties to the Israeli military. A former Likud party spokesman said the Israel Defense Forces had a saying, "We're the best high-tech incubator in the world." *Investor's Business Daily* (March 12, 2001): A8. Even as some nations have learned valuable lessons from us, there were impending signs of a disturbing change of focus in the United States. In his first budget speech in 2001, President George W. Bush stated that deep cuts were intended for the Commerce Department's Advanced Technology Program, which makes grants available for com-

panies trying to develop commercial technologies in sectors such as electronics. *Wall Street Journal* (February 28, 2001): A1.

45. Rutgers student Chandra Brickner, summarizing what she had learned in my Honors Seminar, in her term paper titled "Capitalism: The Petroleum Industry," submitted April 1999. I'd also like to thank all the students in that Honors Seminar for giving me an opportunity to define, refine, and discuss "entrepreneurial capitalism," a concept new to all of us!

46. These Third World concerns were articulated by U.N. Secretary General Kofi Annan in an Op/Ed article titled "Help the Third World Help Itself" *Wall Street Journal* (November 29, 1999): A28.

CHAPTER 2: DEFINING ENTREPRENEURIAL CAPITALISM AND ITS IMPACT ON CORPORATE AMERICA

1. Source: *Investor's Business Daily* (February 26, 2001): A4. In fact, the first Internet-related initial public offering to come to market in March 2001, Loudcloud, actually lost money for late-stage venture capital investors who had bought shares at $12 per share, only to see the company go public at $6 per share!

2. For both time periods under consideration, the pace of innovation increased. From 1980–1997, U.S. patents filed increased by 106 percent compared to a rate of increase of only 43 percent for the prior twenty-year period. Similarly, during the laissez-faire era (1890–1920), the number of U.S. patents filed increased 105 percent compared with an increase of 52 percent for the period from 1870–1890. Source: *Statistical Abstract of the United States: National Data Book* (Washington DC: Government Printing Office: Department of Commerce: U.S. Census Bureau, 119th ed., 1999), 564. For earlier data, *Historical Statistics of the United States Colonial Times to 1970*, Part 2 (Washington DC: Government Printing Office, Department of Commerce, Bureau of the Census, 1975), 957.

3. The Exxon–Mobil merger was followed by the British Petroleum/Amoco cross-border merger, as well as several others. Nineteen of the twenty largest mergers up to that date occurred between 1998 and 1999. The total value of mergers worldwide skyrocketed tenfold during the 1990s. By 1999, the value was estimated at over $3 trillion dollars versus under $3 billion in 1992. *Wall Street Journal* (December 8, 1999): C1. Critics point to these statistics as evidence of a return to the consolidation of the laissez-faire era.

4. John Gray, *False Dawn: The Delusions of Global Capitalism* (New York: The New Press/W. W. Norton, 1998), 94. Gray's concerns were echoed by other observes, including George Soros in *The Crisis of Global Capitalism* (Public Affairs Books, 1999); Edward Luttwak in *Turbo-Capitalism: Winners and Losers in the Global Economy* (New York: Harper Collins, 1999), who detected both a new form of capitalism and an increase in monopoly (see p. 12); and Louis Galambos who in a 1994 paper titled "The Triumph of Monopoly" warned that "competitive oligopolies" were now corporate America's preferred business structure and might emerge as the wave of the future. *Wall Street Journal* (Monday March 9, 1999): B1.

5. Bill Gates, in a *Wall Street Journal* Op/Ed piece titled "Why the Justice Department Is Wrong," had complained about this subtle shift in the Clinton Administration's antitrust policy: "U.S. anti-trust laws exist not to prop up competitors but to ensure that consumers benefit from the widespread availability of goods and services at fair prices." Source: *Wall Street Journal* (November 10, 1997): A18. A few years later, Gary S. Becker and Kevin M. Murphy echoed Gates' concerns in "Rethinking Anti-Trust." They found troubling the Clinton Administration antitrust emphasis on "unfair competition" as opposed to evidence of harm to consumers. *Wall Street Journal.* (February 26, 2001): A22.

6. Robert W. Crandall "Whistling Past Big Steel's Graveyard," *Wall Street Journal* (March 19, 1999): A18.

7. Thomas McCraw, ed. *Creating Modern Capitalism: How Entrepreneurs, Companies and Countries Triumphed in Three Industrial Revolutions*, paperback ed. (Cambridge: Harvard University Press, 1998), 327.

8. Pankaj Ghemawat and Fariborz Ghadar, "The Dubious Logic of Global Mergers," *Harvard Business Review* 78 (4) (July/August 2000) summarized in the *Wall Street Journal* (July 13, 2000): A1. A subsequent *Wall Street Journal* article, titled "Big Mergers of 90s Prove Disappointing to Shareholders" confirmed their findings by suggesting that companies such as MCI Worldcom and AT&T, following acquisition binges, had found that their stocks underperformed both the S&P 500 as well as their peer group stocks by substantial amounts. *Wall Street Journal* (October 30, 2000): C1.

9. Edward Luttwak, *Turbo Capitalism*, 1999, 11–12. Luttwak states: "Free markets have a natural tendency to become unfree, because they allow the most successful businesses to grow so large that they become monopolies or near enough. Turbo-capitalism, of course, accelerates the process."

A separate but related point will be of interest to those familiar with the "elitist"/"pluralist" debate. The "elitist" position was staked out by C. Wright Mills in *The Power Elite*, published in 1956 by Oxford University Press and kept alive by activists such as Ralph Nader and by scholars such as Michael Parenti, whose book *Democracy for the Few*, was published in five editions, the fifth in 1988 by St. Martin's Press. C. Wright Mills had claimed that large corporations constituted one of the three hierarchies (the government and the military being the others) that ruled America. Mills, *The Power Elite*, p. 5. Not only did corporations influence public policy in their own interests, they shielded themselves via their lobbyists from the full forces of the marketplace. I am making the case, however, that entrepreneurial capitalism has changed the rules of the game. New entrants with new technologies, having been given incentives by the federal government, are challenging even corporate giants, now stripped of regulatory protections. Ironically, under the rules of the New Economy, even the biggest corporation is exposed to the same brutal market forces formerly reserved for the smallest, weakest, street-level entrepreneur. For now, therefore, pluralism prevails in an America which has undergone a "stealth" revolution, brought on by government pushed into action by globalization that threatened to undermine the strength of the American economy (which had become uncompetitive) and ultimately American global leadership.

10. Sten Thore, *The Diversity, Complexity and Evolution of High-Tech Capitalism* (Boston: Kluwer Publishing Company), 3.

11. Carl Shapiro and Hal Varian, *Information Rules: A Strategic Guide for the Networked Economy* (1998). This book was the subject of a lead article in the *Wall Street Journal* (June 21, 1999): A1.

12. Kevin Kelly, *New Rules for the New Economy* (New York: Viking, 1998), Chapter 2, p. 27.

13. Robert Baldock, *The Last Days of the Giants: A Route Map for Big Business Survival* (New York: John Wiley, 2000).

14. *Wall Street Journal* (February 24, 2000): C13.

15. Brett Swanson, "Change or Die," *Wall Street Journal* (April 18, 2001): A22. The entry of so many new companies in the Nasdaq Stock Market accelerated its upward progression by early 2000, even in the face of rising interest rates and a collapsing Dow Jones Industrial Average. Analysts suggested that as old technology favorites fell from favor, there was no shortage of new entrants to take their place, even some, like InfoSys Technology, from abroad. "Rotation, rotation, rotation" kept the Nasdaq aloft until it crashed in late 2000–2001. *Wall Street Journal* (February 14, 2000): C1. By 2001, this devastating bear market led sixty-four IPOs to be withdrawn, compared to thirty-four that were registered as of March. *Wall Street Journal* (March 19, 2001): C15.

16. Agilent Technologies, *Annual Report 1999*, 31.

17. *Financial Times* (November 23, 1999): 11.

18. *Wall Street Journal* (February 15, 2000): C1.

19. *Financial Times* (November 23, 1999): 11.

20. *Investor's Business Daily* (February 14, 2000): A4.

21. Interview on *Nightly Business Report*, February 29, 2000.

22. Reported in the *Wall Street Journal* (July 20, 1999): B6Y.

23. *CNBC Interview*, February 24, 2000.

24. *Financial Times* Electronic Business Supplement, (March 24, 1999).

25. Despite the "international" in their names, agencies like Robert Half, with a few exceptions, have had their growth stymied by Europe's inflexible labor laws, which outlaw the growth of temporary and contingent labor via outsourcing. Holland was one exception, with the highest proportion of temporary workers in Europe. It was reported that the Dutch government, intending to protect Dutch workers, had introduced legislation which included a provision that after a worker served three temporary contracts, s/he would be entitled to join the staff. Faced with this restriction, employers promptly terminated temporary positions, forcing the Dutch government to withdraw this provision after it became aware of its unintended impact. Reported in the *Financial Times* (February 26, 2000): 3.

26. Geoffrey A. Moore, *Living on the Fault Line: Managing for Shareholder Value in the Age of the Internet* (New York: Harper Business, 2000).

27. *Financial Times*, Information Technology Supplement (April 7, 1999): vi.

28. Alvin Toffler and Heidi Toffler, *Creating a New Civilization: The Politics of the Third Wave* (Atlanta: Turner Publishing, 1995), 46–47.

29. *Financial Times*, Supplement (March 24, 1999): 1.

30. A study by Peter Golder at New York University's Stern School of Business questioned the long-term value of brand names. Going back to 1923, he found that of 100 top brands then, only 23 were still product leaders. *Wall Street Journal* (February 10, 2000): A1.

31. Richard Tompkins, "Fading Stars of the Global Age," *Financial Times* (March 5, 1999): 30.

32. Ibid., 30.

33. Ibid., 30. This statement was made by Julian Saunders, CEO of Conquest.

34. Ibid., 30.

35. Ibid., 30.

36. *Wall Street Journal* (March 11, 1999): A1.

37. Ibid.

38. *Wall Street Journal* (February 3, 2000): A18.

39. Ibid.

40. Ibid. Information on oil company ramp-ups in production from the *Wall Street Journal* (March 12, 2001): A19.

41. *Wall Street Journal* (December 1, 1999): A12.

42. *Financial Times* (November 18, 1999): 24.

43. *Wall Street Journal* (February 11, 2000): C11.

44. Adapted from a chart compiled by Professor Kay. See *Financial Times* (March 3, 1999): 10.

45. Ibid.

46. Ibid. By February 2000, GM, Ford, and Daimler–Chrysler made a bid for the auto assets of bankrupt Korean company Daewoo, but in the opposite direction BMW announced in March 2000 that it would divest its Rover acquisition.

47. This section is based on an article in the *Wall Street Journal* (December 8, 1999): C1.

48. *Wall Street Journal* (November 29, 1999): C1.

49. Tony Jackson, "Breaking Up is Hard to Do," *Financial Times* (March 19, 2000): 21. Source for data on the conditions for the Exxon–Mobil merger: *Investor's Business Daily* (March 6, 2000): A2.

50. Alvin Toffler and Heidi Toffler, *Creating a New Civilization*, 4.

51. "More Parents are Setting Units Free," *Wall Street Journal* (February 2, 2000): C1.

52. *Wall Street Journal* (March 1, 2000): A1.

53. J. W. Botkin and J. B. Matthew, *Winning Combinations: The Coming Wave of Entrepreneurial Partnerships Between Large and Small Companies* (New York: John Wiley, 1992), 53.

54. *Investor's Business Daily* (February 14, 2000): A6.

55. By 1999 the tables were turned, with European companies actively shopping in the United States for acquisition targets. *Wall Street Journal* (August 15, 1999): A1.

56. *Wall Street Journal* (January 20, 2000): C1.

57. See "Intel Rolls Dice on Tech Upstarts and Hits Jackpot" in the *Wall Street Journal* (February 8, 2000): C1. By 2001, however, the headlines were sadly reversed during the depths of the stock market slide. "Many Technology Companies See Portfolios Shrink" was one headline in the *Wall Street Journal* (April 4, 2001): C1, C19. Having booked over $3.7 billion in portfolio profits in 2000, Intel in 2001 reported selling stakes in ten of its holdings: seven were down more than 90 percent and three were down 50 percent. It was reported that an Intel spokesman reiterated that investment decisions had not only been based on a desire for financial gain but in order to gain access to strategically important technology.

58. *Financial Times* (November 18, 1999): 12.

59. *Wall Street Journal* (February 7, 2000): A1. Eastman Chemical's plans cited in the *Wall Street Journal* (March 22, 2000): A6.

CHAPTER 3: THE GENESIS OF ENTREPRENEURIAL CAPITALISM

1. Bruce R. Scott and George C. Lodge, eds., *U.S. Competitiveness in the World Economy* (Cambridge: Harvard Business School Press, 1985), 1–2.

2. Ibid., 2.

3. Martin K. Starr, *Global Competitiveness: Getting the U.S. Back on Track* (New York: Norton, 1988). See also Paul R. Krugman and George N. Hatsopoulos, "The Problem of U.S. Competitiveness in Manufacturing," Federal Reserve Bank of Boston, *New England Economic Review* (January/February 1987): 18–29.

4. Paul Kennedy, *The Rise and Fall of the Great Powers* (New York: Random House, 1987), Preface.

5. Ibid., 421.

6. Ibid., 422.

7. Ibid., 429.

8. Ibid., 418.

9. Ibid., 417.

10. Ibid., 440.

11. Ibid., 514.

12. Ibid., 538.

13. Ibid., 523.

14. Ibid., 529.

15. Bruce R. Scott, "U.S. Competitiveness: Concepts, Performance and Implications," in Bruce R. Scott and George C. Lodge, eds., *U.S. Competitiveness in the World Economy*, 13.

16. *Business Week* no. 2995 (April 20, 1987): 45–49, 52, 54–66, 68–69.

17. Paul Kennedy, *The Rise and Fall of the Great Powers*, 534.

18. Ibid.

19. Henry Nau, *The Myth of America's Decline: Leading the World Economy in the 1990s* (New York: Oxford University Press, 1990), 11.

20. John G. Ruggie, *Winning the Peace: America and World Order in the New Era* (New York: Columbia University Press, 1996).

21. Paul Kennedy, *The Rise and Fall of the Great Powers*, 358.

22. Ibid., 368.

23. Ibid., 359. The military, too, wanted to secure control of strategically critical materials such as oil, rubber, and metal ores and so also supported liberal trade policies.

24. Thomas McCraw, ed. *Creating Modern Capitalism* (Cambridge: Harvard University Press, 1997), 314.

25. Gus Tyler, "The Case for Protectionism," in Donald Altschiller, ed., *Free Trade versus Protectionism* (H. W. Wilson and Company, 1988), 39.

26. Paul Kennedy, *The Rise and Fall of the Great Powers*, 359.

27. Mancur Olson, *The Rise and Decline of Nations: Economic Growth, Stagflation and Social Rigidities* (New Haven: Yale University Press, 1982), 92.

28. Paul Kennedy, *The Rise and Fall of the Great Powers*, 432.

29. Ibid.

30. Bruce R. Scott and George C. Lodge, eds., *U.S. Competitiveness in the World Economy*, 2.

31. Ibid., 30. (Productivity numbers from Paul Kennedy, *The Rise and Fall of the Great Powers*, 434.)

32. Ibid., 2.

33. Ibid., 32.

34. Ibid., 2–5.

35. Ibid., 6.

36. Ibid., 10.

37. Ibid., 71.

38. William Firin and Annette M. La Mond, "Sustaining U.S. Competitiveness in Microelectronics: The Challenge for U.S. Policy," in Bruce R. Scott and George C. Lodge, eds., *U.S. Competitiveness in the World Economy*, 145.

39. Harvey Brooks, "Technology as a Factor in U.S. Competitiveness," in Scott and Lodge, eds., *U.S. Competitiveness in the World Economy*, 330.

40. Paul Kennedy, *The Rise and Fall of the Great Powers*, 463.

41. Ibid., 422.

42. Bruce R. Scott and George C. Lodge, *U.S. Competitiveness in the World Economy*, 488.

43. Paul Kennedy, *The Rise and Fall of the Great Powers*, xv. See also Ralph Landau and Dale W. Jorgenson, eds., *Technology and Economic Policy* (Cambridge: Ballinger Publishing Company, 1986).

44. Edwin Mansfield with Anthony Romeo, Mark Schwartz, David Theece, Samuel Wagner, and Peter Brach, *Techonolgy Transfer, Productivity and Economic Policy* (New York: Norton, 1982).

45. Ralph Landau and Dale W. Jorgenson, *Technology and Economic Policy*. During the 1980s, reflecting the intense concern over U.S. economic decline, Westview Press devoted a special series to the subject of science, technology, and public policy. See, for example, Martin Fransman, *Technology and Economic Development* (Boulder, CO: Westview Press, 1986); Francis W. Rushing and Carole Ganz Brown, eds., *National Policies for Developing High Technology Industries: International Comparisons* (Boulder, CO: Westview Press, 1986); and *The Micro-Electronics Race: The Impact of Government Policy on International Competitiveness* (Boulder, CO: Westview Press, 1988). See also Ralph Landau and Nathan Rosenberg, eds., *The Positive Sum Strategy: Harnessing Technology for Economic Growth* (Washington DC: National Academy Press, 1986). The book presented a dialogue between engineers and economists on the ways technological innovation could be made to better serve the goal of faster economic growth.

46. Wendy H. Schacht, *Trade, Technology and Competitiveness*, Issue Brief prepared for the Congressional Research Service and regularly updated during the period 1985–1988. In 1997, William C. Boesman at the Science Policy Research Division of the Congressional Research Service served as coordinator of a broad overview of technology policy: *Analysis of Ten Selected Science and Technology Policy Studies*. This report contained many recommendations on how the U.S. science and technology system, especially the U.S. government R&D establishment,

could respond. Source: http://www.house.gov/science/1.97–836.htm. One year later, the Senate Committee on the Budget asked the Congressional Budget Office (CBO) to provide fresh empirical evidence that increases in federal spending on R&D, as well as on infrastructure and education and training, could lead to a significant increase in economic growth. The CBO had provided Congress with an earlier study on the economic value of federal investments in these areas in 1991, *How Federal Spending for Infrastructure and Other Public Investments Affects the Economy*. In 1998, the CBO, in updating the evidence in a new study—*The Economic Effects of Federal Spending on Infrastructure and Other Investments*—reconfirmed the positive impact of federal investments in these areas on economic growth. Source: http://www.cbo.gov/owdoc.cfm?/index=601&sequence=0& from=1.

47. Harvey Brooks, "Technology as a Factor in U.S. Competitiveness," in Bruce R. Scott and George C. Lodge eds., *U.S. Competitiveness in the World Economy*, 329.

48. Ibid., 332.

49. Robert Reich, "The Rise of Techno-Nationalism," *Atlantic Monthly* 259 (May 1987): 63–69.

50. John A. Young, "Technology and Competitiveness: A Key to the Economic Future of the United States," *Science* 241 (July 15, 1988): 313–316.

51. Paul Kennedy, *The Rise and Fall of the Great Powers*, 442. Daniel S. Greenberg, "A Hidden Cost of Military Research: Less National Security," *Discover* 8, (January 1987): 94–101. See also "Military Research and the Economy: Burden or Benefit?" in *Defense Monitor* 14, no. 1 (1985): 1–8.

52. William C. Boesman, *Federal Support of Basic Research and the Establishment of the National Science Foundation and Other Research Agencies* (Library of Congress, Congressional Research Service Report 88–777, June 28, 1988).

53. Final Report: *The Role of Science and Technology in Economic Competitiveness* (Washington DC: National Science Foundation, 1987). In 1988, the role of the NSF in promoting U.S. competitiveness internationally was described in "Out of the Laboratory and into the World Market," *Government Executive* 20 (January 1988): 22–26.

54. Wendy Schacht, *Commercialization of Technology and Issues in the Competitiveness of Selected U.S. Industries: Semiconductors, Biotechnology and Superconductors* (Library of Congress: Congressional Research Service Report 88–879, 1988), 2.

55. Ibid., 2–3.

56. Ibid., 3.

57. Ibid., 4.

58. Congressional hearings during this period are cited in B. F. Mangan, *Science, Technology and International Competitiveness of American Industry: Selected References 1985–1988* (Washington DC: Congressional Research Service, August 1988). I have made extensive use of Mr. Mangan's bibliographical references in this chapter.

59. See *Using Federal R&D to Promote Commercial Innovation* (Washington DC: Congressional Budget Office, 1988): 82.

60. Claude Barfield, "The National Laboratories," in *Government Executive* 19 (October 1987): 34–35.

CHAPTER 4: LEGISLATING ENTREPRENEURIAL CAPITALISM

1. *Wall Street Journal* (December 1, 1999): C1.

2. See Jean Wells, *Financial De-Regulation in the United States: An Introduction* (Washington DC: Library of Congress: Congressional Research Service Report 85–41E, February 13, 1985).

3. See Julius Allen, *Cost–Benefit Analysis in Federal Regulation: A Review and Analysis of Developments, 1978–1984* (Washington DC: Library of Congress: Congressional Research Service Report, May 15, 1984), crs–62.

4. Jeff Kisselhoff, *The Box: An Oral History of Radio and Television 1920–1961* (New York: Viking Press, 1995), 6.

5. Harry M. Shooshan, ed. *Disconnecting Bell: The Impact of the AT&T Divestiture* (New York: Pergamon Press, 1984), 10.

6. Ibid., 10.

7. Peter Huber, *Law and Disorder in Cyberspace* (New York: Oxford University Press, 1997), 4.

8. Ibid., 3.

9. Jeremy Tunstall, *Communications De-Regulation: The Unleashing of America's Communications Industry* (New York: Basil Blackwell, 1986), 1.

10. See Robert Howe, *Telephone Industry De-Regulation: Selected References 1984–1988* (Washington DC: Library of Congress: Congressional Research Service Report, 88–75 IL, December 1988), crs–3.

11. See Julius Allen, *Cost-Benefit Analysis in Federal Regulation: A Review and Analysis of Developments, 1978–1984* (Washington DC: Library of Congress: Congressional Research Service Report, May 15, 1984), crs–2. It is important to recognize that social regulation has increased even while economic regulation has decreased in the years following the above report. See "Rule of Law or Just Rules" in *Investor's Business Daily* (May 8, 2000): A30. Based on data from the Center for the Study of American Business, it was reported that almost 25,000 federal employees were engaged in economic regulation versus over 100,000 engaged in social regulation. Social regulation increased substantially during the Clinton Administration from 1993–2000.

12. Julius Allen, *Cost–Benefit Analysis in Federal Regulation*, crs–90.

13. Julius Allen, *Costs and Benefits of Federal Regulation: An Overview* (Washington DC: Library of Congress Congressional Research Service Report, 78–152E, July 19, 1978), crs–1.

14. Julius Allen, *Estimating the Costs of Federal Regulation: Review of Problems and Accomplishments to Date* (Washington DC: Library of Congress: Congressional Research Service Report, September 26, 1978), crs–23.

15. Ibid.

16. Ibid., crs–15. Robert de Fina, under the direction of Murray Weidenbaum.

17. *Investor's Business Daily* (December 7, 1999): A8.

18. Roland McKean, *Avoidance and Enforcement Costs in Government Regulation* (St. Louis Center for the Study of American Business, October 1976), 9–10.

19. Julius Allen, *Costs and Benefits of Federal Regulation*, crs–31.

20. Ibid., crs–36.

21. Julius Allen, *Estimating the Costs of of Federal Regulation*, crs–24.

22. Ibid., crs–14. The Center for the Study of American Business reported that federal spending on its regulatory activities had increased as well, more for social regulation and estimated $12 billion by 1999 versus $1.5 billion in 1980 compared with $3 billion for economic oversight in 1999 versus under $1 billion in 1980. Source: *Investor's Business Daily* (May 8, 2000): A30. See also Stephen Vogel's *Freer Markets: More Rules* (Ithaca, NY: Cornell University Press, 1996), a comparative study of deregulation.

23. Julius Allen, *Costs and Benefits of Federal Regulation*, crs–32.

24. Ibid., crs–3.

25. Sam Peltzman, "An Evaluation of Consumer Protection Legislation: The 1982 Drug Amendments" *Journal of Political Economy* 81 (September 1983): 1090.

26. Julius Allen, *Costs and Benefits of Federal Regulation*, crs–81.

27. Harry Shooshan, ed. *Disconnecting Bell*, 25.

28. Peter Huber, *Law and Disorder in Cyberspace*, 3.

29. Ibid., 3.

30. Jeremy Tunstall, *Communications De-Regulation*, 5.

31. Former FCC Chairman William Kennard in an Op/Ed piece published in the *Wall Street Journal* (August 24, 1999): A18. Subsequent comments by George Gilder and Brett Swanson appeared in another Op/Ed piece, "The Broadband Economy Needs a Hero," addressed to incoming FCC Chairman Michael Powell, published in the *Wall Street Journal* (February 23, 2001): A14. Ironically, AOL had first raised the issue of "open access" in Portland, OR after AT&T had begun assembling its cable broadband empire, but dropped its lobbying efforts after announcing its own merger with Time Warner, through which it acquired its own cable access. Now it was being "hoisted on its own petard" by being required to ensure open access on its own cable lines.

32. Harry Shooshan, ed., *Disconnecting Bell*, 27.

33. Ibid., 4.

34. Ibid., 19.

35. Richard Wiley, "The End of Monopoly: Regulatory Change and the Promotion of Competition," in Harry Shooshan, ed., *Disconnecting Bell* 27.

36. Jeremy Tunstall, *Communications De-Regulation*, 38.

37. Ibid., 45.

38. Ibid., 52.

39. Ibid., 56.

40. Peter Huber, *Law and Disorder in Cyberspace*, 22–23.

41. Senate Bill 652, 104th Congress, The Telecommunications Act of 1996, Library of Congress, thomas.gov. This act mandated that local Bells would have to provide access on their lines to new entrants called CLECs (Competitive Local Access Carriers) in exchange for being permitted to enter the long distance business. Local Bells have resisted sharing their lines, forcing CLECs to litigate instead of spending their time acquiring customers. This has forced several, including Northpoint, Winstar, and Teligent, into bankruptcy. In consequence, FCC Chairman Michael Powell, asked Congress for authority to increase fines to combat anticompetitive practices to $10 million per violation from $1.2 million and also requested enhanced regulatory oversight over Baby Bells who failed to

open their lines to these smaller new rivals. See the *Wall Street Journal* (May 8, 2001): B5. Wall Street wags had jokingly begun to refer to CLECs as entities whose "Current Liabilities Exceed Cash"!

42. William Firin and Annette M. La Mond, "Sustaining U.S. Competitiveness in Microelectronics," in Bruce R. Scott and George C. Lodge, eds. *U.S. Competitiveness in the World Economy* (Cambridge: Harvard Business School Press, 1985), 158.

43. Charles Bell, quoted in Harry Shooshan, ed., *Disconnecting Bell*, 73.

44. Rowina Oligario, "IBM and the Two Watsons" in Thomas K. McCraw, ed. *Creating Modern Capitalism: How Entrepreneurs, Companies and Countries Triumphed in Three Industrial Revolutions* (Cambridge: Harvard University Press, 1997), 379.

45. Ibid., 381.

46. *Wall Street Journal* (June 9, 2000): B6.

47. Peter K. Eisenger, *The Rise of the Entrepreneurial State: State and Local Development Policy in the United States* (Madison: University of Wisconsin Press, 1988), 9.

48. Ibid., 334.

49. www.sba.gov/regulations/the act 97sbaact.txt

50. Wendy H. Schacht, *Co-Operative R&D: Federal Efforts to Promote Industrial Competitiveness* (Washington DC: Library of Congress: Congressional Research Service Issue Brief, August 12, 1997), crs–1.

51. *Promoting Technology Transfer by Facilitating Licenses to Federally Owned Inventions* by Dan C. Brand, chair, Federal Laboratory Consortium for Technology Transfer, Report Prepared for the Committee on Science, Sub-Committee on Technology, U.S. House of Representatives, September 25, 1997 (www.federallabs.org).

52. Lawrence Rudolph, acting general counsel to the National Science Foundation, *Overview of Federal Technology Transfer*, p. 3 (www.fplc.edu/RISK/Volume 5/spring/rudolph.htm).

53. Wendy Schacht, *The Omnibus Trade and Competitiveness Act: Technology Development Provisions* (Washington DC: Library of Congress: Congressional Research Service Report 89–93, February 3, 1989), crs–5.

54. www.federallabs.org/flc/ftpsrc/hr 2544.htm.

55. *Technology Innovation: Chapter 63, United States Code Annotated, Title 15, Commerce and Trade, Sections 3701–3715*, prepared for the Federal Laboratory Consortium for Technology Transfer, Special Reports Series No. 1, Eagan, MN: West Publishing Company, August 1994), viii. Information about the impact of the Bayh–Dole Act obtained from: http://www.nttc.edu/training/guide/seca02.html.

56. "When NIH Helps Discover Drugs Should Taxpayers Share Wealth?" *Wall Street Journal* (June 1, 2000): B1.

57. Interviews with Elizabeth Zygmunte and Andrea Mulrine, Electronic Commerce Resource Center, University of Scranton, August 20, 1999.

CHAPTER 5: FINANCING ENTREPRENEURIAL CAPITALISM

1. *Wall Street Journal* (August 8, 2000): C1. This estimate, provided by the National Venture Capital Association, is higher than government estimates of

$46.6 billion and compares with $20 billion in private-venture capital raised in 1998. Estimates for 2000 by Pricewaterhouse Coopers predicted that private-venture capital would plateau at $70 billion. See *Investor's Business Daily* (August 14, 2000): A6. Yet, during the first ten months of 2000 only $52.1 billion had been raised, suggesting that the declining stock market had dampened enthusiasm. *Wall Street Journal* (November 1, 2000): C1.

2. See Jacob M. Schlesinger, "Why a Long Boom?" *Wall Street Journal* (February 1, 2000): A1.

3. www.edgar-online.gov.

4. Schlesinger, "Why a Long Boom?" *Wall Street Journal*, A1.

5. John W. Kingdon, *Agendas, Alternatives and Public Policies* (New York: Harper Collins, 1984), 49.

6. Peter K. Eisinger, *The Rise of the Entrepreneurial State: State and Local Economic Development Policy in the United States* (Madison: University of Wisconsin Press, 1988), 342.

7. Source: *Investor's Business Daily* (June 3, 1998): A32.

8. Ibid.

9. Josh Lerner, "The Government as Venture Capitalist: The Long-Run Impact of the SBIR Program," *Journal of Business*, 72 (July 1999): 96. Lerner, however, acknowledged that this superior performance was not universal and that in areas without new venture activity, there may have been greater direct or indirect political pressures, leading to the selection of inferior firms.

10. Ibid., 295.

11. Ibid., 296.

12. William C. Boesman and Michael E. Davey, *U.S. Civilian and Defense Research and Development Funding: Some Trends and Comparisons with Selected Industrialized Nations* (Library of Congress, Congressional Research Service Report, rev. November 1994), crs–49.

13. William C. Boesman, *International R&D Data Trends: Some Comparisons and Implications for the U.S. R&D System* (Library of Congress, Congressional Research Service Report, February 1997), crs–35.

14. Michael E. Davey, *Federal R&D Funding Trends in Five Agencies*, (Library of Congress, Congressional Research Service Report, January 1997).

15. *Investor's Business Daily* (June 3, 1999) A1.

16. Wendy H. Schacht, *Commercialization of Technology and Issues in the Competitiveness of Selected U.S. Industries: Semiconductors, Biotechnology and Superconductors* (Library of Congress, Congressional Research Service Report, rev. August 1988), summary.

17. William C. Boesman, *International R&D Data Trends*, crs–18. See also William C. Boesman and Michael E. Davey, *U.S. Civilian and Defense Research and Development Funding*, crs–42.

18. William C. Boesman and Michael E. Davey, *U.S. Civilian and Defense Research and Development Funding*, crs–42.

19. Ibid.

20. William C. Boesman, *International R&D Data Trends*, crs–8.

21. Michael E. Davey, *Federal R&D Funding Trends in Five Agencies*, crs–3.

22. Ibid., crs–26.

23. Michael E. Davey, *Research and Development Funding FY 1998*, (Library of Congress Congressional Research Service Report, June 1997), crs–1.

24. Wendy H. Schacht, *Commercialization of Technology and Issues in the Competitiveness of Selected U.S. Industries*, crs–10.

25. Ibid., crs–12.

26. Gary L. Guenther, *Semiconductor Devices: The Changing Competitiveness of U.S. Merchant Producers, 1977–1987* (Library of Congress Congressional Research Service Report, rev. June 1988), crs–6.

27. See Josh Lerner, "The Government as Venture Capitalist," *Journal of Business*, 1999. Department of Defense figures from SBIR Program Booklet, 8.

28. William C. Boesman, *International R&D Data Trends*, summary.

29. *Investor's Business Daily* (June 3, 1998): A32. Pharmaceutical companies, it was reported in the *Wall Street Journal* (June 22, 2000), spent $20 billion on R&D in 1999.

30. *Investor's Business Daily* (March 22, 1999): A2. Given the emphasis on the life sciences, the Clinton Administration was advised by his Information Technology Advisory Committee to increase funding for information technology R&D by 10 percent annually, and by $1 billion by 2004. (See PITAC Report to the President at http://www.ccic.gov/ac/report/exec_summary.html.)

31. Gary L. Guenther, *Semiconductor Devices: The Changing Competitiveness of U.S. Merchant Producers 1977–1987*, crs–8.

32. Ibid., crs–4.

33. Ibid., crs–7.

34. See Glenn J. McLoughlin, *Sematech: Issues and Options* (Library of Congress, Congressional Research Service Issue Brief, June 12, 1996), crs–10.

35. Ibid., crs–10.

36. Wendy Schacht, *Cooperative R&D: Federal Efforts to Promote Industrial Competitiveness* (Library of Congress, Congressional Research Service Issue Brief, August 12, 1997), crs–5.

37. *Wall Street Journal* (July 25, 1997): A7A.

38. Michael Davey, *Federal R&D Funding Trends in Five Agencies*, crs–2.

39. Wendy H. Schacht, *Cooperative R&D*, crs–1.

40. Ibid., crs–3.

41. "The Process and Analysis Behind Ace-Net," *Catalog of Small Business Research, 1995* ed., published by the Office of Advocacy, SBA. Data obtained from the National Venture Capital Association, Rosslyn, VA.

42. SBIC Program Statistical Package, June 1996, prepared by the Investment Division of the U.S. Small Business Administration, Washington, DC.

43. http://www.acenet.sr.unh.edu. See *Creating New Capital Markets for Emerging Ventures* by Freear, Sohl, and Wetzel (Durham, NH: Center for Venture Research, Whittemore School of Business and Economics, University of New Hampshire, June 1996).

44. Information on the SCOR form can be obtained from the NASAA, Washington, DC. See also "The Process and Analysis Behind ACE-Net."

45. www.sec.gov/news/speeches/spch118.txt.

46. SBIR booklet, Department of Defense, 7.

47. Ibid., 4.

48. Statistics for 1980s from Peter Eisenger, *The Rise of the Entrepreneurial State*, 246. Statistics for 1990s from U.S. Census Bureau, Statistical Abstract of the United States, 2000.

49. Interview on public radio program *Success Stories*, May 1995. Series produced in association with Rutgers–Camden School of Business.

50. SBIR booklet, Department of Defense, 8.

51. See Wendy Schacht, *Cooperative R & D*.

52. Figures from phone interview with Small Business Technology Transfer Program Department of Defense officials on August 7, 1997.

53. *Investor's Business Daily* (March 6, 2000): A2.

54. Michael Milken, "Prosperity and Social Capital," *Wall Street Journal* (June 23, 1999): A20. Milken argued that the turning point was the spike in interest rates and the Wall Street crash of 1974, when large financial institutions, faced with problems of their own, stopped lending to all but a few of their most high-grade borrowers, creating a credit crunch and junk bond status for less creditworthy borrowers. Reflecting Milken's general argument, Jacob M. Schlesinger of the *Wall Street Journal* made a similar case one year later in an article asking the question "Why the Long Boom?"

Many economists argue that the more evolved financial markets are . . . better at nurturing new companies with good ideas. Clubby bankers, who are more likely to support large, established companies than struggling start-ups, have less control over capital, venture capitalists . . . have more."

See Jacob M. Schlesinger "Why a Long Boom?" *Wall Street Journal* (February 1, 2000): A1.

55. Schlesinger, p. A1.

56. Source: Nasdaq Stock Market.

57. *Financial Times* (March 24, 1999): 17.

58. *Wall Street Journal* (July 2, 1998): A1.

59. *Wall Street Journal* (March 23, 1999): B2.

60. *Investor's Business Daily* (February 28, 2000): A2.

61. International Institute for Management Development (IMD) and the World Economic Forum, *The World Competitiveness Report 1994* (Lausanne, Switzerland: IMD, September 1994), 16.

62. *The World Competitiveness Yearbook 1996* (Lausanne, Switzerland: IMD, June 1996), 16.

63. *Wall Street Journal* (July 14, 1999): A18.

CHAPTER 6: THE GLOBAL IMPACT OF ENTREPRENEURIAL CAPITALISM

1. John Gray, *False Dawn: The Delusions of Global Capitalism* (New York: New Press/W. W. Norton, 1998), 194.

2. Ibid., 175.

3. Edward Luttwak, *Turbo-Capitalism: Winners and Losers in the Global Economy* (New York: Harper Collins, 1999), xii.

4. Ibid., xiv.

5. *Financial Times* (November 23, 1999): 7.

6. See Geoffrey A. Moore, Paul Johnson, and Tom Kippola, *The Gorilla Game: An Investor's Guide to Picking Winners in High Technology* (New York: Harper Collins, 1999).

7. Ian Hendry, *Innovating for Failure: Government Policy and the Early British Computer Industry* (Cambridge, MA: MIT Press, 1990), 163. Source for quote by German CEO: *Wall Street Journal* (January 28, 2001): A1.

8. Harris Collingwood, "How to Position Your Portfolio to Benefit from Discontinuous Innovation and Growth Tornadoes," *Worth* magazine (April 1999): 94.

9. Ian Hendry, *Innovating For Failure*, 9. Source for information on the Technology Foresight Programme: *Financial Times* editorial (March 28, 1995): 15. The editorial also made a point similar to one I have been making about the role of government in areas where the private sector may not find it profitable to act alone: "Although the private sector will in many cases carry out the recommended research, simply out of self-interest, Foresight may still make a difference at the margin. There are many areas of research which companies neglect because of the unreliability of returns on investment." Some years later, this public/private partnership precedent was amplified by the Labor Government, which made plans to subsidize venture capital for parts of England that found it hard to attract private venture capital, despite European Commission warnings restricting state aid for business. *Financial Times* (March 12, 2001): 6.

10. J. W. Botkin and J. B. Matthew, *Winning Combinations: The Coming Wave of Partnerships Between Large and Small Companies* (New York: John Wiley, 1992).

11. Thomas McCraw, ed. *Creating Modern Capitalism* (Cambridge, MA: Harvard University Press, 1998).

12. Kenneth Flamm, *Targeting the Computer* (Washington DC: The Brookings Institution Press, 1987), 125.

13. Ibid., 175.

14. *Wall Street Journal* (June 12, 2000): A21.

15. See David Wessel, "American Economy Offers a Model Others Both Fear and Envy," *Wall Street Journal* (January 18, 2001): A1.

16. Kenneth Flamm, *Targeting the Computer*, 175. Market forces are being permitted to enter other countries, but to a limited extent. For example, the Indian United Front government in 1997 suggested it would focus on nine large state-owned companies—their "crown jewels or navratnas." These big public-sector companies were promised enhanced freedoms to build world businesses but would not be privatized. See Krishna Guha, "Indian Investment See Saw Tips from Public to Private," *Financial Times* (February 26, 1999): 22.

17. *Financial Times* (March 3, 1999): 2.

18. Ibid.

19. Tony Barber, "Germany's Blame Game," *Financial Times* (February 24, 1999): 15.

20. Ralph Atkins, "Steering an Uncertain Course," *Financial Times* (March 9, 1999): 17. Wim Duisenberg's comment was reported in the *Wall Street Journal* (December 7, 1999): A27.

21. This question was raised in an International Monetary Fund Economic Forum held on December 12, 2000. The topic was "The Information Economy:

New Paradigm or Old Fashion," and one of the participants, Thomas Duester-berg, president of the Manufacturers Alliance, made several important linkages between innovation, productivity, and economic growth—though he did not take the specific position I have taken about the impact of labor market inflexibility in Europe limiting economic gains. Source: http://www.imf.org/external/np/tr/2000/tr121200a.htm.

22. Source for information on the Eureka Project: http://www.eureka.be.

23. "Social consensus" is the cultural tradition forged after the war in which interlocking directorates of banks (which own huge blocks of shares in companies and vice versa), government officials, and unions make up half the boards of large companies. The presence of these interlocking groups effectively makes change difficult to achieve, even if it becomes a desirable goal. It is a key part of the "Rheinish model," viewed much more favorably than the "Anglo Saxon" model, which is perceived as heartless.

24. The Neuer Mitte initiative, which would undermine this ethos, was re-ported in the *Financial Times* (December 8, 1999): 2.

25. *Financial Times* (February 24, 1999): 15.

26. Source for investment data: *Wall Street Journal* (December 18, 1999): A2. By 2001, a report in the *Wall Street Journal* headlined "Germany Tackles Joblessness but Misses" focused on moves made by Schroeder to further regulate labor mar-kets, despite reforms of the tax system designed to help business. His govern-ment boosted sick pay and worker protections against layoffs. It also imposed restrictions on employers who hire workers on fixed-term contracts, created a legal right to part-time work, and extended the powers of company works coun-cils. These steps have not bolstered long-term job creation but have won the support of trade unions and the party's traditional left wing. See the *Wall Street Journal* (May 8, 2001): B11A.

27. *Financial Times* (December 8, 1999): 1.

28. *Financial Times* (November 20–21, 1999): 8.

29. *Financial Times* (March 4, 1999): 5

30. In a report published in the *Wall Street Journal* (December 8, 1999): A27.

31. In an interview with Jim McGinnis, analyst at Dresdner, Kleinwort, Benson, *Financial Times* (March 9, 1999): 130. *Financial Times* (February 20–21, 1999): 24.

32. *Wall Street Journal* (March 24, 1999): A23.

33. John Gray, *False Dawn: The Delusions of Global Capitalism*, 169.

34. *Financial Times* (October 19, 1999): 20.

35. John Gray, *False Dawn: The Delusions of Global Capitalism*, 171.

36. *Financial Times* (October 19, 1999): 29.

37. *Financial Times* (August 31, 1999): 25. For a more detailed discussion of Japan's structural problems, see Michael E. Porter et al., *Can Japan Compete?* (Cambridge, MA: Perseus Books, 2000).

38. Indeed, one of the concerns about American consumers was that at the end of the 1990s was that they were not saving at all. By 2000 consumer debt was projected at over $6 billion, with a negative savings rate recorded since late 1998. *Wall Street Journal* (July 5, 2000): A11.

39. *Wall Street Journal* (July 10, 2000): A24. Canada had the highest immigration

rate per 1,000 at 5.6. Germany, however, has not fully embraced immigration despite a shrinking labor market, nor is it an attractive destination for guest workers. Its Green Card program has 20,000 five-year cards on offer but only 4,441 have been issued. Right wing politicians have stressed educating "kinder" (their children), not importing "Inder" (Indians) as a way to obtain more high-tech workers. Source: *Wall Street Journal* (January 18, 2001): A1.

40. Reported in the *Wall Street Journal* (July 17, 2000): A29.

41. George Melloan, "France's Antiglobalism Masks a Different Reality," *Wall Street Journal* (July 11, 2000): A27.

42. *Financial Times* (December 8, 1999): 2.

43. Ibid.

44. Source: David Wessel, *Wall Street Journal* (January 18, 2001): A1. The "euro" economy may, however, bring about change more quickly than anticipated. Olivetti's surprising and successful 1999 takeover of formerly state-owned Telecom Italia, which had been privatized in 1997, was made possible by access to European capital markets and foreign investment banks. See report by Dan Roberts, "Northern Invader Brings Change to Rome," *Financial Times Supplement*—The Challenge of Globalization (February 2, 2001): 3.

45. At the IMF Economic Forum referred to earlier (See Note 21), Lawrence Mishel, vice-president of the Economic Policy Institute, offered a strong dissenting opinion about the value of economic growth in the United States, which he believed masked rising inequality of incomes and a flat rate of per capita income growth per worker. Source: http://www.imf.org/external/np/tr/2000/tr121200a.htm. Hence, many European governments seem unlikely to permit the efficiencies of entrepreneurial capitalism to undermine social harmony. Indeed, Sweden has carved out a unique path of expanding, not cutting, its welfare state, using revenues obtained from implementing new technologies. For example, the Swedish government hired Oracle to provide electronic procurement software to its state-owned companies, hoping that efficiencies in government would further enhance its revenues. See the *Wall Street Journal* (July 17, 2000): A1.

CHAPTER 7: BACKLASH: THE LIMITS OF ENTREPRENEURIAL CAPITALISM

1. George Melloan, "Global View," The *Wall Street Journal* (July 18, 2000): A27.

2. *Wall Street Journal* (December 16, 2000): A1.

3. Ibid.

4. See the revised, updated edition of Daniel Bell, *The Coming of Post-Industrial Society*, originally published in 1974 and republished in 1999. Summarized in the *Financial Times*, November 19, 1999, i. In the latest edition, Bell updates the dimensions of the changes he predicted, which make strong labor unions unlikely in the twenty-first century. Not only has the manufacturing sector shrunk even further in the past twenty-five years but manufacturing itself has changed from "smokestack industries to silicon chip and pharmaceutical industries." Concomitantly, there has been an extraordinary rise in professional and technical employment to 60 percent of the workforce, while skilled and semiskilled jobs account for only 25 percent. This reflects a more educated workforce than ever

before. Whereas in 1960 only 41 percent of the population had completed high school, by 1996, 81 percent had, while people reporting "some college" had increased from 7.7 percent to 25 percent.

5. *Wall Street Journal* (December 16, 1999): C1.

6. Patrick Buchanan, *The Great Betrayal: How American Sovereignty and Social Justice are Being Sacrificed to the Gods of the Global Economy* (Boston: Little Brown, 1998), 37.

7. Ibid., 7.

8. Ibid., 50.

9. Ibid., 43.

10. Ibid., 44.

11. *Wall Street Journal* (December 10, 1999): A10.

12. Ethan Kapstein, *Sharing the Wealth: Workers and the World Economy* (Madison, WI: University of Wisconsin Press, 1999), 7–8.

13. Ibid., 10.

14. Ibid., 17.

15. Ibid., 9.

16. Kofi Annan, secretary general of the United Nations, made an impassioned plea on behalf of Third World nations that would be adversely impacted by the imposition of labor and environmental standards. See Op/Ed, "Help the Third World Help Itself" *Wall Street Journal* (November 29, 1999): A28.

17. *Wall Street Journal* (April 6, 2001): A1.

18. *Wall Street Journal* (July 14, 2000): A8.

19. *Wall Street Journal* (July 17, 2000): C23.

20. *Wall Street Journal* (July 14, 2000): A1.

21. Michael J. Mandel, *The Coming Internet Depression: Why the High-Tech Boom Will Go Bust, Why the Crash Will be Worse Than You Think and How To Prosper Afterward* (New York: Basic Books, 2000). Mandel compared technology overcapacity to the automotive overcapacity of the Roaring Twenties. While it is difficult to fault Mandel's prescience in predicting the full dimensions of the technology bust, I am not sure the analogy with conditions in the 1920s is really relevant. When consumers purchased cars, they purchased products with a "useful life" of at least ten years. Technological obsolescence, however, is much more rapid, given the pace of technological innovation today. New software with new applications reduce the "useful life" of equipment at a faster rate than ever before, requiring the purchase of faster computers or other technology products in three years or less. Of course, an economic slowdown, or a focus on profitablity by businesses, may cause capital expenditures to be reduced or deferred. Since those reductions can be put into effect with greater speed than ever before, periods of technology overcapacity may therefore become the Achilles heel of the New Economy.

22. *Wall Street Journal* (July 18, 2000): C1.

23. *Wall Street Journal* (April 18, 2000): A18.

24. Lawrence Kudlow, http://www.cnbc.com, *Market Analysis* (April 14, 2000). The shift in antitrust focus was first pointed out by Bill Gates in a *Wall Street Journal* Op/Ed piece titled "Why the Justice Department is Wrong," in which he complained that "U.S. anti-trust laws exist not to prop up competitors but to

ensure that consumers benefit from the widespread availability of goods and services at fair prices." *Wall Street Journal* (November 10, 1997): A20. This theme was echoed in a subsequent and more lengthy Op/Ed article, "Rethinking Antitrust" by Gary S. Becker and Kevin M. Murphy. The authors made the case that the Clinton Justice Department under Joel Klein had actually reversed antitrust policy in force since the Reagan Administration. They pointed out three areas of reversal: an emphasis on "unfair competition" as opposed to evidence of harm to consumers; a focus on avoiding "market dominance"; a focus on "market engineering" through the imposition of structural remedies. See the *Wall Street Journal* (February 26, 2001): A22.

25. *Wall Street Journal* (August 11, 1999): B6. Not everyone agrees with the Microsoft position. See, for example, Ken Auletta, *World War 3.0: Microsoft and Its Enemies* (New York: Basic Books, 2001), and John Heilmann, *Pride Before The Fall: The Trials of Bill Gates and the End of the Microsoft Era* (New York: Harper Collins, 2001).

26. *Financial Times* (February 26, 1999): 7.

27. *Financial Times* (March 19, 1999): 28.

28. Amy Harmon, "The Rebel Code," *New York Times Magazine* (February 21, 1999): 36.

29. *Wall Street Journal* (March 18, 1999): A1.

30. *Financial Times* (March 19, 1999): 27.

31. Linux server market share data based on a report in the *Wall Street Journal*, (April 9, 2001): B1.

32. Microsoft was not the only market-dominating entrepreneurial giant on the government's antitrust list. In 1999, the Federal Trade Commission also unveiled anticompetitive charges against Intel, which quickly worked to resolve the issue. Since the case was ultimately settled before it went to trial, the government's contention that Intel was using its monopoly power unfairly went unchallenged publicly. Nevertheless Intel, like Microsoft, had begun to face several competitive threats to its market dominance. Competitors Advanced Micro Devices and Cyrix gained market share at the lower-end chip market in 1998 (50 percent of low-end computers were manufactured without Intel chips, and in 1999 new $299 computer Webz would use Cyrix chips) even while competing chip technologies continued to be developed elsewhere and non-PC competitors emerged.

33. John Gray, *False Dawn: The Delusions of Global Capitalism* (New York: New Press/W. W. Norton, 1998), 198.

34. *Wall Street Journal* (December 21, 1999): C1.

35. During the first year of the George W. Bush Administration, for instance, there seemed to be a pulling back from federal efforts to help commercialize defense technologies as well as a reversion back to federal funding of basic, rather than applied, research. In Congress, the "Tauzin Bill" was under consideration, a move to amend the 1996 Telecommunications Act by reversing the requirement that Baby Bells open their markets to competition and eliminating the requirement that they lease parts of their high-speed data networks to competitors at wholesale prices. Competitive Local Access Carriers (CLECs), a product of deregulation, many in or near bankruptcy, would be adversely affected, as would consumer choice. Source for telecom legislation: *Wall Street Journal* (May 15, 2001): A28.

Historical Timeline of Innovation Legislation: Select Provisions Providing Incentives for Small Business and Entrepreneurs, 1980–1998

1980	Stevenson–Wydler Technology Innovation Act	*focused on dissemination of information leveled playing field
	Bayh–Dole Patents & Trademark Amendments Act	*permitted small businesses (as well as universities and non-profits) to obtain title to inventions developed with government support
1982	Small Business Innovation Development Act	*required agencies to provide special funds for small business R&D connected to agencies' missions
1984	Trademark Clarification Act	*permitted private companies regardless of size to obtain exclusive licenses
1986	Federal Technology Transfer Act	*allowed laboratories to make agreements with small companies on title and license to inventions resulting from cooperative R&D agreements (CRADAs) with government laboratories
		*allowed current and former federal employees to participate in commercial development

		*established a principle of royalty sharing for federal inventors and set up a reward system for other innovators
1987	Executive Orders 12591 & 12618	Facilitated and promoted access to student technology
1988	Omnibus Trade & Competitors Act	*mandated technologies developed under National Institute of Standards & Technology programs to be transferred to small and mid-sized businesses
		*authorized Training and Technology Transfer Centers administered by Department of Education
1989	National Institute of Standards & Technology Authorization Act	*clarified the rights of guest worker inventors regarding royalties
1991	Defense Authorization Act of FY 1991	*established model program for national defense laboratories to demonstrate successful relationships between federal, state, and local governments and small businesses.
	American Technology Preeminence Act	*included intellectual property as potential contributions under CRADAs
1992	Small Business Technology Transfer Act	*required each of five agencies (DOD, DOE, HHS, NASA and NSF) to fund cooperative R&D projects involving a small company and a researcher at a university, federally funded research and development center, or nonprofit research institute
1993	National Department of Defense Authorization Act	*Facilitated and encouraged technology transfer to small businesses
	Defense Authorization Act for FY 1993	*extended the streamlining of small business technology transfer procedures for non-federal laboratory contractors
1994	Federal Acquisitions Streamlining Act	*mandated use of e-commerce as the main procurement method to increase efficiency and included a

specific mandate to be fair and to support small business.

*extended use of ECRCs (Electronic Commerce Resource Centers) to train entrepreneurial vendors. DARPA ran this program.

| 1995 | National Technology Transfer and Advancement Act | *incentives provided for prompt commercialization of technologies developed under CRADAs |
| 1998 | Technology Transfer Commercialization Act | *Section C: First preference in the granting of any exclusive licenses in this section shall be given to small business firms having equal or greater likelihood as other applications to bring the invention to practical application within a reasonable time |

Source: 1980–1993: Technology Innovation: Chapter 63, United States Code Annotated Title 15, Commerce and Trade, Sections 3701–3715, Prepared for the Federal Laboratory Consortium for Technology Transfer, Special Reports Series No. 1, by West Publishing Company, August 1994. 1994–1995: www.federallabs.org/flc/chap63.html. 1998: 111.federallabs.org/flc/ftpsrc/hr2544.html.

Select Bibliography

Altschiller, Donald A., ed. *Free Trade versus Protectionism*. New York: H. W. Wilson and Company, 1988.

Auletta, Ken. *World War 3.0: Microsoft and Its Enemies*. New York: Basic Books, 2001.

Baldock, Robert. *The Last Days of the Giants: A Route Map for Big Business Survival*. New York: John Wiley, 2000.

Barlett, Donald L., and Steel, James B. *America: Who Stole The Dream?*, paperback ed. Kansas City, MO: Andrews and McMeel, 1996.

Botkin, J. W., and Matthew, J. B. *Winning Combinations: The Coming Wave of Entrepreneurial Partnerships Between Large and Small Companies*. New York: John Wiley, 1992.

Boutellier, Roman; Gassman, Oliver; and Zedtwitz, Maximilian Von. *Managing Global Innovation: Uncovering The Secrets of Future Competitiveness*, revised ed. New York: Springer Verlag, 2000.

Buchanan, Patrick. *The Great Betrayal: How American Sovereignty and Social Justice are Being Sacrificed to the Gods of the Global Economy*. Boston: Little, Brown, 1998.

Cohen, Linda R., and Noll, Roger G. *The Technology Pork Barrel*. Washington, DC: The Brookings Institution Press, 1991.

Eisinger, Peter K. *The Rise of the Entrepreneurial State: State and Local Economic Development Policy in the United States*. Madison, WI: University of Wisconsin Press, 1988.

Flamm, Kenneth. *Targeting The Computer: Government Support and International Competitiveness*. Washington DC: The Brookings Institution Press, 1987.

Flamm, Kenneth. *Creating the Computer: Government, Industry and High Technology*. Washington DC: The Brookings Institution Press, 1998.

Fransman, Martin. *Technology and Economic Development*. Boulder, CO: Westview Press, 1986.

Fransman, Martin. *Japan's Computer and Communications Industry: The Evolution of Industrial Giants and Global Competitiveness*. New York: Oxford University Press, 1996.

Gates, Bill. *Business @ The Speed of Thought: Succeeding In the Digital Economy*. New York: Warner Books, 2000.

Gladwell, Malcolm. *The Tipping Point: How Little Things Can Make A Big Difference*. Boston: Little, Brown, 2000.

Gray, John. *False Dawn: The Delusions of Global Capitalism*. New York: New Press/ W. W. Norton, 1998.

Grove, Andrew S. *Only the Paranoid Survive: How to Exploit the Crisis Points that Challenge Every Company and Career*. New York: Doubleday, 1996.

Heilmann, John. *Pride Before The Fall: The Trials of Bill Gates and the End of the Microsoft Era*. New York: HarperCollins, 2001.

Hendry, Ian. *Innovating for Failure: Government Policy and the Early British Computer Industry*. Cambridge, MA: MIT Press, 1990.

Huber, Peter. *Law and Disorder in Cyberspace*. New York: Oxford University Press, 1997.

Johnson, Chalmers. *MITI and the Japanese Miracle: The Growth of Industrial Policy 1925–1975*, paperback ed. Palo Alto, CA: Stanford University Press, 1983.

Kapstein, Ethan. *Sharing the Wealth: Workers and the World Economy*. Madison, WI: University of Wisconsin Press, 1998.

Kelly, Kevin. *New Rules for the New Economy*. New York: Viking Books, 1998.

Kennedy, Paul. *The Rise and Fall of the Great Powers*. New York: Random House, 1987.

Kingdon, John W. *Agendas, Alternatives and Public Policies*. New York: Harper Collins, 1984.

Kisselhoff, Jeffrey. *The Box: An Oral History of Radio and Television 1920–1961*. New York: Viking Press, 1995.

Krugman, Paul. *The Age of Diminished Expectations: U.S. Economic Policy in the 1990s*, rev. 3rd. ed. Cambridge, MA: MIT Press, 1997.

Kuttner, Robert. *Everything For Sale: The Virtues and Limits of Markets*. New York: Alfred Knopf, 1997.

Landau, Ralph, and Jorgenson, Dale W. *Technology and Economic Policy*. Cambridge, MA: Ballinger Publishing Company, 1986.

Luttwak, Edward. *Turbo-Capitalism: Winners and Losers in the Global Economy*. New York: HarperCollins, 1999.

Mandel, Michael J. *The Coming Internet Depression: Why The High-Tech Boom Will Go Bust, Why the Crash Will be Worse Than You Think and How To Prosper Afterward*. New York: Basic Books, 2000.

McCraw, Thomas, ed. *Creating Modern Capitalism: How Entrepreneurs, Companies and Countries Triumphed in Three Industrial Revolutions*. Cambridge, MA: Harvard University Press, 1997.

Moore, Geoffrey. *Living on the Fault Line: Managing for Shareholder Value in the Age of the Internet*. New York: Harper Business, 2000.

Nau, Henry. *The Myth of America's Decline: Leading the World Economy in the 1990s*. New York: Oxford University Press, 1990.

North, Douglass C. *Institutions, Institutional Change and Economic Performance.* New York: Cambridge University Press, 1990.

Olson, Mancur. *The Rise and Decline of Nations: Economic Growth, Stagflation and Social Rigidities.* New Haven, CT: Yale University Press, 1982.

Porter, Michael; Sachs, Jeffrey; Warner, Andrew; and Schwab, Klaus. *The Global Competitiveness Report.* New York: Oxford University Press, 2000.

Porter, Michael E.; Sakakibara, Marika; and Takeuchi, Hirotake. *Can Japan Compete?* Cambridge, MA: Perseus Books, 2000.

Rushing, Francis W., and Brown, Carole Ganz, eds. *National Policies for Developing High Technology Industries: International Comparisons.* Boulder, CO: Westview Press, 1986.

Scott, Bruce R., and Lodge, George C., eds. *U.S. Competitiveness in the World Economy.* Cambridge, MA: Harvard Business School Press, 1985.

Shapiro, Carl, and Varian, Hal. *Information Rules: A Strategic Guide to the Network Economy.* Cambridge, MA: Harvard Business School Press, 1998.

Shooshan, Harry M., ed. *Disconnecting Bell: The Impact of the AT&T Divestiture.* New York: Pergamon Press, 1984.

Starr, Martin K., ed. *Global Competitiveness: Getting the U.S. Back on Track.* New York: W. W. Norton, 1988.

Thore, Sten. *The Diversity, Complexity and Evolution of High-Tech Capitalism.* Boston: Kluwer Publishing Company, 1995.

Thurow, Lester. *The Future of Capitalism,* paperback ed. New York: Penguin Books, 1996.

Toffler, Alvin, and Toffler, Heidi. *Creating a New Civilization: The Politics of the Third Wave.* Atlanta: Turner Publishing, 1995.

Tunstall, Jeremy. *Communications De-Regulation: The Unleashing of America's Communications Industry.* New York: Basil Blackwell, 1986.

Vogel, Ezra. *Japan as Number One: Lessons for America.* 1980. Out-of-print; now available through iuniverse.

Vogel, Stephen K. *Freer Markets, More Rules: Regulatory Reform in Advanced Industrial Countries.* Ithaca, NY: Cornell University Press, 1996.

Yergin, Daniel, and Stanislaw, Joseph. Tergin Daniel. *The Commanding Heights: The Battle Between Government and the Marketplace That Is Remaking the World,* paperback ed. New York: Simon and Schuster, 1998.

Index

About the Author

KIM EZRA SHIENBAUM is Assistant Professor of Political Science at Rutgers University's Camden Campus and has written on a variety of subjects ranging from American Elections to the American Presidency. For over a decade she also has created, hosted, and produced the Rutgers public affairs radio series "Head to Head" sponsored by TIAA-CREF and broadcast on over seventy-five public radio stations across America.

DATE DUE

GAYLORD

PRINTED IN U.S.A.